COLOSSAL
CANADIAN
FAILURES

COLOSSAL CANADIAN FAILURES

A Short History of Things that Seemed Like a Good Idea at the Time

Randy Richmond
and
Tom Villemaire

A HOUNSLOW BOOK
A MEMBER OF THE DUNDURN GROUP
TORONTO · OXFORD

Copy-Editor: Artemis Creative Consulting
Design: Jennifer Scott
Printer: Transcontinental

National Library of Canada Cataloguing in Publication Data

Richmond, Randy, 1958-
Colossal Canadian failures : a short history of things that seemed like a good idea at the time
/ Randy Richmond and Tom Villemaire.

Includes bibliographical references and index.
ISBN 1-55002-416-7

1. Canada — History — Miscellanea. 2. Failure (Psychology). I. Villemaire, Tom II. Title.

FC25.R54 2002   971   C2002-902291-6   F1005.R54 2002

1   2   3   4   5   06   05   04   03   02

We acknowledge the support of the **Canada Council for the Arts** and the **Ontario Arts Council** for our publishing program. We also acknowledge the financial support of the **Government of Canada** through the **Book Publishing Industry Development Program** and **The Association for the Export of Canadian Books**, and the **Government of Ontario** through the **Ontario Book Publishers Tax Credit** program.

Care has been taken to trace the ownership of copyright material used in this book. The author and the publisher welcome any information enabling them to rectify any references or credit in subsequent editions.

J. Kirk Howard, President

Printed and bound in Canada.⊛
Printed on recycled paper.

www.dundurn.com

Dundurn Press
8 Market Street
Suite 200
Toronto, Ontario, Canada
M5E 1M6

Dundurn Press
73 Lime Walk
Headington, Oxford,
England
OX3 7AD

Dundurn Press
2250 Military Road
Tonawanda NY
U.S.A. 14150

COLOSSAL
CANADIAN
FAILURES

TABLE OF CONTENTS

ACKNOWLEDGEMENTS

Just in case this book is a failure, we'd like to share the blame.

We mean, here are all the people we'd like to thank:

Those who emailed, phoned, talked to us and called CBC's "Ontario Today" radio show with ideas and tips. And CBC's Dave Stephens himself, of course. Tipsters and helpers included Duncan Marshall, Shane Roberts, Bob LePage, John Row, Adrian Lewis, Jim Evans, Hector McNeill, P.J. Harston, Julie Carl, Chip Martin, Lisa Sardi, Larry and Don Dube, and Gordon Kent.

The curators at the Canada Science and Technology Museum — Dr. Randall Brooks, Bryan Dewalt, Garth Wilson, and David Monaghan — all worried we would make too much fun of inventors.

The mostly patient staff at Dundurn Press, especially those who suffered through this book — editorial boss Barry Jowett, editor Janis Lee, designer Jennifer Scott, publicist Mike Millar, and cheque signer Kirk Howard.

Our employers, Osprey Media and London Free Press, for giving us time to work, whether they knew it or not.

All the historians and writers whose books on Canada grace our shelves.

Anyone else we've failed to mention.

Friends, especially those who kept asking, "Isn't that thing out yet?"

Our families, especially Sandra, Janice, Rebecca, Sawyer, and Molly.

Every Canadian who tried hard (and left good notes).

INTRODUCTION

"Cross the ocean," everybody in Europe said.

"Send out ships, keep going straight and we'll hit China or India. There's nothing, absolutely nothing, between us and gold, spices, tapestries, and riches."

So they sailed and sailed.

Then they hit land. It was neither China nor India, but a big rock with trees.

"That's okay," everybody in Europe said, "this new land is full of gold."

It wasn't.

"No problem," everybody said, "this new land has a giant river that will take us to the ocean that leads us to China and India. Gold, tapestries, spices!"

The river didn't. It led to a few lakes.

"So what?" everybody said. "The lakes must lead into the

ocean that goes to China and India. Gold, tapestries, spices!"

The lakes led to more land.

"No matter," everybody said, "we'll just settle this new land rich in furs and trees and prairies. Look how nice the summers are. It'll be easy."

It wasn't. Instead of riches, they got winter, scurvy, and starvation. Not to mention mosquitoes.

And for helping the newcomers out, the people who already lived in this new land got smallpox, war, and missionaries.

Welcome to Canada, a country steeped in failures.

This book celebrates some of our best blunders, mistakes, and bungles. The word "colossal" in the title is used occasionally to describe the scope of the failures (some were massive), but more often the vast gulf between the intent and the result. Some of the failures led to the loss of lives. So we'd like to make it clear we're not poking fun at the victims; rather we're ridiculing the dumb ideas that led to the disasters. We'd also like to make it clear that in many cases, it wasn't the people who were failures, but their ideas. In fact, many of the failures can be attributed to people who were successful in other ways.

And that brings us to the reasons why we figure Canada's failures must be celebrated.

First, as more than one scientist and historian pointed out to us during our research, anybody trying something different is bound to fail a few times. Success, especially in inventing, is often built on failure. A good track record of failures means a country is thinking ahead. Canada has so many failures, it must be doing something right.

Second, our peculiar failures made Canada what it is today. Failures made us humbler than the Americans, British, and French — all of whom tried at one time or another to take over North America. Who can focus on conquering when you can't walk outside for the blackflies? Failing to be like anyone else, we created our own country. Which we still fail to define, except that we all like to laugh a lot.

And that's the third reason to celebrate our blunders. Because if we can't laugh at ourselves, we fail to be truly Canadian.

CHAPTER 1

A BETTER LAND
(SOCIAL EXPERIMENTS)

Many Canadians try to make their world a better place.
Some of them should just relax.

Let's make a place with no rules. Hey, how come no one is following the rules?

"Hey man, you know what would be cool? A school where there's no, like, teachers or students, just learners."

"Yeah, and a place to hang out with nobody harassing us about our hair and the dope or nothing."

And so, one can imagine, began one of the greatest social experiments and, to some, greatest social disasters, in Canadian history — Rochdale College.

Okay, so the introduction to this failure is a little unfair. It wasn't a group of pot-smokers who came up with the idea for a self-run, eighteen-floor combination college and community residence in the late 1960s, even though it seemed like that later. Like many projects of that era, the idea came from good-intentioned and intelligent, if a tad too idealistic, people.

Partly in response to the lack of affordable and nearby housing for University of Toronto students and partly in response to a growing awareness of the limitations of structured classroom learning, a long-standing housing co-op attached to the university created Rochdale College. The idea was to build a self-run residence/college where like-minded, community-minded and well, nice, people would explore new ways of thinking and learning and doing.

With a low-interest mortgage from the Canada Mortgage and Housing Corporation (CMHC), the co-op built a high-rise on Bloor Street near the university. Philosophically, the high-rise that became Rochdale had firm roots. Author Dennis Lee helped to create the college's educational program.

As soon as the building went up, though, there were problems. First, it wasn't ready in time. Early residents suffered a range of mechanical and maintenance problems, from plumbing breakdowns to heating woes. Second, within months of opening, a Metro Toronto commission ruled Rochdale College was not an educational institution and owed taxes of $134,000 — money the co-op did not have. But the biggest problem was the people. About 800 students had been pre-selected to live in Rochdale, students interested in community living and a new style of education. Unfortunately, the building's late opening prompted many of them to bail out and find other places to live. At the same time, Yorkville merchants and police were pushing the hippies out of the village thanks to an anti-war riot that got out of hand in the summer. So Yorkville — the hippies, pushers, bikers, users, scammers, and freaks — simply moved a few blocks away into a really cool new place where you could crash for free and where there were almost no rules: Rochdale.

The crashers, as they were called, buried the ideals of Rochdale under a mess of amphetamines, disregard for rules of any kind — even the vague, always changing, love everyone rules of Rochdale — and serious dope dealing. Of course, there was a lot of smoking in Rochdale — this was the 1960s — and probably no more dealing than at your average high school or college campus. But Rochdale soon turned into a drug distribution centre for North America, with hundreds and hundreds of kilograms of marijuana hidden in rooms guarded by attack dogs and bikers. The rent-paying Rochdale residents and a twelve-member council pushed the speed freaks out by the end of 1969 but the other drugs remained. Celebrated ex-con and broadcaster Rosie Rowbotham told Bob Mackowycz and Henry Mietkiewicz, the writers of *Dream Tower: The Life and Legacy of Rochdale College*, that he oversaw deals worth $50 million between 1969 and 1974. All that money, and very little of it was going to pay the building's mortgage or maintenance. Some people who didn't like rules flaunted all of them at Rochdale, including throwing garbage into the halls or out the windows, or letting dogs defecate in the hallways.

Alarmed by the drug use, Metro Toronto police began steady raids on Rochdale by 1970. The raids were more like forays into enemy-controlled streets in the Middle East than an apartment building in Toronto. Residents would shut down the elevators, turn off the lights, and surround police in the stairwells. By the time police got to a stash room where drugs were kept, the merchandise would have been moved and their warrants were rendered useless. But police managed to arrest a lot of buyers and annoy a lot of residents. Tensions peaked in August when, after a drug raid, about 1,500 people confronted 150 police officers. The raids continued in the fall and turned one floor into a war zone. Rochdale's supporters eventually voted to toss the dealers out.

Of course, not much changed. And that was another of Rochdale's problems. The sheer mass of people was difficult to control, especially by a council that loathed controlling anyone. Trying to keep on top of the various factions was like trying to keep track of postwar governments in Italy or the changing alliances in soap operas. Classes came and classes went, depending on the interests of students wandering in. And no one could take control, because taking control meant you were just part of the establishment, man.

Meanwhile, the rent money was due and because so few people paid rent, there was never enough. The CMHC threatened to shut Rochdale down as early as 1969 and in 1970 concluded the place would never pay its way. When it was full, it was full mainly of non-paying crashers, freethinkers who didn't believe in private property, and assorted others fleeing rent.

Political pressure to close the haven for dealers, runaways, and all kinds of weirdos mounted after the drug raids of 1970. But it was the inability to pay the bills that killed Rochdale.

By June 1971, Rochdale was $330,000 behind on its mortgage, and by August, $450,000. College administrators managed to make only eleven of thirty mortgage payments. The federal government decided to foreclose on the mortgage, less than three years after the college opened. Legal and public relations battles stretched out the project's demise. In 1972, receiver Clarkson Company took over the building. For three more years, a dwindling band of residents fought the inevitable, with moderates trying to work with the receiver and others making death threats against the receiver's employees who were trying to manage the building. If there was any doubt Rochdale was dead, it disappeared in 1974 when an inquest into one of the many suicides at the building concluded the college should close. In February 1974, the federal government and Clarkson began the slow task of evicting the final 408 residents. The response from the peace-and-love generation? More death threats, dropping eggs on the heads of the receiver's employees, and at one point turning fire hoses on them. Residents claimed the security guards hired by the receiver and police roughed them up and the building's new owners shut off heat and elevators just for fun.

In 1976, Metro Toronto bought the former college for $9 million and eventually turned it into the Senator David A. Croll Apartments.

Not all of the Rochdale experience was bad. When she looks back on it, Ann Pohl, a former resident, gives a wry laugh. "What happened inside there was not all that great. We didn't put enough effort into keeping the place alive and well. We were young and immature," says Pohl, who ran the health clinic in Rochdale and remains an activist in Toronto. "But there were a lot of good things that came out of it. Just imagine the birth of the universe. There is chaos but all these galaxies and stars are created. What is left is dust and debris."

For some, especially those who set up communes on certain floors, the college provided a haven. Other supporters say

Rochdale allowed people to try everything without fear of failure or social censure. There were concrete successes. Toronto's Theatre Passe Muraille got its start in Rochdale. Science fiction fanatic Judith Merril started what would become Toronto Public Library's Space Out branch — a world-class collection of science fiction literature — in Rochdale. It's a small who's who list of notables. But take a look at some of the photos from Rochdale College, then ask the question, did it work. Pictures of the college's armed guards give the answer.

Utopias, a great way to meet women

Major William Kingdom Rains was thirty-six when he quit the British Army and his wife. He wanted something better. He wanted a new life.

So Rains headed for Ontario with two women, sisters, actually. They settled on Lake Simcoe, but Rains wasn't satisfied. He wanted something perfect. So he leaned on some friends in government and was granted permission to establish a settlement on St. Joseph Island, up in the neck of the Great Lakes, where Lake Superior flows into Lake Huron. Nice little spot.

Rains and the two sisters gathered up some other believers in better things and created a community called Milford Haven. Everything was going swimmingly until money troubles arose — Rains and his business partner had a disagreement. So Rains abandoned his search for utopia and moved to a point on the island with his women, where he lived out his days. He had walls of books, two wives, and twenty-five children. All reports are he was a cultured, interesting, although somewhat tired and disheveled-looking man who lived in a shack until his dying day. That's not to say he wasn't happy with his lot, but it probably wasn't quite the utopia he'd been looking for.

A number of proto-utopias were started on the West Coast, for reasons that are obvious, or so the people who live there now will have you believe.

For example, Sointula, on Malcolm Island in British Columbia, began as a planned utopia. The name Sointula means "harmony" in Finnish. In 1902, Matti Kurikka arrived on Malcolm Island with a band of followers from Nanaimo. Kurikka had tried to establish a utopian community in Australia in 1899, but it failed. Apparently word of his attempt preceded him and Finns working in the coal mines invited him to British Columbia.

Kurikka had first come to Nanaimo in 1901 and was given the job of editing and publishing Canada's first Finnish language newspaper, *Aika*, which means "Time" in Finnish. Kurikka had been a social activist and playwright in Finland. Finland was part of Czarist Russia when Kurikka was born in Tuutari in 1863. By the end of the 1800s, the taxes and hardships imposed on Finns by the Czarist state were inspiring many to leave in search of a better life. In Canada, communities of Finns were established in clusters from coast to coast, including Thunder Bay, Ontario and through areas of British Columbia.

After a year of editing the paper, Kurikka and his band headed northeast for Malcolm Island, right across from Port McNeil and Telegraph Cove.

Kurikka was charismatic and handsome, with lots of long, thick, dark hair and a full, bushy beard. It may have been that he was quite popular with the ladies and this influenced his views on free love (he loved it).

It's harder to say what exactly made him such a lousy administrator. For example, once he headed across the strait to Vancouver Island to buy some needed engine parts. He came back with a piano.

Engine, piano — well, both need to be tuned.

Life in Sointula, which had a population of about 2,000 at its peak, was never quite utopian. Finns of all types were living in the settlement. Many did not have the skills to survive in the rugged, remote island locale, where their skills as tailors, seamstresses, or poets did not translate well. The poor leadership and hard life made for low tolerance. The Finns were willing to work and learn how to survive, but they couldn't take their leader's odd priorities and philosophies. By 1904, the plan had petered out. Only about thirty-five families stayed behind.

Undeterred, Kurikka set out to establish his third attempted utopia and headed for the Fraser Valley, near Webster's Corners. This community was even more short-lived than Sointula.

Kurikka eventually left Canada and returned to Finland, where he married and had a daughter. He came to North America again, this time going no further than Rhode Island in the United States, and spent his remaining years there, presumably either experiencing or dreaming of utopia. Perhaps when he died in 1915, he found was he was looking for.

If we build it, they will come

Ontario treasurer John White had a dream — a vision of the perfect city, with beautiful schools and nice parks and shopping centres and housing that young families could afford.

All he needed was the people.

So in 1974, the province spent $56 million to buy 9,100 hectares of land in Southwestern Ontario.

The dream city would be called Townsend. The province got the punctuation wrong. It should have been Town's End.

The disastrous plans began in the early 1970s when Ontario's Conservative government came under pressure for failing to ease a provincial housing shortage. A task force concluded in 1974 that the province needed to create a million houses in ten years. A year later, the new Housing Ministry hadn't even met its first year target of 100,000 houses. With an election looming in the fall, the province had to look like it was doing something. The solution? Create new cities outside existing urban areas to speed up growth and at the same time take pressure off small places that wanted to stay small. It was mostly White's idea. He refused to be pinned down on the number of new cities. "I don't know if we're going to have 3 or 300," he told reporters. "I haven't the faintest idea." To say the least.

To be fair, it was reasonable for White and the Conservative government to expect that new industrial development along the shores of Lake Erie would bring the workers to fill the new city. Ontario Hydro's coal-fired generating station, Stelco's new steel plant, and Texaco Canada's refinery were all being built near the small hamlet of Nanticoke. Stelco's 6,600-acre property, which was to include an industrial park, straddled the counties of Haldimand and Norfolk. So the province first "encouraged" the counties to form a regional government.

Then the province picked a site for the new city. A group of developers counted on a different site, bought up land nearby, and began pushing White to put the new city there. White refused, saying no developer was going to make money in Townsend. Meanwhile, though, the location of the province's chosen site had leaked. There were rumours speculators were buying land nearby. So, secretly, White began assembling land about thirty kilometres away from Townsend in the area of South Cayuga, about an hour's drive to the east, as a kind of an insurance policy.

So now there were three sites: the one the government picked, the one the developers owned (the actual Townsend), and the secret one being assembled at South Cayuga. White couldn't use the government site because so much land was in the hands of speculators. And he couldn't tell anyone about South Cayuga. So it had to be the developers' site. He refused, though, to let developers get their hands on the new city. It was the government's project, and only it knew how to make the dream city a reality. Finally, in May 1974, the developers who owned Townsend gave in, selling their parcels for about $1.7 million, largely to cover costs. White happily announced Townsend was a go. Except, he kept buying land in South Cayuga. About a hundred farmers reluctantly sold their family farms to real estate agents who warned them the government might expropriate the property or surround their acreages with houses and malls. The farmers didn't complain to anyone, yet. So it was a surprise to Ontario when White announced in November 1974 that he had also bought a whole lot of land in South Cayuga.

Now everyone was confused. Had the province paid $33.5 million for 13,440 acres in Townsend, then $28.3 million for another 12,690 acres in case the first site didn't work?

Why not have two cities of 250,000 people each? White replied to his critics. He was quickly moved out of the treasurer's post to a ministry without portfolio. He was going to leave politics soon anyway, White assured reporters.

White didn't run in the 1975 election, which was just as well. The Conservatives lost their majority and lost Haldimand-Norfolk for the first time since the 1940s. The party set about to repair the damage White had done. Letting the farmland in South Cayuga sit around seemed silly, so the Conservatives came up with a surefire way to use the property and calm everyone's nerves at the same time. They decided to put a liquid hazardous waste site there. It was such a perfect spot, with a variety of waterways that could carry liquid waste straight to Lake Erie, that the province decided not to hold a full environmental assessment hearing. That was too much for the good farmers and merchants of South Cayuga. They fought the waste proposal and eventually won. In the 1980s, the province announced it would start selling the land back.

Reality took longer to tear the dream city from the Conservatives' sleepy grasp. A consulting firm was hired to design the city and in March 1977, the Townsend Community Plan was unveiled. The city of 100,000 would not only accommodate the growth of the region, expected to jump from 88,000 to 181,000 by 2001, but become its cultural, recreational, and civic heart. Townsend could contain seventeen public elementary schools, seven separate elementary schools, and six public high schools. The public elementary schools would be distributed so that no child would have to walk more than 500 metres to get to class. The separate school students would only have to walk 1,000 metres or less.

Two kinds of parks would be created. A twenty-five-acre park would be built for every 15,000 to 20,000 people, meaning no one would be more than a ten-minute walk from an open space. Each of these bigger parks would include a combination of baseball diamonds, soccer and football fields, recreation hall, indoor pool, and tennis courts. Smaller neighbourhood parks of five to seven acres would be built for every 4,000 to 5,000 people. These could include playgrounds, gardens, and wading pools.

Five mixed service centres, including the town centre, would be built. Each would have a large supermarket and a range of stores from hair salons to bakeries. About 500 people could be expected to find work at the five centres. Another fifteen to twenty areas would be designated for convenience stores. Two industrial sites would be built. "Depending on the type of uses, each area can reasonably accommodate between 3,000 and 6,000 jobs," the report concluded.

But the best part would be Townsend's downtown. It "has the opportunity to become the main commercial and social centre for both the new community and the region." The downtown would boast three or four department stores, specialty shops, 300 apartment units, office space, government buildings, a theatre, cinemas, hotels, an art gallery, a hospital, a library, an indoor sports centre, and bus depot.

Whew.

Economic slowdowns from the 1970s through the 1990s stalled that ambitious plan. Neither the politicians nor ordinary people in the communities around Townsend gave it much support. The regional government decided in 1981 to move its headquarters there but the city of Nanticoke, which included Townsend, refused. The earliest settlers in Townsend enjoyed its pretty surroundings and new facilities, but suffered from waves of tour buses, the noise of construction crews, and accusations from residents in communities nearby that they were traitors or small town pretenders.

Today, twenty-five years later, Townsend has some nice offices, a few stores, a pond, a baseball diamond, and about 800 people.

"Honey, get me the Finishing Cluster!"

The tip came into the Canadian daily newspaper just before nine o'clock in the morning. A caller whispered that the city was going to raise parking fees and put in new meters across the city.

In the old days, an editor would bark the information to the city hall beat reporter, who would make some calls and get the story. Meanwhile, a photographer would be assigned to take a photograph of someone parking a car. The photo and story would go to other editors, who would slap a headline on the package and put it on a page for the next day's paper. At the last minute, the city hall reporter, drowning his sorrows at a local bar, would hear that the mayor stood to make thousands because his company got the contract to update the parking meters. He would call the office. "Honey," he'd say to the telephone operator, "get me rewrite!"

But this wasn't the old days. This was the brave new world of 1993.

When the tip came in, Zero Option operators passed it over to the Startup Cluster Leader, who passed it on to the Public Spirit Cluster Leader.

The Public Spirit Cluster Leader presented the tip to his Fact Gatherers.

The Fact Gatherers spent several days talking about the tip. Then they spent several more days working the tip into a series of colourful charts, maps, and graphs that explained the history of traffic flow in the city, the effect of malls on the downtown shopping core, and the debate over angled versus parallel parking.

The Fact Gatherers approached several Information Processors for some real estate for the package. An Information Processor specializing in Work/Wealth offered prime real estate — the front of a section — and won the package. Everyone in the newsroom took a well-deserved break.

The person who called in the tip wondered why no one covered the story about rising parking fees.

Only the tip in this story is made up. The rest of it, strange names included, is true.

The brave new world was *The London Free Press* in the 1990s, when beats became clusters, editors became cluster leaders, and information processors and reporters became fact gatherers. To any employee who has survived the countless reorganizations that litter corporate Canada, who has suffered through interminable meetings with consultants and facilitators expressing their feelings about the best strategies for achieving goals and benchmarks, or who has wondered if all managers signed over their brains upon promotion, *The Free Press*'s cluster system should bring a smile of relief. No one went through a stranger experiment in changing the workplace. Some journalists at the paper defended the reorganization as an attempt to give the grassroots at a newspaper more power. Most shudder when they hear the word "cluster." The experiment is already shrouded in mythology, and misty-eyed reporters get into long arguments about what exactly happened and when. Here's one version of the legend.

Like other newspapers in the 1990s, *The Free Press* faced stagnant circulation and increased competition from television news. Newspapers dallied with a variety of solutions, from heavy doses of colourful charts and illustrations to endless readership surveys. No one went further than *The Free Press.*

"We walked out on the edge," recalled one reporter, "and right off the plank."

The experiments began in 1989, when the editor in chief, Phil McLeod, overhauled the front page and turned it into a giant and colourful index for the rest of the paper, full of charts and small boxes of point-form information. Reporters said they realized only years later the topics in the index were colour-coded to sections inside the paper. Others recall being told the newspaper was declaring war on the narrative. Entire, well-crafted stories with subjects, verbs, and objects became point-form "fact boxes." During the Gulf War, one reporter covering the latest developments was urged to "think like a poet." He gathered all the material he could and turned the war into a play. Great work, the managers said. I work for lunatics, the reporter thought.

Making the newspaper look like a television set did little to solve the financial problems, so *The Free Press* managers took a close look at what were called pods in several U.S. newspapers. Pods were made up of an editor, some reporters, a photographer, and graphic artists. Pods were consultative. Pods thrived on words like "community" and "facilitate" and "evolve." In a pod, anyone could pitch a story idea. The ideas were then discussed and an entire proposal of words, photos, and graphics was developed before anyone started working.

It was great in theory. Warm and kind of fuzzy. Except reporters didn't want to be called pods. So *The Free Press* managers came up with Home Communities, then Home Base Clusters, then simply, clusters. Through 1990 and 1991, *The Free Press*'s top editors and a few lucky reporters theorized about clusters. Charts with dozens of circles bisecting other circles were drawn up to explain how clusters would put out a paper. Managers and reporters went on three-day workshops and worked through "grope, gripe, and group cycles" (thinking, complaining, then by consensus, solving) to consider "structural infirmities." The old beats were thrown out. Clusters would incorporate what people really cared about and get names that reflected the new reality.

The business, labour, and finance beats were replaced by the Work/Wealth Cluster. The court, cop, and social services beats were combined into the Justice Cluster. The city hall and other political beats became the Public Spirit Cluster. The environment was covered by the Well-being/Ecology Cluster. Education, amateur sports, and health were combined into the Family Cluster.

The people who read press releases and took news tips in the morning, then distributed them to the appropriate clusters, were called the Startup Cluster. And the people who put out the pages at night were called the Finishing Cluster.

But the best cluster of all was a combo-cluster. In order to shake things up and get the best out of people, the managers took all the hard-bitten jocks in the sports department and all the artistic theatre critics, music critics, and arts writers in the entertainment department, then jammed them into one group called the Applause Cluster. Or, as participants quickly renamed it, the Clap Cluster.

Not only was there great potential for conflict, the arts writers were expected to cover sports — "The Toronto Blue Jays provided a delicate balance between style and content in yesterday's game" — and the sports reporters were now expected to cover the arts — "Hamlet and enemies settle for tie!" To complicate matters, the Applause Cluster covered only professional sports. University, high school, and other amateur sports were covered by the Family Cluster.

By 1993, the newsroom had been converted to clusters. Many reporters and editors welcomed the change from the top-down hierarchy of old. Clusters would have worked, they said, if there had been enough people. But there weren't enough employees to go around. Too often, photographers, reporters, and editors were borrowed for other clusters or to work on the Finishing Cluster at night. Some days, a cluster would consist of a reporter, a cluster leader, and the section editor.

There were many other problems. Some days the clusters would talk a lot but accomplish little. One veteran compared clusters to group projects in high school where six people did nothing but socialize while one person worked desperately to get something done. One survivor pointed out that a newspaper works by passing on a package of information — a story idea — from person to person, from morning to midnight, when the last person puts the information on a page. But in the cluster system, everyone started at nine, strategized, then went home at five, often with little done.

The editors of the newspaper's sections — such as business, sports, entertainment, and news — owned what was called real estate, the pages of their section. Each day, the clusters were supposed to get the best real estate they could for their stories, and the section editors would try to get the best stories by offering up the best space. Although section editors were responsible for filling their pages, they could not assign a story or in some cases even talk to the reporters. That was too hierarchical, too old school. Let the clusters alone, let everyone consult, and the best ideas would float to the surface, the managers said.

"I was reprimanded twice for talking to reporters," recalled one business editor. He resorted to sending a newsletter out to try to encourage the Work/Wealth Cluster to do stories.

And that was the biggest problem. Newspapers can't survive on big projects alone, or on the will and whim of journalists. Someone has to order up a story. Someone has to write news. Reacting to breaking news, reported one section editor in an office memo about clusters, "went into the ditch."

After a series of errors in early 1993, the editors of *The Free Press* tried to explain the new system to readers. "We are devoting less space to what happened yesterday, more space on our agenda," said editor Gary May, kind of a cluster leaders' cluster leader. "In a general sense, we are planning the paper two days in advance. We'll be able to respond to emergencies but there's little that falls into that category."

In a later story, editors explained they were trying to rid the newspaper of its bias toward stories that appealed mainly to white, middle-class professional men and attract more women and members of minority groups. It was a noble aim and a change *The Free Press* likely needed. But all readers — men, women, and minority groups — wanted news in their newspaper.

Armies of memos about the cluster system moved back and forth across the newsroom for the next five years. Task forces reconsidered, re-evaluated, and reassessed. New titles were pondered. Perhaps different labels would make people think differently. Section editors were to become Information Processors. Reporters were to become Fact Gatherers, collecting the bits that would meld into a greater whole. No one took to the new names. The really disgruntled found foxholes to hide in — a bureau job two hours away, a night job on the Finishing Cluster. The rest just tried to survive.

Every year, mid-sized and small papers in Ontario honour the best of each other's work with awards and a dinner. *The Free Press* was used to getting dozens of nominations a year. Papers one-eighth of the size routinely get three and four. One year during the cluster era, *The Free Press* got one reporting nomination.

There are disagreements about when the clusters died. Some reporters were brought back to beats, which of course couldn't be called beats, but Superbeats, to differentiate them from the regular clusters. Other newsroom staffers seemed to simply ignore the system and go back to regular reporting. When the paper was sold to The Toronto Sun in 1997, the traditionalists from the tabloid chain were aghast at what they saw. Consult? Evolve? Facilitate ideas? Editors barked orders and reporters grumbled while they followed them — that was how a newspaper was supposed to work. The cluster system was destroyed.

But newcomers to *The Free Press* get a jolt from the past when they learn what the newsroom receptionists are called. As the cluster system was dying and the managers continued to look for new ways to save money, the position of receptionist was eliminated. Who needed receptionists when answering machines and reporters could answer the phones? Of course, a lot of the time reporters were out, so it was nearly impossible for callers to get a live person on the other end. After one high-ranking manager calling into the newsroom let the phone ring an enraging seventeen times before giving up, the receptionists' positions were brought back. But calling the workers receptionists caused problems with the union and the people let go, so managers instead created a new position. The title reflects all that was great about clusters. Callers unable to reach reporters or editors had the option of pressing zero to reach an operator. So the receptionists were called Zero Option Operators. Unhappy about having the word "zero" in their job title, those who answered the phones soon took on new, unofficial titles: Zed girls and Zed boys. The names have stuck, and are all that remain of the cluster revolution.

What time is it in your house?

Sometimes two grave problems that seem unrelated to ordinary people present one common solution to the great thinkers. So it was for Mayor William Frost and newspaper publisher Charles H. Hale of Orillia, Ontario. The two were wondering how to make Orillia stand out from the hundreds of small towns dotting Ontario. And one day, they got to pondering the plight of the working man in summer. No sooner had he got off work and had his dinner but darkness fell on his evening activities.

"The bone and sinew of the town, who work from 7 to 6, day in and day out, find it dark almost as soon as tea is over," Hale noted in his newspaper, *The Packet*.

What if, he wondered, one just moved the clock one hour ahead in the summer so that seven o'clock had as much light as six o'clock? "Moving the clock one hour ahead would give these men an opportunity to enjoy another hour's daylight in the evening … Life will have a new zest … because they will sleep in the dark hours and have an hour more sunlight added to the waking period."

Not only would people get an extra hour of zest, the town itself would stand out from the rest. Hale took his idea to the Orillia board of trade, which grew enthusiastic. After all, he was the president. We can call Orillia, Hale said, "The Town Ahead." The next year, Hale was elected to council. He and Mayor Frost convinced their fellow politicians to try the daylight savings that summer and declared ten o'clock, Saturday, June 22, 1912 as the time Orillia moved ahead.

The bone and sinew of the town did not want to move ahead.

If you put the clock ahead one hour, you will lose that hour permanently, the mathematical reasoned.

Worse than that, said the theologians, you will push Saturday into Sunday, violating the Lord's Day Act.

Who cares about that? said the sinners. Daylight savings will force us to get up and eat breakfast too early in the day.

As the hour of doom approached, opposition grew. The Bricklayers Union voted against the proposal and petitions against it circulated through several factories. Daylight savings was a plot to make men work extra hours, labour leaders said.

No, no, no, said Hale. You don't understand time. The hours of a clock were set arbitrarily, he wrote in *The Packet*. Six o'clock came at the same time every morning because everyone agreed it was six o'clock. Putting the clock ahead did not mean you lost sleep, because you still went to bed at ten and got up at six.

Although Port Arthur, Ontario had already switched to daylight savings, Orillia was credited with trying a grand experiment and newspapers across Ontario watched closely.

"All eyes are on Orillia," *The Packet* proclaimed just before the day of change arrived. "Manifest the Orillia Spirit." At ten o'clock on the evening of Saturday, June 22 the town bells rang to remind everyone to turn their clocks ahead one hour. Time and Orillia jumped ahead.

Mayor Frost awoke the next morning, had his breakfast, got dressed and went to church. All eyes watched him enter. He was late. The minister was already an hour into his service, thanks to the mayor's own proclamation, which he had promptly forgotten.

"The confusion," Hale recalled, "was beyond belief." The church bells rang at different times. The town clock rang, not at seven in the morning as it always did, but an hour earlier at six. On Monday morning, meticulous merchants arrived an hour late at their stores, having forgotten to move their clocks one hour ahead.

Some crafty workers figured out a loophole in the system. The employees of Hewitt Brothers trucking arrived at seven o'clock, the normal start time, then insisted on waiting an hour for standard time to catch up. They laughed at nearby workers starting their jobs at the "new" seven o'clock. The Hewitt workers figured they could begin at eight o'clock daylight savings, because it was still only seven o'clock standard time. We'll then leave for lunch at noon, the new daylight savings time, and cut an hour off our morning, they exulted. At noon they quit for lunch, but to their dismay their employer had a better sense of time. You owe me another hour, he said and ordered them back to work.

Some companies adopted daylight savings, but others rejected the plan. Shipping schedules could not be kept. No one knew when the important evening baseball games were supposed to start. Employees working under daylight savings time got off an hour before everyone else. As they wandered to the ball diamonds, they teased the men still at work, causing some bad feelings in town. Still other workers thought the new hours meant they had to go to work at six o'clock in the morning and waited for an hour for everyone else to show up.

A standard greeting became, "Do you go on God's time or Bill Frost's time?"

All of this Frost and Hale could have ridden out. Factory owners could be pressured, workers could be convinced, but the two leaders forgot about the most powerful element in town — the boarding house owners. Hundreds of working men roomed in these boarding houses and they expected three squares a day. Because factories operated on two different times, the boarding house owners had to serve two sets of breakfast, two sets of lunch, and two sets of dinner. That was intolerable. The boarding house operators told Mayor Frost and publisher Hale to fix it. After only two weeks of being "The Town Ahead," Orillia returned to "The Town the Same as the Rest." Frost got an embarrassing nickname. But time heals all wounds, or at least allows everyone to catch up. When Canada adopted daylight savings time in the summers several years later, Frost began wearing his nickname, Daylight Bill, with pride.

CHAPTER 2

YOU SAY YOU WANT A REVOLUTION?

Canada is known as a peaceful land. We send peacekeepers around the world. We believe in compromise over conflict. And revolutionaries we're not.

Shouldn't somebody stay and fight?

During the rebellion of Upper Canada, rebel forces were marching, after a fashion, down Yonge Street towards York (which is what Toronto was called then). It was December 1837, and the rebels were mostly armed with picks and poles, but there was a small cadre of riflemen.

It had taken their leader, William Lyon Mackenzie, no little effort to get to that point. Mackenzie had wanted to hit York's armoury in October, when two constables were all that stood between rebel forces and weapons and gear for 6,000 men. His followers needed more time to warm up to the idea of rebellion, so he set a date of December 7, 1837.

But while Mackenzie was out beating the bushes and farms for supporters, some of his lieutenants arbitrarily changed the date to December 4. When Mackenzie returned to the rally point, men were already filing in to fight. There were few weapons and little food, so things were postponed until the original date of December 7.

By then, word was out and every citizen loyal to the crown was headed to York for the big showdown. By the time the rebel force made it to the toll bar at Yonge and Bloor, it had managed to capture a captain of artillery, a lawyer, and the sheriff's horse.

At that point, Mackenzie had two parties of riflemen move down either side while the rest of the rebels marched down the middle of the road. As he recounts: "Our riflemen ahead saw 20 or 30 of the enemy in the road and fired at them. The 20 or 30 or some fired at us and took to their heels and ran."

In military jargon, that's a retreat. But what was different about this retreat was that Mackenzie's men were running away, as well.

Among the rebel forces, each rifle platoon, to use the term loosely, drilled separately. Colonel Sam Lount's riflemen, for example, used a drill similar to that used by the British. The men formed into three rows and when the front row fired, it fell to the ground, allowing the second row to fire and fall to the ground, and then the third row to fire.

Many of the rebel forces were not familiar with the British drill. What they did know, though, was that many of the loyalists they were facing were members of the militia and some were half-pay officers from the British army. They were professionally trained and would be crack shots. The rebels in the back of the charge who saw Lount's men dropping to the ground thought they had been killed or wounded by the loyalists. So they ran.

For their part, the loyalists could see that they were outnumbered. They were only a few dozen men, but the rebels a few hundred. And the rebels were literally swarming down the road, bent on death and destruction. So when the rebels fired, the loyalists fired and fled, not having the numbers to hold off such a force for long.

Oh, no, it's Pirate Bill

No doubt you have heard of Blackbeard. He was a pirate — a much-feared and pretty successful one, at that.

This story isn't about him. This is about Pirate Bill.

Not really a scary moniker, Pirate Bill.

Still, if you venture into the throat of the St. Lawrence River, where it leaves Lake Ontario, you are likely to stumble across his name here and there. And while Pirate Bill was a good navigator, smuggler, pirate, and escape artist, his abilities as the commander of a navy suffered somewhat from the inescapable fact that he sometimes just wasn't very good with large boats.

Pirate Bill was born William Johnston in Quebec in 1782. His family was dirt poor, and no doubt poverty provided a certain impetus to Bill's life.

As a young man, Johnston built a boat and used it to transport goods around the Thousand Islands at the north-east end of Lake Ontario. This is an area in which it is easy to get lost or shipwrecked, but the French who had settled the area — and Johnston — came to know it well.

English navy ships often lost their bearings in the maze of islands during the Seven Years' War campaign against the French. Sometimes an English captain effectively removed himself from battle when, thinking he could sneak up on the enemy by navigating around an island, he instead found himself lost and the other ship nowhere in sight.

Bill became quite cocky about his navigational abilities. He made many friends on the American side of the border and developed tight trade ties with Yanks and Yankee smugglers. Just before the War of 1812, Bill sold his boat and used his money to establish a business in Kingston. When the war broke out, Bill's ties to the States made him a suspect. His unwavering refusal to stop trade with the enemy almost landed him in jail.

But Bill, as he would prove a number of times, was a great escape artist. With the possibility of jail threatening him, he took to the water and crossed Lake Ontario in a canoe.

Working for the Americans, he prowled the waters, capturing British and Canadian communications and behaving like, well, a pirate. Civilian transport was also fair game for Bill and he supported his lifestyle by seizing anything he could that was British or Canadian.

Once the war ended, Bill found it too hard to give up his new lifestyle. He and his daughter, Kate, continued to pillage as opportunities arose. Bill would invariably be caught and tossed in jail. He would just as invariably be released or escape and return to his wicked ways.

By 1837, Upper and Lower Canada were embroiled in political turmoil. Lower Canada's rebellion was a bloody slugfest. In Upper Canada, the first march on York by William Lyon Mackenzie ended in a mutual retreat and Mackenzie fled to Buffalo. Eventually, he made his way to Navy Island, in the middle of the Niagara River above the falls.

A boat, called the *Caroline*, was used by Mackenzie's men to supply Navy Island and the provisional government of Upper Canada that Mackenzie had established there. However, when the *Caroline* was on one of its supply missions, it was captured by forces loyal to the crown, set ablaze, and left to drift over the falls.

Pirate Bill was angered when he heard of this incident, and he later made, "Remember the *Caroline*!" his war cry. Most people who heard this had no idea what he was referring to.

Perhaps it was this incident that influenced Pirate Bill to go legit almost half a year after the first rebellion. He declared himself Admiral and Commander-in-Chief of all the so-called patriot forces. Not that there was much in the way of forces. Mostly they were Hunters, men who joined "hunter lodges" in the United States, giving them an excuse to carry guns and practice shooting. This is where most of the patriots trained.

Pirate Bill wasn't so concerned about the land forces, which he left to the soldier types. He decided to focus on creating a patriot navy. The first thing he would need would be some kind of boat.

With a couple of dozen supporters encouraging and emboldening him, Bill decided to nab the nicest boat on that part of the lake — a steamer. The *Sir Robert Peel* was a fine craft that was not a military ship, but a boat of commerce, owned by Brockville businessmen. It was a ferry and transport vessel that plied the same waters Bill had travelled during his early pirating days.

One of the boat's regular stops was Wellesley Island. Bill and his men hid at the wharf and waited, dressed as Mohawks, for the boat to arrive. It was raining and cold, but Bill was in high spirits, and later he described how fierce he and his compatriots felt in their war paint and how they hoped things would hurry up and happen before their make-up ran.

When the steamer chugged up to the dock the rebels swarmed it. Whooping like Native warriors (except Bill, who yelled, "Remember the *Caroline*!"), they captured the ship quickly and roused the sleeping passengers, pushing them ashore.

Once everyone, including the crew, was on the docks, in the rain, Bill and his men set about to leave. But no one, including the self-proclaimed admiral, had a clue how to operate a steamboat.

As time ticked by, Bill became more and more impatient. Finally, he decided he had wasted enough time and he ordered his sailors to pillage the boat and the passengers and then burn the boat. Then they rowed off into the night.

That was the first naval action of Pirate Bill's admiralty days. It was not the last.

With a $1,000 reward on his head from Canada and a $500 reward from the American government, Bill had to move in secrecy. Bounty hunters searched the islands, looking for Bill and his men. In less than a week, nine of two dozen were nabbed, but Bill remained free.

By this time, there were nine regiments of British troops in Upper Canada, in addition to the militia. There were also Royal Marines and sailors from the Royal Navy. Still, raids by the so-called patriots continued along the southern Great Lakes and Pirate, excuse us, Admiral Bill was not one to be left out of a good raid.

Mind you, not everyone would characterize the seizure by Bill's navy of the two schooners, the *Oswego Charlotte* and the *Toronto Charlotte*, for the purpose of attacking Fort Wellington, as "a good raid."

The schooners, filled with men and supplies, were making their way to Sacket's Harbour on the southeast side of Lake Ontario. Meanwhile, an American steamer headed for Ogdensburg stopped in at Sacket's Harbour early on November 11, 1838, and picked up 400 "passengers," who were really rebel patriots. More joined at Cape Vincent, Clayton, and Millen's Bay. As the captain of the steamer prepared to leave Millen's Bay, he was asked to take the two schooners in tow. This was the signal for the patriot troops to show themselves on deck.

In her book, *Battlefields of Canada*, Mary Beacock Fryer describes Bill's navy this way: "The Hunters emerged, clad in a bewildering array of home-made uniforms, no two alike."

With the breeze picking up, men made their way to the two schooners. Bill took control of the *Oswego Charlotte* and headed towards Prescott, Ontario. He managed to run the schooner aground near the Oswegatchie River. The other *Charlotte* sailed back and forth, waiting for her sister assault ship to free itself from the silty bottom.

Finally, the *Toronto Charlotte* left, sailed into the Prescott harbour, and tied up at the dock. Then the rope broke and the *Toronto Charlotte* began to drift.

By now, the militia was starting to form up and march towards the wharf. Just before two o'clock in the morning on November 12, the militia dragged a cannon down and got a shot off before the *Toronto Charlotte* was out of range. There was no report of any damage.

But the shot was heard in Fort Wellington, the objective of Pirate Bill's invasion, and the commander there, a British regular forces lieutenant colonel, organized the garrison of thirty-five Glengarry militia and the 200 Grenville militia in the nearby village.

The shot was also heard in Brockville by the head of the Orange Lodge, Ogle Robert Gowan, and his new militia, the Queen's Loyal Borderers. Ogle and two companies began to march on Prescott, about seventeen kilometres away, by ten o'clock.

Back on the water, another boat arrived from Ogdensburg and began to off-load the gear and men on the grounded *Oswego Charlotte*. The *Toronto Charlotte* took the loaded boat in tow. It was then that an argument broke out between the patriot leaders. It continued until the *Toronto Charlotte* grounded near a windmill downstream from Prescott.

The other patriot leader, Nils Von Schoultz or Szolteocky, thought the area was defensible and ordered his men ashore to take over the windmill. Things degenerated quickly, to the point where people were being killed in the assaults on the windmill by the British regulars, marines, and militia.

When a patriot commander ordered Pirate Bill to create a diversion with a faux landing upstream, no one could find the admiral. The quintessential escape artist had once again disappeared.

Bill, it is suggested, ran as soon as things got thick, because of the price on his head. He hid out in a cave on Devil's Oven Island, with his daughter, Kate, running supplies out to him. Eventually, he was captured by the Americans. Kate offered to serve time with him and within half a year, the slippery couple had escaped.

Admiral Bill was eventually pardoned in the United States and served his twilight years as a lighthouse keeper, watching the ships go by.

A family embarrassment

Nils Von Schoultz, or Szolteocky, was a Swede. He served for a time with the Polish army in the early 1800s before coming to Upper Canada. Here he joined up with the people who followed William Lyon Mackenzie and wandered back and forth between Canada and the United States, taking part in training with the Hunters' Lodges that were forming in the States.

The Hunters' Lodges were an imitation of the French Canadian lodges known as the *Société des frères chasseurs*. The American government tolerated, and in some cases encouraged, these lodges as a way of opposing the British who ran Canada at the time.

Von Schoultz, with his military background, was welcomed by the rebels. He told them a story of being a Polish exile. He claimed to have fought the Russians, and said that he saw the poor people of Canada as being in the same boat as the Poles who were always under the Russian boot.

What really happened is that once he left Sweden, he abandoned his family in London, England and took a boat to New York City. He got a job in Salina at a salt plant, after lying about his credentials as a chemist.

Von Schoultz led a group of men in an assault near Prescott in 1838, trying to gain a cache of arms at Fort Wellington that would help re-ignite the Rebellion of 1827. After the attack, Nils's men surrendered honourably. He did not. He was caught hiding along the St. Lawrence River and was taken to Fort Henry, where he was hanged after facing a trial.

His family in Sweden was so embarrassed by his actions that when a package of his papers arrived in Stockholm, it was ignored for 130 years.

This is why naval battles are fought on lakes and oceans

The government's stern-wheeled paddleboat steamed ahead, bristling with soldiers and guns. The sharpshooting rebels waited with rifles ready and a crafty plan to stop the boat cold. This would be the naval battle to decide the future of Canada's West.

On a river. In the prairies.

Well, no legend is perfect.

The South Saskatchewan River was the only sizable body of water the Canadian government and the Métis and Cree had in the 1885 Rebellion. When the Métis and their Cree allies began gathering at their stronghold of Batoche on the river in May 1885, Major General Fred Middleton began marching his troops to the same spot. As long as he was going to fight by a river, he figured, he might as well use the steamer *Northcote* to help out. The Hudson's Bay Company boat had been ordered down from Medicine Hat, Alberta, to bring supplies and help ferry troops across the river.

Much of the time, the *Northcote* walked. It drew sixty-six centimetres of water, but parts of the river were only fifty centimetres deep. In order to get over the shifting sandbars of the river, steamers had spars on either side of their bows. The spars were lifted out of the water most of the time. When a steamer got stuck on a sandbar, the spars were lowered and the vessel "walked" until deep water was reached.

It took the steamboat a week to travel from Medicine Hat to Saskatchewan Landing, where troops were waiting to be ferried across the river. They cheered when the *Northcote* came around the bend, then watched it get stuck on a shoal. With a winch and cable hooked up to a tree on shore, the steamboat got going again. Sort of. The river wasn't getting

Who would blink first? The crews on the heavily armed steamer Northcote *or the crafty Métis on the riverbanks at Batoche, Saskatchewan? As it turned out, everyone blinked first. From a sketch in* Canadian Pictorial and Illustrated War News, *1885.*

any deeper and the *Northcote* took fourteen days instead of the usual four to travel from Qu'Appelle to Middleton's camp at Fish Creek. Middleton put thirty soldiers on the steamer with the intent of landing below Batoche and attacking on one side, while the land force rode in from the prairie side. On May 7, as the *Northcote* travelled down river, the main force of 850 men, four cannons, a Gatling gun, and 150 wagons started toward Batoche.

The rebels knew they were coming. Their military leader, Gabriel Dumont, and his prairie fighters could have easily harassed and picked off members on the cumbersome march. But their spiritual and political leader, Louis Riel, had a vision from God that said they should hold up in Batoche. Presumably, God told him how a band of 300 guerrilla fighters with antiquated weapons, best at small forays and prairie skirmishes, was going to stave off a well-armed and overwhelmingly larger troop of soldiers perfectly suited and trained to lay siege to a town. Dumont and the other rebel leaders made the best of it and dug trenches around Batoche.

Meanwhile, the *Northcote* proceeded down the river. At Gabriel's Crossing, about fifteen kilometres upriver from Batoche, Dumont's own stables were torn down. The wood and some bags of grain were used to fortify the upper deck of the *Northcote*.

On May 9, the double-barrelled attack began. The troops headed out before sunrise, and the *Northcote* left at about seven o'clock. The troops and wagons, picking their way cautiously, took four hours to reach Batoche. The *Northcote* steamed merrily ahead, for once hitting no sandbanks, and arrived at Batoche at eight o'clock. The troops were still an hour away and could only listen to the whistle of the *Northcote* in the distance announcing its arrival.

Meanwhile, Dumont had prepared a trap for the ship. As men on either bank fired on the steamer, other rebels would lower the cable that ran the Batoche ferry back and forth on the river. The cable would trap the boat, the crew and soldiers would have to surrender, and hostages would be taken to use as bargaining chips with the Canadians.

As the *Northcote* approached, the Métis fired. Hearing the first shots, the helmsman on the steamboat threw himself to the floor, and with no one at the wheel, the *Northcote* started to drift toward a sandbank. Dumont had ordered his men to lower the cable. They thought it was low enough, but they, too, were victims of the shallow Saskatchewan. "The cable barely touched the steamboat," Dumont recalled years later. As the *Northcote* slipped by, the cable tore off a smokestack then slipped over the stern. The smokestack started a small fire that was quickly put out, and the *Northcote* drifted out of rifle range. The major in charge of the ground troops urged the *Northcote*'s captain to turn the boat around and head back upstream to join the battle, but the captain refused. Dumont left to fight the main army. He eventually lost that battle and the rebellion.

No side could claim victory in the only naval battle fought on the prairies. In fact, both sides should have declared defeat.

CHAPTER 3

PLANES

With Canadians' smarts, this country could rule the air.
If it weren't for the politicians.

The plane that wouldn't float, or fly

The first indication something wasn't right with the seaplane prototype was when it almost sank at the dock. Perhaps it was the just the heavy snow that had fallen the night before.

There was no reason just to abandon the Vickers Velos yet.

The Department of National Defence wanted a plane for photographic surveying, and manufacturer Canadian Vickers wanted to complete its contract. National Defence's original specifications, issued in 1926, called for a two-engine aircraft capable of converting from land to ski to seaplane and carrying a pilot, surveyor/navigator, and photographer. The photographer had to be able to shoot from a variety of angles, so the first versions of the plane had an elongated nose. The photographer would sit farthest up in the nose, followed by the surveyor, and then in back by the pilot. All of them were to sit in an open cockpit. Someone connected the idea of a ski-plane with the idea of an open cockpit and realized the poor crew would be trying to fly and shoot photographs in winter without any protection. So the cockpit was enclosed. A copilot was added to the arrangement and the photographer, pushed back into the plane, only had the ability to shoot straight down.

By the time the Velos was ready to fly, it was seriously overweight. Perhaps it was the new, more powerful engines installed. Or perhaps there was too much steel. Or perhaps it was just a bad design.

In any case, the machine was 786 kilograms heavier than expected. When snow fell the night of October 20, 1927 onto the Velos moored outside the Vickers plant, the plane almost sunk. Engineers went back to the drawing board and seven months later unveiled the new, better Velos, which was even heavier though presumably stronger.

A series of brave test pilots took the Velos into the air. It was more at home in the water.

Royal Canadian Air Force (RCAF) Flight Lieutenant R.S. Grandy flew the Velos in August 1928 and noted a few flight problems. The plane was so sluggish a pilot could barely fly it. The seat was broken from previous pilots straining against the controls. There was hardly any room to move around in the cabin because there were so many tubes bracing the plane together. The cabin doors led straight to the propellers, so anyone leaving while the propellers were going "would be chopped to pieces." Overall, Grandy wrote, "it is considered that this aircraft is most unsuitable for any operation carried out in the Royal Canadian Air Force." If he had to fly it again, Grandy said, he would do so under protest.

Grandy didn't have to worry about it. In late November 1928, the Velos was moored outside the Vickers plant when twenty-five centimetres of snow fell. By morning, the plane had sunk. The aircraft was raised and the engines salvaged.

Aviation historians K.M. Molson and H.A. Taylor say there's no clear answer why the Velos failed so miserably. A few months before the Velos sank, engineers realized a model built for wind tunnel testing had a tail almost a metre longer than the version that took to the air. One RCAF engineer blamed the design on a committee of bureaucrats trying to put too much into one plane.

It's unclear what the two-year exercise cost the RCAF and Canadian Vickers. Employees called the plane "The Dead Loss." Molson and Taylor, who have written an exhaustive study of all Canadian aircraft, awarded the Vickers Velos the honour of being the worst aircraft in our country's history.

Maybe if we build something ugly, they'll let us keep it

To summarize Canada's topnotch aeronautical developments of the 1950s: We developed North America's first commercial jetliner. The United States was shocked and envious. Jetliners were the future. The skies belonged to Canada. We scrapped the jetliner.

Then we developed the most advanced jet fighter in the world. It cost hundreds of millions of dollars. The skies belonged to Canada. We scrapped the fighter.

So we built a flying saucer … but that's another story.

The sad tale started after the Second World War, when Hawker-Siddley Aircraft of England bought a bomber-making company in Malton called Victory Aircraft. For several years the newly named company, A.V. Roe Canada, worked on a twin-engine, thirty-six-passenger jetliner for Trans Canada Air. On August 10, 1949 the Avro Jetliner took flight and launched Canada into the forefront of a new era of aviation.

Its first test flight from Toronto to New York in April 1950 made front-page news in *The New York Times*. "The Avro jetliner, the first turbojet transport plane ever flown in the United States, arrived yesterday at New York International Airport," *The New York Times* wrote. "The sleek new airliner received a prolonged welcome from the several hundred spectators."

Canada, U.S. commentators said, had proved to be ahead of the United States, which was still experimenting with jets. England had flown the world's first passenger jet only fourteen days earlier. "This should give our nation a good healthful kick in its placidity," wrote one U.S. reporter.

But the Jetliner was almost too far ahead of its time. Nobody seemed to trust it or know what to do with it. Some air traffic controllers reportedly refused to let the Jetliner land, fearing that the engines would spew fire all over the airport. Trans Canada Air cancelled its order for the passenger jets. Government officials said the jet wasn't well designed, although its designer won a U.S. award for the plane.

The United States Navy, Air Force and the RCAF expressed much interest but didn't offer any contracts. One U.S. airline company ordered four of the jetliners, but the Canadian government wouldn't let Avro fill the contract until it had built jet fighters. In 1951, work on the second Jetliner was stopped. The first was flown in air shows for a few years, then cut apart and scrapped in 1956.

Avro survived though, soon putting into production its jet fighter, the CF-100 Canuck. The two-seater turned into a popular and durable fighter for the RCAF.

But it wasn't perfect and by the early 1950s, the Canadian government was already looking for a more advanced fighter. The Soviet Union was developing a force of long-range bombers and the West needed jet interceptors. In 1954, Avro got approval to build a new supersonic, all-weather jet fighter. If the fighter met the Royal Canadian Air Force specifications — high speed, with good manoeuvrability, long range, and heavily armed — it would be the most advanced in the world. Only four years later, the first Arrow was rolled out of the shops at Malton. Test flights of the CF-105 Arrow pleased pilots and thrilled the 14,000 employees of Avro. With its swept-back wings and needle-sharp nose, the Arrow looked like the future.

But costs were much higher than the Liberal government expected. In the late 1950s, military leaders began thinking that the greatest threat was not long-range bombers, but the Intercontinental Ballistic Missiles (ICBMs) the Soviet Union was going to send our way. Jets that intercepted bombers seemed kind of useless when the skies were filled with missiles. Besides, army and navy brass weren't happy about the air force getting more and more money out of a shrinking defence budget.

Although the Liberal government fretted over the Arrow, it wasn't until Conservative John Diefenbaker was elected prime minister in 1957 that the jet fighter ran into serious trouble. The farm boy from Saskatchewan was going to clean house and save money, and the Arrows were cluttering up the toy box. Each Arrow was supposed to cost $1.5 million but it was looking like each one would cost about $9 million. The RCAF was told to justify a $200 million project that was quickly rising to about $500 million. (Reports on the final costs for the Arrow vary from $400 million to $700 million). Well, for one thing, the RCAF said, the Arrow could attack missiles, probably better than the U.S. Bomarc missiles under consideration for Canada. Diefenbaker didn't buy it. Instead, he cancelled the Arrow program on February 20, 1959. More than 13,000 workers were immediately laid off. Eventually many of the top engineers left Canada for the United States and Britain. Diefenbaker ordered the destruction of all the Arrows, technical drawings, designs — anything that had to do with the jet fighter. Not only did Canada lose the jobs and the jet, but also all the knowledge built up over the course of the project. And a souvenir of a heady time.

The Bomarc missile, by the way, was a flop. Canada bought the nuclear missiles. But Diefenbaker did not want nuclear weapons on Canadian soil. Nor did many Canadians. So the nose cones of the missiles were filled with sand. Diefenbaker's government barely won re-election in 1962. The controversy over nuclear weapons and support for the United States led to a non-confidence vote and new election in 1963. This time, the Liberals earned a minority government. The same thing happened again in 1965. His own party kicked Diefenbaker out in 1968. He died eleven years later in Ottawa. His body was sent home to Saskatchewan by train.

Years later, the Arrow still sparks debate. Movies, magazines, radio shows, documentaries, books, and articles discuss the Arrow. Rival teams near London are vying to salvage a scale model of the Arrow from the bottom of Lake Ontario. The Arrow is either the greatest Canadian mistake of the century, or the most overblown Canadian story of the century. Diefenbaker killed it because it was a Liberal plan and the arrogance of Avro executives got on his nerves. No, he killed it because it was a waste of money. Either way we lost a great technological edge, our national dream, no less. Maybe we had no business spending that kind of money on a jet fighter in the first place. The debate goes on and on, and will ever more.

The biggest problem with the Arrow? We just can't get over it.

It's a bird, it's a plane . . . it's a flying hubcap

Sometimes an idea comes along that's so good, and so fraught with risks, Canada happily shares it with its friends. Then everyone can enjoy the failure.

Such was the case with the Avrocar, a flying saucer developed in Canada for the U.S. military by John Frost, an ingenious designer with many successes to his credit over his lifetime.

Born in England in 1915, Frost came to Canada in 1947 as the chief designer of Avro Canada's fighter jet project, the XC-100, the predecessor to the Avro Arrow.

Frost wasn't keen on the design of the XC-100, and in 1952, he set up the Special Projects Group for Avro. Frost headed a hand-picked team of designers and researchers in a building at Avro's headquarters in Malton,

Ontario kept hidden from the rest of the workers by guards and secret passes.

Frost's team immediately began work on a new kind of engine and design that would allow a supersonic aircraft to execute vertical take-off and landing, or VTOL, and reach speeds of 2,400 kilometres per hour. The shape was like a giant stingray, almost a saucer with a blunt back end. Frost made forty-five centimetre models of his saucers, and shooting compressed air through them, flew them around the lab.

Although the first prototypes weren't truly round, word got out about Avro's flying saucer experiments.

The second stage of the design used the true saucer shape and by then, late 1953, the U.S. military was showing interest. A year later, Canada bailed out of the project because of an estimated $100 million development cost. In all, Canada spent about $2 million in research before handing the project over to the United States Air Force (USAF).

Money was no object to the U.S. military.

The United States commissioned two studies of the saucer, one mildly positive and one strongly negative. But hey, this was the era of flying saucers and UFOs and the race with the Soviet Union to control the world. In the minds of U.S. military leaders, a supersonic flying saucer was worth trying.

The flying saucer would work basically like this: Air would be sucked in through ducts circling the upper surface and thrust downward for vertical takeoff. There was no need for landing gear because of the ground cushion produced by the downward exhaust.

During flight, air would be sucked in by ducts on the forward section of the disc, and thrust through ducts around the outside edge of the saucer. The thrust would control the aircraft. A cockpit in the centre of the saucer was surrounded by the fuel cells and a turborotor.

The project split into two versions in 1957. The USAF wanted an armed, twenty-five metre, circular-winged fighter jet with a top speed of 1,600 kilometres per hour. The U.S. Army heard about the saucer and asked Avro to design a flying saucer that could takeoff and land vertically, skim the ground or fly at high altitudes, go faster than helicopters, and with its rounded surface, slip by radar systems. Drawings show the flying jeeps as skimming around rocks to blast away tanks.

Both saucer projects suffered when the Canadian government cancelled the Avro Arrow project on February 20, 1959. In the jumble of layoffs, the design team for the saucer fighter changed and took on men who favoured more traditional styles of aircraft. The new team pushed to drop the saucer shape while the USAF pushed back, insisting the saucer was the way to go. The United States let the funding for that project run out in 1960.

Frost, meanwhile, more or less abandoned the saucer fighter and focused on the Avrocar. He had dreams of not only the Avrocar, but a family Avrowagon (the recreational off-road vehicle, so to speak), the Avroflier, and the troop transport and fighting machine, the Avrocruiser.

The Avrocar, said company chair Sir Roy Dobson at the October 1959 annual meeting, "could well be a breakthrough in the advancement of aeronautical science."

The United States tested that theory with two prototypes in 1959. During the first flights, the Avrocar was tethered to the ground but finally, on December 5, 1959, test pilot Spud Potocki took off in the flying saucer … sort of. The Avrocar reached an altitude of one metre. In subsequent tests, it never flew any higher. That wasn't its biggest problem. Although the Avrocar could zip around at thirty kilometres per hour, stop quickly, and handle well just slightly above the ground, as soon as the saucer reached a half metre, it was difficult to control. The saucer had no rudder or tail fin like traditional aircraft and the side thrusters didn't allow for the same kind of control. Test showed that in the air, the saucer would dip and twist, what Avro engineers called "hubcapping," the same effect as a hubcap thrown through the air.

Try as they might, U.S. and Avro engineers couldn't figure out how to control the saucer in flight. Today's computers might have solved the problem, suggests Bill Zuk, author of *Canada's Flying Saucer*, the most complete account of the Avrocar. The development of the Avrocar might have continued, had it not been for the cost of redesigning and the fact that helicopters, which did the same job, grew more advanced. In December 1961, the U.S. funding for the Avrocar ended. It cost that country about $7.5 million.

"It was," a U.S. defence official confided to the *Financial Post*, "probably just a little too far out."

CHAPTER 4

TRAINS

A criss-crossing of railways from sea to sea became Canada's national dream. Or in some cases a nightmare.

If it works for moving cases of beer and grocery boxes, why not entire railway trains?

That's the simple thinking behind one of Canada's greatest inventions that never was, a failure attributable only to the stubbornness, paucity of imagination, and blindness of our leaders.

In 1874, D.R. Gouldie proposed in a lengthy and fantastic pamphlet that the country's struggling railway system had to be supplanted by his "Perpetual Sleigh Road." He didn't get the idea from beer or grocery stores, of course, but from watching ice-boats run over the frozen surface of Lake Ontario.

"It was while watching with intense admiration, some ten years ago, the swift and graceful motions of the ice-boats, as they went sweeping over the glassy surface of Lake Ontario, that the idea first sprung up in my mind, that if it were only possible to form a 'permanent way' as smooth, level and firm as the frozen lake, we would have perfection, or as near it as man could ask, in a railway."

He came up with the perpetual sleigh road, "simply a mechanical substitute for the frozen river and the ice-boat, though unlike most other imitations, it will be found very much superior to the original."

Gouldie proposed building a track of rollers across the country, upon which train cars on sleigh runners would zip at faster speeds and lower costs than the traditional railway. Posts would be sunk into the ground below the frost level, with about half a metre above the surface. Beams would then be attached to the posts, and lubricated rollers or steel wheels would be attached to the beams. The engine of this new style of train would have a wheel that rested below the rollers on a track. It would pull train cars that had not wheels on their bottoms, but sleigh runners. Instead of wheels running on track, the sleigh runners would zoom on top of the rollers.

"A ride in a car, on this plan, will more resemble a sail on a perfectly smooth sea, or a sleigh ride over well packed snow, than the jolting, thumping, swaying motion of our railway cars," Gouldie proposed.

And there was even better news. "I wish it to be distinctly understood," Gouldie noted, "that for long journeys (say across continent) and where cheap freight is (as it must always be) a matter of vital importance to producers and the public, that wind power should be used, wherever practicable."

His sleigh road would cost 70 percent less to build than traditional railways, Gouldie promised. Instead of blasting through hills, draining ditches, or filling in hollows to make an even grade, engineers could just build longer or shorter posts to keep the perpetual sleigh road level. Because the cars on the perpetual sleigh road would be lighter and wouldn't jostle against the rails, expensive bridges could be replaced by steel ropes holding the wood that supported the rollers. And when the train engine travelled over a stream or hollow, its driving wheel would be lifted so the cars could "slide sweetly and smoothly by [their] previous acquired momentum."

Even before he described his sleigh road, Gouldie spent forty-five pages dissecting the problems of traditional railways, such as the cost of construction and the dangers of snow and ice on the tracks. The weight of the engine and the train cars lessened the efficiency and raised the costs of transport. Friction makes the engine work but slows the cars, so why have them on the same track? Gouldie posed. The cars rattled and move sideways, damaging the tracks and making the ride unpleasant for passengers. The simplest fault or miscue could send engines, cars, freight, and passengers tumbling off the tracks.

His cars couldn't leave the track, and the "pleasant sliding motion … will allow of the passengers sleeping, reading or writing undisturbed by the dreadful thumping and swinging motion now experienced on the railways, while the absence of the terrible noise now endured will permit conversation to be carried on with comfort and convenience."

Because his roadway would be elevated, snow and water would not delay trains. In towns and cities, the perpetual sleigh road could be built high enough to allow traffic to go underneath.

Gouldie backed up his claims extensively and went into great, mind-numbing detail about everything from friction and finances. Aside from the question of whether his perpetual sleigh road would even work, Gouldie himself posed the other key query of his lengthy proposal: "Why this repetition, this amplification and superfluous explanation?" Because his idea is so important and radical, Gouldie answered.

"I have, therefore, aimed to present certain facts and ideas, in a number of places and in quite a variety of aspects, in the hope that should they fail to impress you on one page, you may comprehend and appreciate them in another."

Gouldie approached engineers and mechanics to assess his idea. One hopes their replies were mere efforts to get Gouldie to stop talking. "So unanimous has been the commendation of the idea," Gouldie wrote, "that I have been sometimes tempted to think they were hardly sincere."

All he needed was $150,000 for a test road. And some help overcoming mixed metaphors: "I have launched the idea upon the great ocean of human thought," Gouldie concluded, "confident that it will take root and bear fruit for the world's benefit."

The great ocean of human thought let Gouldie's idea sink without a sound. His proposal appears in a letter to the federal government seeking a patent and money. The federal government didn't offer any money, so Gouldie tried to gather private investors. He printed up a pamphlet in Toronto containing the full range of his ideas on the subject and offering any engineers or investors a chance to view his proposal. Gouldie sold each pamphlet for a dollar. He made more money from the pamphlets than he did the sleigh road.

And that was a shame. Each roller or set of rollers on his railway would have been about one and a half metres from the next. That works out to about 650 rollers a kilometre. Even if the railway went in a straight line from the Atlantic to the Pacific Ocean, there would have been at least five million rollers spinning across our great land, with sleigh cars crisscrossing it like the wind. Gordon Lightfoot could have written *The Great Canadian Sleigh Road Trilogy*. Pierre Berton could have written about the pounding of the Last Roller. We could have had one giant beer case roller belt running from sea to shining sea. What could be more Canadian than that?

We need all the curves to make the train go 'round

The Dominion government sent Thomas Swinyard to Prince Edward Island in 1874 to assess the railway before the government took it over. Travelling by train on the few completed sections, inspecting the stations, fences, rolling stock, and examining the contract, Swinyard arrived at some surprising conclusions, when he arrived at all.

The ninety-kilometre trip from Summerside to Alberton, on what was supposed to be a completed section of the railway, took eleven and a half hours, "we having frequently to stop and pack up the road bed in soft places and at culverts and rivers before the engine could pass over." On his entire

trip through the province, Swinyard found only one real gravel bed holding up the tracks. The road bed on the western
section wasn't built high enough and the work trains bringing equipment and men were bending the rails. The fences
along the tracks that were to keep cattle away were poorly
built, with some posts simply stuck into the ground.

Of the new station at Summerside, Swinyard reported, "a
worse location it could hardly be possible to conceive." The
province's main highway crossed the tracks between the
engine and car sheds and the passenger station. People driving their horses to the wharves or station would have to jostle with engines and rail cars shunting back and forth along
the rail line. To add to the confusion, the station was built at
right angles to three wharves with their three roads also crossing the tracks. All the goods and people going to and from
the wharf had to cross the tracks near the station. "To
increase the danger, the station is approached in both directions by share curves," Swinyard noted. The western curve
was on a downhill grade, and houses blocked the view of the
busiest wharf road from the conductor. The farthest train
crews could see ahead as they came into Summerside, often in
the fog or rain, was forty yards.

"Crowning all this," Swinyard said, the tracks were so
close to shipyards, sparks from the engine had already set
fires in the wood chips and shavings and threatened to burn
entire buildings down. Many of the other stations along the
track had no waiting rooms, no washrooms, and no places
for stationmasters to sleep, quite a failing in the days when
they were supposed to be on call for emergencies twenty-
four hours a day. Between Charlottetown and Summerside,
most of the eighteen stations were built on an incline.
Starting in one direction and stopping in the other became
more challenging.

If nothing else, however, there were plenty of stations. No one in Prince Edward Island had to go far to climb aboard a train. On a track 320 kilometres long, the contractor built seventy stations — on average, one station for every four and a half kilometres.

No one had to go out of their way to get to a station, either. The line is "very circuitous," Swinyard noted. An entire one-third of the tracks laid down were curves. An engineer replying to Swinyard's report argued there were so many curves because the contractor was trying to avoid the rough terrain and creek gullies of Prince Edward Island and save money. Swinyard had his own idea about the many curves and gradients that were built. The contractors, Collingwood Schreiber for the main line and Schreiber and Burpee for the branch lines, were paid by the mile. And the route of much of the track was left up to — you guessed it — the contractor. With about $14,000 a mile coming from the government, it's no wonder the track wandered so much.

"This power given to the Contractors, combined with the contract having been let at a certain price per mile without any definite limit as to length, was certainly not one to ensure the attainment of the most perfect alignments and gradients," Swinyard wrote. Even the most honest contractor would prefer to put down a curved track to avoid an obstacle rather than undertake costly grade work that would cut his profits. Matters weren't helped by the politicians, Swinyard noted. "There is no doubt that political and local influences greatly tend to increase the unnecessary length of the railway."

The unfinished, station-heavy, and curvy railway put the province $3 million in debt. That's where the happy ending to this story comes. Prince Edward Island had rejected Confederation in 1867 because voters saw no financial gain in the deal. Seven years later, between the railway debt and the cost of buying the island from absentee landlords, the province had few options. The new Dominion of Canada offered to assume the debt and hand over money to pay off the landlords. In return, Prince Edward Island and its wandering railway joined Confederation.

It's either that, or cut Nova Scotia adrift

To a ship captain, Nova Scotia is an example of poor planning. Continental drift, God, the Creator, whatever — the province sticks way out in the middle of the Atlantic Ocean.

Ships heading from the richest country in the world, the United States, to another of the richest countries in the world, Canada, have to veer way out into the ocean to get around Nova Scotia and into the Gulf of St. Lawrence. All because of a twenty-seven-kilometre wide strip of land linking Nova Scotia to New Brunswick called the Chignecto Isthmus.

If Nova Scotia weren't there, or at least if it had the grace to be an island, ships could hug the coast and save hundreds of kilometres in travel and fuel.

As early as 1622, someone in the New World took a look at the isthmus and thought a canal was a good idea. In 1825, the government of New Brunswick calculated the cost at a whopping, in those days, $7.1 million. One of the biggest problems was the high tides of the Bay of Fundy to the south compared to the lower ones in the Northumberland Strait that leads to the St. Lawrence.

Sixty years later, the cost seemed less prohibitive. The Maritimes were sailing high on shipbuilding and trading. And along came Henry Ketchum of New Brunswick. A commanding man, large in size and energy, Ketchum was no slouch at engineering or building. With several Maritime railway projects behind him, Ketchum helped build the San Paulo Railway in Brazil. While he was there, he got the idea for a ship railway from a British engineer. He carried the idea back to Canada, enthused enough to create a plan by 1875 for a ship railway across the Chignecto Isthmus.

There were setbacks, perhaps clues that the idea wasn't going to be easy to implement. His first plans were destroyed in a fire in 1877 in Saint John. Ketchum carried on, and by the 1880s had completed a survey, ignited government interest, and raised a $150,000 a year subsidy from the government for twenty-five years, as long as the railway was up and running in seven.

The government and newspapers praised the ship railway. The construction costs would be a third of a canal's. The Chignecto Marine Transport Railway Company was incorporated in England and £650,000 were raised. The contract, signed in 1886, was sent on the ship *Oregon*, which sank off the coast of New York. Fortunately, or unfortunately for Ketchum, the mailbag containing the contract was recovered by divers and sent to Ottawa.

Work began in 1888, and the ship railway seemed destined to become one of Canada's greatest engineering feats. Here's how it was supposed to work:

Ships would enter one of the two basins at either end. To get an idea of the size, the Bay of Fundy Basin was to be 150 metres long and ninety metres wide, with a gate eighteen metres wide and nine metres high to keep water in when the tides of Fundy went out. Each ship, as heavy as 200 tons, would be floated over top of an iron cradle and raised by hydraulic presses onto the rails. Then a locomotive would pull the ship the twenty-seven kilometres over land on a double track, sixty wheels under the cradle on each side to distribute the weight. At fifteen kilometres per hour for the largest ship, it would take about two hours to raise each vessel, ship it across, and deposit it in the waters of the other basin.

The project was largely Canadian. The heavy rails were built in England, but the locomotives were constructed in Kingston and the cradle wheels in Saint John.

For the next three years, teams of men with horses, steam shovels, hand shovels, and picks graded the rail bed across the isthmus, through rock and over bogs that were eighteen metres deep. In one, crews had to dump rock fill into the bog and up another six metres before it settled to the level of the rail bed. By 1891, less than two kilometres of rail bed was unfinished, near Tidnish, Nova Scotia, where workers were busy building a culvert to divert a river and allow the riverbed to be filled in for the railway. Two-thirds of the fill had been dumped into the riverbed but the tides had eroded the filling. The filling collapsed and men, horses, and machinery fell into the riverbed in a mess of shouts. No one was hurt.

But in July 1891, with all of the bed but one and a half kilometres graded, twenty kilometres of track laid, and the locomotives ready, the project stopped.

It came down to money and politics, of course. The company had difficulty floating the rest of the bonds it needed to fund the project, which so far was estimated to have cost $700,000 with another $1.5 million needed. In 1895, officials with the company asked the government for an extension to complete the railway. The government refused, perhaps under pressure from Halifax's rich merchants. If the railway succeeded, Halifax would lose business from all the ships that had to go around Nova Scotia.

For years, buildings, machinery, and the walls in the basins survived. Eventually tides, time, and workers knocked most of it away. Ketchum died in 1896, at the age of fifty-seven.

If the Chignecto ship railway had succeeded, it might have changed the world. Engineers planning the Panama Canal were closely following the proceedings in Nova Scotia. If the Chignecto project worked, they would build not a canal through the Americas, but a giant ship railway. Canada could have inspired the world.

Or maybe not. There is a ship railway at the narrow rapids called Big Chute about an hour and a half north of Toronto on the Trent-Severn Waterway. The rail car takes pleasure boats in a sling, then carries them over the rocks and rapids to the next lake. It's a thrilling sight, but almost every year, sometimes for days at a time, boat traffic along the Trent-Severn Waterway stops cold, because the railway has broken down.

If there's a train, there has to be a tunnel, right?

Not necessarily, but that didn't stop Brockville from building what is now the oldest railway tunnel in Canada.

In 1852, Brockville agreed to participate in building a railway line — the Brockville and Ottawa Railway — to connect Ottawa with the St. Lawrence River.

There were at least two ways of linking the riverfront with the inland rail lines. One was to create a tunnel running half a kilometre under the city. The other, favoured by the railway's supervising engineer, Samuel Keefer, was to build a railway line through what was then the western part of the city. It was said this could be done in half the time and at half the expense of the tunnel.

So they built the tunnel. Because a tunnel kept the trains out of sight.

Started in 1854 and officially opened in 1860, the tunnel was used until 1954.

It was an aesthetic success, but as Thomas F. McIlwraith, in his book, *Looking for Old Ontario*, notes, it "hardly reflected sound business practice."

In 1983, the city bought the tunnel and in 1992 both the north and south entrances were designated as historic sites. There is now a museum at the south end of the tunnel.

Diesel, schmiesel, the future's in steam

When Canadian National Railways (CNR) Engine Number 9000 rolled out of Kingston on November 28, 1928, the era of the steam locomotive had ended. The dawn of the diesel age had begun. The future pulled into the station, then left without anybody aboard.

Only four years earlier, CNR had sent engineer C.E. "Ned" Brooks to Scotland to examine diesel engines. They weren't well-known in North America and only a few rail services were experimenting with the new power. Brooks found a diesel engine used for airships that could be converted to trains. The next year, fourteen diesel-electric cars were built for CNR to carry a couple of coaches on branch lines to compete with buses. The cars looked more like trams or today's commuter passenger trains than locomotives.

On November 1, 1925, CNR put the diesel to a real test. Engine Number 15820 left Montréal and arrived in Vancouver in a quick sixty-seven hours. Three years later, Brooks unveiled the first real diesel locomotives, Engines Number 9000 and 9001. They were built to pull cars across the country, unlike the smaller, self-propelled diesel trams. The two engines were put on the run between Montréal and Toronto, making the 530-kilometre trip in seven hours and forty minutes. The diesel engines were proving to be more powerful and faster than steam engines. It appeared CNR was well on its way to diesel, years before anyone else in North America.

But there were doubts about spending all that money, especially during the Depression. After years of battling federal politicians over spending money on CNR, Sir Henry Thornton was fired as president in 1932. His replacement, Samuel Hungerford, began to make deep cuts in the railway and slashed spending. Thornton died a year later, as did Brooks. The two deaths, the Depression, and Hungerford's retrenchment of service put the brakes on converting steam to diesel. In the mid-1930s, the United States began putting diesel engines into regular service. Left behind, CNR didn't begin replacing steam with diesel until the 1940s and wasn't finished until the 1960s.

The people running CNR's great rival, Canadian Pacific Railway (CPR), weren't much smarter. In 1928, even as CNR showed off its new diesel locomotives, CPR began rebuilding bridges along its Montréal to Toronto route. The bridges had to be stronger because CPR was embarking on a program of building bigger and more streamlined steam engines to haul greater loads. The future, CPR brass figured, was in steam.

The mountains are nice, but it sure is hot in here

Canadian Pacific Railway started to take advantage of the tourist trade in the 1890s by adding observation cars for its western run through the mountains. The first cars were simply open passenger cars, with no roof, waist-high sides, and safety bars between the sides and roof supports.

This was so popular that CPR managers decided to enclose the observation cars in 1902. The first, Car Number 517, had a cupola roof, like a caboose, that offered views all

National Archives of Canada/PA-209307

Call it a moving greenhouse. The first observation cars Canadian Pacific Railway tried, such as Car 84, tended to bake travellers.

around. It also featured upholstered chairs that revolved to allow views through all the windows. This car, perhaps the world's first dome car, was such a success, CPR decided to launch a whole line of improved observation cars. The next three included windows in the ceilings and came out in 1906. The older observation cars were also refitted.

Unfortunately, the windows in the ceilings turned the cars into roasting ovens. Passengers baked like plants in a greenhouse. Within seven years, all the cars were scrapped. Several years later, CPR went back to the first style of observation cars, without any roof at all. Perhaps it was the rain or the cinders from the engine, but by 1923, not even the open cars were running. It took the inventions of polarized glass and air conditioning before CPR could introduce a successful dome car in 1953.

Where did we put the locomotives?

Spend $2.5 million in order to make $65,000. That was the British Columbia government's approach to building a commuter rail system in the 1980s. Oh yes, and don't build the rail system, either.

The Social Credit (Socred) government bought five locomotives in 1981 for a commuter rail project in Vancouver, paying $374,500. The General Motors locomotives came from the Quebec North Shore and Labrador Railway, so before they could make it out west, they were moved to the Ontario Northland Rail Yard in North Bay, Ontario. From 1981 to 1984, the Urban Transit Development Company — the crown corporation that was going to build the commuter system — spent $1.3 million updating and fixing the locomotives. It also cost about $20,000 a year to insure and store the units.

The locomotives, though, were stored outside and unguarded. Vandals tore some of them up. The cold damaged the engines, which, despite the $1.3 million, were never winterized.

In the meantime, the government also spent $316,000 on three generators to heat the passenger cars the engines were going to pull. Fortunately, the passenger cars were never bought or leased. Unfortunately, the generators were damaged in an accident at the Ontario Northland yards. (The generators were eventually used for another BC Rail service, Skytram, then sold in 1994 for $15,000.)

By 1988, it was clear there wasn't going to be a commuter system, at least not yet. The chairperson of the transit board warned the Socred minister of municipal affairs to sell the locomotives. They'd already cost $2.1 million to keep idle 4,800 kilometres away. The locomotives, the bureaucrats figured, could get $500,000 on the market. The

Socreds ignored that advice and the advice of others over the next several years.

When the New Democratic Party (NDP) came into power a few years later, it took a look at the locomotives. Not only were they damaged, they were under-powered. Train experts said the locomotives could have easily pulled the passenger trains in a commuter system's early years. The NDP sold the units for $65,000 to an Ontario rail broker, who then promptly resold two of them to the New Brunswick Southern Railway for double the price. All he had to do was add batteries and to one, a new air-brake system. Adding up repairs, storage, insurance, and interest on borrowed money, the five locomotives ended up costing the British Columbia government $2.5 million. And they never made it farther west than the middle of Ontario.

CHAPTER 5

AUTOMOBILES

Few nations have embraced the automobile like Canada with its honking big landscape. We weren't always heading in the right direction, though.

Thomas Turnbull sat in the seat of the Andromonon Carriage and took hold of the handles on either side. Machinery three years in the making sat hidden beneath him. Two strong men held the car in front of him. And all around, the curious had gathered on a cold January day to watch.

Turnbull pushed and pulled the levers and the two men pushed against the front of the car. Try as they might, the men couldn't resist the force of the machinery and had to give way. The carriage moved forward.

"Every Man His Own Horse," declared the Saint John, New Brunswick *Morning News* two days later on January 31, 1851. "Highly Important Invention — Railroads About to Be Superseded."

Turnbull, an ordinary carpenter, had stood the world on its head. He had invented a carriage that required no horses, no steam, and only the slight motion of two hands to propel. He named it Andro, for "man," and Monon, for "alone." About 300 people, including the *Morning News* reporter, had witnessed for themselves that man alone could propel the carriage.

"The carriage is of the ordinary size and appearance, except that it contains a single wheel in front. The rider propels himself along by seizing hold of the two upright handles, placed on either side of the seat, which he moves backward and forward, as if in the act of rowing a boat — and yet so great is the motive power of the machinery, that after the vehicle is started, it requires scarcely any exertion to keep it in motion," the reporter wrote.

Whatever it was that made the thing move was hidden, probably because Turnbull had not patented the system yet. It certainly didn't appear to be a steam boiler. More likely the two levers operated a system of flywheels and gears that propelled the car. No one ever did find out.

It was too cold and snowy on that January day to test the Andromonon Carriage outside, but Turnbull promised it would travel fifty kilometres per hour on level streets, the same speed as railway locomotives.

"As soon as the carriage is more fully tested on the street, every man in Saint John who can afford to pay thirty pounds, which is almost the cost of it, may keep his carriage and act as his own horse, free of all expenses," the *Morning News* reporter enthused. Doctors would especially benefit, because they were on the move so much. Imagine what could be done with a few men or a larger machine — one or two could easily carry a dozen passengers.

The *Chatham Gleaner* was equally enthusiastic about Turnbull and his invention two weeks later. "He has the most perfect control over the carriage," wrote a reporter in the February 11,1851 edition. "He can drive it backwards or stop it at once when at its full speed."

The *Morning News* suggested the province exhibit the Andromonon at the 1851 Great Exhibition in London, saying: "There have been inventions of a similar description to this… but they have always failed for want of machinery correct and powerful enough." Instead, the province sent over some samples of fish and lumber. Perhaps road tests were unsatisfactory or Turnbull could not raise the money to make improvements. He had already spent three years and a lot of money on the machine.

It's not clear what eventually happened to the Andromonon Carriage. But it did not supersede the railway.

It didn't go far, but it was good on gas

The three-wheeled vehicle Tom Doherty built in Sarnia, Ontario in 1895 consisted of a simple engine, and it produced a simple result.

Doherty was an entrepreneur who built a foundry in Watford, Ontario then moved to Sarnia in 1882. In the small city beside the St. Clair River, he created the Doherty Manufacturing Co. Ltd., which made stoves.

But producing stoves every day wasn't much of a challenge for Doherty. He grew interested in the horseless carriages that were making news. Inventors before him had experimented with steam and gas, but Doherty had a better idea — one that wouldn't cost much and was a lot quieter. He developed a three-wheeled vehicle that was steered by a tiller and propelled by a large coil spring. The clockwork spring was attached to the rear axle. With a lot of muscle and sweat, the driver or his helper wound up the spring with a lever. Then he released the lever and the spring uncoiled. The "springmobile" quickly reached speeds of three to five kilometres an hour. But it only travelled a block or two, then it stopped.

So Doherty turned to fuel. With the help of a machinist named Tom Montgomery, he built a gas automobile. The car's engine had two pistons working in one cylinder, instead of the traditional one piston per cylinder. When one piston moved out of the cylinder, the other moved in. One piston was attached to the crankshaft and the other to a rocker arm, also presumably attached to the crankshaft.

Doherty's first car with the novel engine was banned from the streets after it frightened a horse, throwing a woman from her carriage and breaking her arm. Doherty's response to the ban? Build a bigger car. He patented his opposing piston engine and built a two-cylinder, four-piston model. But no one wanted to buy his new engine because, despite his claims to the contrary, it was noisier than the previous one. Doherty eventually gave up on cars and turned to politics, and he became mayor of Sarnia.

The mechanic is working on horses until Monday

If it's Thursday, we can take the car.

If it's Friday, we'll have to take the horse.

So went travel planning for Prince Edward Island drivers from 1913 to 1919. Even though a steam-operated horseless carriage had appeared on the island in 1866, the province stumbled toward an acceptance of the automobile long after everyone else in Canada. By 1907, seven drivers had cars operating on the island. But seven was plenty for many islanders. They scared and occasionally hurt horses, alarmed gentlewomen and good children, and spit out noise and smoke in equal increments. Only the rich could afford them, anyway.

People everywhere complained about the noisy automobile when it was first introduced, but few politicians listened as closely as those in Prince Edward Island. On March 26, 1908, members of the provincial legislature voted unanimously to ban the car from the peaceful island. The handful of automobile owners in the province appealed to the province's Supreme Court. When that court upheld the law, they tried the Supreme Court of Canada. The higher court refused to intervene, but auto fanatics did not give up. Citing studies that showed Prince Edward Island was losing motoring tourists to other Maritime provinces, they pressured the provincial government to alter the ban.

The province compromised in 1913, passing legislation allowing motoring on Mondays, Wednesdays, and Thursdays.

The system allowed regular folk to head safely to the market on Tuesday and Friday, the stores on Saturday, and church on Sunday. The new legislation had to be accepted by plebiscite in individual constituencies. Residents in urban centres, such as Charlottetown and Summerside, voted to allow automobiles three days a week. Residents in rural constituencies voted against any compromise. That meant the drivers of the twenty-six registered cars in the province had to watch where they were going, and when. If a vehicle broke down on a Thursday, the driver had to wait until Monday to drive it home. And getting caught was serious business. The penalty for an infraction was a $500 fine or six months in jail.

The First World War helped change the rules. Trucks and cars were needed to move troops and by the end of the war in 1918, the number of registered vehicles had jumped to 303. That same year, despite lingering disgust with automobiles, the province rescinded the Automobile Act.

It took years for Prince Edward Island to catch up with the rest of the country in terms of the number of car drivers, losing a lot of money attached to the automobile business in the meantime. The first paved road wasn't finished until 1934, when the island's long-suffering car owners — 7,000 of them by then — could finally look forward to a smooth ride.

Just sign here, no need to look under the hood

Oh, but it was a beautiful car. Wing doors. Aerodynamic lines. Hot orange and cool green colours. The 1970s personified.

Did it matter that the doors stuck or leaked? That the show model had no radiator? That the hydraulic doors were secretly hooked up to a generator beneath the floor? That no one knew how to fix the car?

Only if you were a grumpy New Brunswick taxpayer. Or someone who expected the Bricklin to run.

For a couple of years in the 1970s, before anyone discovered the truth, the Bricklin seemed destined to revolutionize the automobile industry, bring New Brunswick into the world of the Big Three car companies, and offer consumers a safe and really, really cool car — so cool even *Playboy* magazine wrote about it.

New Brunswick's dalliance with making sports cars began with American Malcolm Bricklin, a promoter and car salesman whose hobby seemed to be collecting creditors and lawsuits. In the early 1970s, with little more experience than test driving Subarus, Bricklin decided to design and sell a new sports car. He built a prototype in 1972, made a short movie about it, then raised $950,000 from banks in New York and Philadelphia in order to turn the prototype into a consumer vehicle. But Bricklin needed a factory. He first tried to get the Quebec government to contribute $7 million in financing and open a factory there. Quebec officials, eyeing a consultant's report that said Bricklin didn't have enough experience, turned him down.

Undaunted, Bricklin then went to New Brunswick, home of the federal-provincial development group, Multiplex Corporation. Multiplex studied the idea for three weeks, watched the short movie, and concluded, with enthusiasm, that 264 jobs could be created at a Saint John plant, eventually producing 32,000 cars a year. Each car would cost a consumer less than $5,000 to buy, still returning 18 to 29 percent on the province's investment.

The federal government's Department of Regional Economic Expansion (DREE) was invited to join in, for a mere $4 million. The federal government balked, worried that a federally subsidized plant would break the rules of the

Auto Pact and annoy the Big Three automakers. DREE eventually agreed to a loan, as long as a majority of the plant's owners were Canadians.

New Brunswick premier Richard Hatfield was much more enthusiastic. He saw in the project the chance for his province to build a beautiful car and become a player in the auto industry. In 1973, he announced the province would guarantee a loan of almost $3 million and buy the majority of shares in Bricklin for $500,000. Bricklin would get another $1 million from the bank.

There was one small problem. Bricklin didn't know how to build the car.

Okay, two small problems. The head office was in Arizona, the design shop in Michigan, the plant making body parts in Minto, New Brunswick, the assembly plant in Saint John, and the accounting office in New York.

No wait, there were three small problems. Bricklin kept hiring family members who didn't get along with the managers who were supposed to run the company.

Of course, there was also the fact no one had ever bonded acrylic to fibreglass, a key feature of the car. And the fact the hydraulics on the doors didn't work. And Bricklin's habit of buying machinery and raw materials just because they were on sale, whether they matched the design or not. And his high-flying lifestyle and luxurious new offices in Arizona. And the old debts he had to pay off from other ventures.

But who's counting?

The car was supposed to be in production by September 1973, but the deadline had to be extended to the end of the year. The startup costs jumped from $6.5 million to $16 million.

It was all too much for Jean de Villers, a top Bricklin executive in Canada. De Villers resigned in October 1973. He called Premier Hatfield to give him the straight goods on Bricklin. Surely the premier would listen. Surely he could sort things out.

Quoted in the book, *Bricklin*, by H.A. Fredericks, de Villers told Hatfield he was resigning.

Hatfield asked, "Have you told the board?"

"Yes," said de Villers.

"Okay," Hatfield said incisively, "goodbye."

Things didn't get much better over the winter of 1973–74. Workers at the design plant in Livonia, Michigan, frustrated by problems with the door and Bricklin's unwillingness to make design changes, planned a palace coup. They hoped to convince New Brunswick to build the Bricklin car without Bricklin the man. They locked up the engineering files so he couldn't take them away when the rebellion took place. But before the workers could get to Hatfield, Bricklin learned of the plan and quickly fired the ringleader.

Meanwhile, the project was running out of money. So the New Brunswick government increased its loan guarantee from $2.8 million to $4 million. DREE announced a loan guarantee worth $2.7 million and the First Pennsylvania Bank gave Bricklin a $3 million credit line. Bricklin Canada — whose biggest shareholder was the province of New Brunswick — also had to give the bank another $1 million in a cash deposit.

Ah, but what's a few more million dollars when you've got a hot car? At media events from New York to Las Vegas in 1974, the Bricklin created a huge buzz. Of course the car bodies of the three prototypes unveiled at a New York show in the spring of 1974 were made by hand, because technicians still didn't know how to bond the fibreglass and acrylic. One of the cars had no radiator. One had to be driven at only fifty-five kilometres per hour from Saint John because of worries the shock absorbers would fall off. The gull-wing doors worked only because they were hooked up to a generator under the platform.

None of that mattered. Automotive magazines praised the new vehicle. *Playboy* magazine gave it a feature article in September. The car made its movie debut in *The Betsy*, based on the Harold Robbins novel. And, finally, the plant in the Saint John Grandview Industrial Park began making cars.

The first one came off the line August 6, 1974 to great fanfare. That first car was actually built by hand. And the next cars to come off the line cost about $16,000 each to build.

Sold to the American Bricklin companies for $5,400, that meant each of the first several hundred cars lost $11,000. None of it mattered, publicly at least, to Premier Hatfield. He needed a symbol of success for a provincial election campaign in 1974. That symbol became a bright orange Bricklin that he drove across the province trying to win votes. Bricklin officials took the opportunity to talk to the New Brunswick government about its financial commitment to the car. One can almost imagine the backroom conversation: It would be a shame, Mr. Premier, if something should ever happen to that nice car of yours. By the time Hatfield drove his orange Bricklin to victory November 18, company officials had driven another $3 million in loans to the bank. All the deals were made in secret. Only a few days after the election, Malcolm Bricklin told a reporter he needed yet another $6 million to $8 million.

Opposition parties and the media started taking a closer look at the project. Provincial officials were also worried, and the government made some effort to take greater control over the project. At the same time it loaned Bricklin even more money, $2.5 million in December 1974 and another $7.5 million the next January. The money poured into the same old sinkhole — production problems, wasted parts, and managers' lifestyles.

The plant was supposed to be making forty cars a day, but couldn't make even twenty. And each car cost $13,000 to build. The political debate intensified. Car dealers in the United States had some nice brochures, but they were still waiting for Bricklins promised two years earlier. Those dealers who had the cars weren't much happier. Many of the 1,800 cars built by the summer of 1975 had leaky windows and doors, if the doors worked at all. The wiring in some cars was faulty. There was no service network, and there were no service people trained to repair the cars.

Still, on September 15, 1975, Hatfield announced another $1.2 million in financing. That commitment didn't last long. A few weeks later, the government received a report from a consulting firm commissioned to take a close look at Bricklin Canada. The company's first year loss was reported at $16.6 million. The next year's loss was projected to be $20.7 million. More than $20 million was owed the New Brunswick government. Bricklin was asking for another $10 million, but the consulting firm didn't think even that would stop the bleeding. Finally, on September 26, the Hatfield government put Bricklin Canada into receivership.

The finally tally: $23 million of New Brunswick taxpayers' money to produce 2,880 cars, or $7,986 a car in 1975 dollars. You could buy a Bricklin over the Internet in 2002 starting at $22,000.

The bump and roll

Al Turcott never came across a good idea he wouldn't try. A business and community leader of Wawa, Ontario for thirty-five years, Turcott had more successes than failures and both were so novel they have to be celebrated. He also helped force

Canada Post and the Algoma Central Railway to admit one large failure. And he created the giant goose that adorns the highway near the northern Ontario town.

Turcott arrived in Wawa in 1939, planning to stay for six months to help get a mining operation underway. He liked the place so much, he stayed. By the 1940s, Turcott had a clothing store to run and a battle of epic proportions to wage. For some reason, in 1947, certain authorities decided to rename the community Jamestown, after Sir James Dunn. The people of Wawa resisted the change in two votes, according to the town's history, written by Turcott's wife, Agnes. That didn't matter. The Algoma Central Railway changed their station name to Jamestown. Canada Post did the same thing to the community's post office.

The Turcotts and other community leaders fought the battle on the political side. Others took a guerrilla warfare approach. When Canada Post put up a new building in 1959 with the words "JAMESTOWN POST OFFICE" in thirty-centimetre high letters, the Wawa pranksters struck. First they took off the J and A, suggesting the post office had created a "MES-TOWN." Then the M, E, and S were taken down, leaving a generic "TOWN POST OFFICE." When the T was taken down, the pranksters had created Wawa's "OWN POST OFFICE." Then they got really creative. Taking down one F, they created a truly appropriate sign for Wawa that winter: "OWN POST OF ICE." Canada Post and the railway gave up and in 1960, went back to calling the town Wawa.

About the same time, Turcott decided to publish a newspaper. He bought some used equipment and had it shipped to town. The only trouble was he had no idea how to run the printing presses. With the help of a few workers, Turcott began publishing *The Echo*. It didn't last long, partly because there weren't many stores willing to advertise in a town where you could just stroll along the street to see what was for sale. But a newspaper wasn't really the point, one of Turcott's employees recalled. Turcott created the paper to raise public awareness of the province's failure to extend the highway to Wawa. The road was finally built in 1959, but the government had used fine sand fill and a number of vehicles got bogged down the next spring. The province set up barricades to control traffic and prohibit vehicles in wet weather. Police had to be called in to guard the barricades after a few violent incidents between barricade keepers and Wawa residents, enraged their long-awaited way out of town was blocked. By September 17, 1960, the road was accessible to all traffic, just in time for the grand opening. A giant statue of a goose — Turcott's idea — was unveiled. The goose was made of plaster and didn't stand up to the weather, but its iron replacement has become a tourist attraction.

Once the highway was open, Turcott began working on another venture and the reason he's in a book about failures — his roller bumper. Sometime during the late 1960s and early 1970s, Turcott came up with a surefire way to lessen the damage and injury in car crashes. He welded a V-shaped frame to the front of a car; his friends remembered it as a 1953 or 1954 model. The point of the V stuck out about forty-five centimetres from the front of the car, recalled Wawa resident Larry Dube. At the point, Turcott placed a steel roller, standing vertically, about a half-metre high. At the corners where the wide part of the V met the bumper, Turcott put two more rollers. Then he did the same thing to another old car. He and a friend got in the two cars and crashed them at about fifty kilometers per hour head on. When the two sets of special bumpers met, the cars were supposed to roll away from each other harmlessly. And it worked.

"The rollers ensured you would never come to a dead stop," Dube said in an interview. "The cars just glanced off each other. It does work."

His brother, Don, remembers being in one of the cars during a test drive. "I had the great pleasure of riding in the old '53 Ford that had the bumper installed. If my memory is correct the other car was a '52 to '54 Chev. It was quite a feeling running head on … but the impact was hardly noticeable, a sideways push and then you kept on going."

Turcott added other safety features to his cars, such as railings all the way around the vehicles, about twenty-five centimetres off the ground. The railings were designed so two cars in a collision would lift each other up slightly, limiting the impact and damage.

Turcott tried to get investors and government representatives interested in his roller bumper. "He had quite a few people interested in it," recalled Larry Dube.

Meanwhile, Turcott was involved in another scheme. In 1969, he obtained one hundred acres on the Michipicoten River and built a fort and museum. It was supposed to recreate the fur-trading days in the area, although it was to feature miniature golf, go-cart racing, stores run by merchants from Wawa, and a chapel made out of empty bottles called The Church of the Departed Spirits. Only the basics of the fort were built, but that was enough to draw school trips and visitors from across Canada and the United States. But not enough business and political leaders backed Turcott's plan, Dube said.

Still, Turcott kept the fort operating and kept working on his roller bumper. In 1974, he died of a heart attack, his last two dreams left unfulfilled. His wife tried to keep the fort going but had to sell the property a few years later. It has since fallen into disrepair. No one's sure where the roller bumpers ended up. As crazy as the bumpers sound, they would have kept cars and drivers safe, Dube said.

"Al didn't have the ears of the right people. But he was a guy who was thirty to forty years ahead of his time."

CHAPTER 6

BOATS

Canada has more contact with water than any country in the world. More ocean coastline, more lake shoreline, and some of the biggest rivers on Earth. Naturally, we are great mariners. With a few exceptions.

Third time unlucky

Poor Charles Robertson.

An army officer put in charge of ships, he tried three times to get from the Niagara River to the upper Great Lakes only to end up on a roasting spit. And his failure to bring ships to several garrisons cost the English heavy losses in the uprising of Native Chief Pontiac.

In 1761, the British lieutenant was given command of building two armed vessels that would be used to maintain communications between wilderness forts on the Great Lakes. Starting construction too late that summer, Robertson managed only to get a six-gun schooner, the *Huron*, finished. He tried to get the schooner to Lake Erie, but couldn't get it through the rapids at the head of the Niagara River.

The next year, Robertson finished a sloop called the *Michigan*. He took both the *Huron* and the *Michigan* up the river and into Lake Erie, only to discover sandbars blocking the channel through Lake St. Clair.

The year after that, in the spring of 1763, Robertson led a party on the schooner *Huron* to find a navigable route through Lake St. Clair. French settlers warned the crew of about eight men that the great Native Chief Pontiac was planning to attack the British. No matter, Robertson had a job to do. The schooner reached the narrow entrance to the Lake St. Clair River, where it came across a band of Pontiac's warriors. The warriors fired on the schooner and on two men who had come ashore in a canoe. Robertson and three others were killed and the rest taken prisoner. Some historians say Robertson's body was roasted and eaten, then the remains buried.

And if that wasn't bad enough, by failing to get any further than Detroit, Robertson doomed the garrisons higher up on the lakes. Just as Robertson had been warned, Pontiac did lead an uprising against the British in 1763. The British garrisons on the upper lakes, waiting three years for Robertson's boats, were unable to get proper supplies or reinforcements. Every one of them fell to the uprising.

It'd be cheaper if we gave them water wings

During the First World War, the federal government, like all governments, was trying to find ways to save money.

One quick-thinking adviser came up with the idea of changing the policy of providing transport home for lighthouse keepers at the end of the shipping season. Why not let them find their own way home? The federal government implemented the new policy in 1916. It changed it back in 1921. It seems the new policy was saving money at the cost of people's lives.

One lighthouse keeper, William Sherlock, almost became the first victim during the initial year of the policy. Rowing their damaged sailboat across Lake Superior from Michipicoten Island, Sherlock and his son and dog managed to make it to shore, but Sherlock had to kill the dog for food. Two years later, Sherlock went missing while crossing from the lighthouse on his own. His body was never found.

What the government and its advisers apparently failed to realize, until it was so graphically pointed out to them, was that the reason a shipping season ends is that it becomes too dangerous to sail — not the ideal time to ask people who are, at best, amateur sailors to sail home from a workplace that is, by its very nature, in treacherous waters.

Five ships, five sinkings ... let's keep him on shore

Naval tradition has it that in the event of a shipwreck, the captain is the last person to leave the ship. Captain John Hackett may have learned that by his fifth shipwreck, but he was apparently unfamiliar with the convention his first time around.

His inaugural shipwreck, the first known wreck in Georgian Bay, was with the ship the *Alice Hackett* in 1828.

The ship and Captain Hackett had been chartered by the government to move the military garrison stationed on Drummond Island to the Naval Establishments at Penetanguishene. The British had originally established a garrison at Penetanguishene, chosen by John Graves Simcoe for its ideal harbour, in the late 1700s. Simcoe also had a road built, which provided for overland communication in case war broke out. War did break out in 1812, and the British garrison from Drummond Island captured Fort Michilimackinac from the Americans before they even knew the war had started.

After the war, the garrison had to hand the fort back to the Americans and a new post was established, first at St. Joseph's Island and later at Drummond Island. But as the years wore on, the British and Americans redrew the borders of what would be Canada and the United States, and eventually the British decided to bring their troops back to the more easily defended and supplied Penetanguishene.

It may have been a sensible decision. What was not so sensible, it turns out, was to decommission the fort in November, with all the fall storms that go with it, and to charter the illustrious Captain Hackett and his ship to carry the passengers — both soldiers and civilians planning to settle in Penetanguishene.

The snow that was falling when they began the journey was the least of their problems. Headed south by southeast, they found there were worse things to sail through in a Georgian Bay November. When the gale hit, the winds drove the ship towards Fitzwilliam Island, which lies between Tobermory and Manitoulin Island. The shoals off the island ripped away at the boat, eventually spearing it.

There was some talk that the captain, his crew, and many of the soldiers had achieved an advanced state of drunkenness before the gale hit that night. Thankfully, though, they weren't far from land. The passengers and crew managed to reach shore safely. While much of the cargo was lost, some was brought ashore, including some livestock and the thirteen barrels of whiskey that passenger Alexander Fraser was bringing with him to open a pub in Penetanguishene.

It was not until the next morning that Pierre Lepine, one of the passengers who had finally recovered from the celebrations the night before, realized his wife and infant child were not ashore. The men made it back to the wreck to find mother and child barely alive. Mrs. Lepine had tied the baby to her body and lashed herself to the mast for safety during the long night.

Hackett went on to sink four more vessels — albeit in less exciting fashion — between 1832 and 1835. When he retired from sailing, he became a lighthouse keeper. Fortunately for him, he would have retired before the government changed the policy on staffing lighthouses, forcing lighthouse keepers on the Great Lakes to find their own way home in the November storms at the end of shipping season.

Where's the steering wheel?

Imagine a squirrel in a revolving cage.

Now cover the cage so it won't leak, and put it in the water.

When the squirrel starts to run, the cage will roll across the water.

And just like that, you'll see the genius of Frederick Augustus Knapp and the vessel that would have revolutionized shipping — Knapp's Roller Boat.

For almost a decade, Knapp, a lawyer from Prescott, Ontario, put all of his energy and hundreds of thousands of his and others' dollars into his vision of a boat that would roll over, not through, the waves.

And it almost worked.

Like all the best ideas, Knapp's arrived in a moment of simple wondering. One day he nudged a pencil on his desk and watched it roll quite easily across the surface. Why not, he wondered, do the same with a boat?

He started making designs and a model and took them to naval architects in Glasgow, Scotland. It might work, they said, but we're not going to give you any money. So Knapp returned to Canada and eventually hooked up with an Ottawa contractor named George Goodwin, who had overseen construction of the Soulange Canal.

"If this thing succeeds, it means millions," Goodwin told him. "Besides, it will be a good advertisement for Canada."

Frederick Knapp's roller boat, tested in Toronto and Prescott, managed to turn over but not turn a corner. That was only one of the problems with his novel idea for navigation.

So Goodwin put up $250,000 and Knapp began building the boat in a Prescott carriage and iron shop.

It took a lot of trial and error to make a cylindrical boat with tools designed for more traditional vessels. Eventually, Knapp pieced together a double tube of steel, thirty-four metres long and seven metres in diameter. Inside each end, attached to the outer cylinder, was a short piece of railway-like track. On each track rested a set of wheels. On each set of wheels rested a platform carrying a 200-horsepower steam engine and boiler. The engine was connected to the wheels. When the engine started, the wheels moved and the little platform, like a locomotive, moved forward and started to climb up the wall of the outside cylinder. Of course, it would only climb a little way before forcing the outside cylinder itself to start to roll. Inside the cylinder, passengers or freight would be safe and sound and level. For the early tests, platforms were built on the outside at either end.

Knapp envisioned making a ninety-metre long, sixty-metre diameter ocean roller that could carry four million bushels of wheat across the Atlantic at twenty knots.

On one of his own voyages across the Atlantic seeking investors, Knapp stopped in Québec City where newspapers, if not the board of trade, embraced his plan to create the world's largest port for shipping grain in roller boats. Success, a reporter concluded, would mean "the expenditure of many millions of dollars in Quebec and the making of this city the largest and wealthiest in Canada."

Some people tried to tell Knapp his roller boat would never work.

A captain and steamboat inspector named Donnelly told the Kingston correspondent of *The Globe* he warned Knapp in 1894 the roller boat wouldn't work. "Mr. Knapp at that time could neither see the objections I offered to the feasibility of the plan nor show any detailed plan for successfully applying the principle he had in view. He has never had any mechanical or practical training in engineering."

None of that mattered to Knapp. In 1897, he finished his hundred-ton craft in the Poison Shipbuilding Yard at the foot of Sherbourne Street in Toronto. The boat tapered slightly at each end, so the ends would stay out of the water. On the first day of tests, the roller boat failed to get out of the slip because of rough weather. However the boat did, exulted *The Globe*, roll in the slip.

Two days later, the weather calmed and Knapp tried again.

As word spread throughout the harbour, thousands crowded the boatworks to watch. Knapp was his usual confident self, telling reporters, "Wait a few minutes and you will see the boat go round, just as I said it would."

Just before two o'clock, Knapp tested the engines with the roller boat tied to the pier. The boat turned over one and a half times.

It was a success, said boatbuilder Frank Poison. It's all yours, he told Goodwin, the financial backer.

Not so fast, Goodwin replied. Let's see if it works on the lake.

Poison refused to budge and Goodwin reluctantly took possession of the roller boat.

A steam yacht towed the roller boat into the glass-smooth harbour about three o'clock. By then, the docks were covered with people and the betting was split evenly on whether the boat would roll or not.

In the centre of the bay, with a whistle and a hiss of steam, the roller boat's engines started. "The great circular tube with its flanges or paddles commenced to revolve in the water and go slowly ahead," *The Globe* reported. "The platforms on either end of the new boat swayed up and down when the revolutions of the flanges commenced, but as soon as the boat got well under way the platforms became level and steady."

Members of the crew stood on the platforms, getting soaked from the steam but no doubt thrilled by the ride. As spectators on a flotilla of boats cheered, the roller boat made its way up the bay.

"Knapp's roller boat has rolled all right," concluded *The Globe* reporter. "Looking for all the world like a gigantic stovepipe painted red and belching forth clouds of smoke and steam, rolling to and fro in the harbour, and making as it rolled curious rumbling noise."

There were a few snags. One of the wooden flanges snapped off. And the boat drew over a metre. But it was just a test run. The flanges or paddles on this version extended only a quarter of the length of the vessel, and would probably have to run from end to end. More flanges would mean more speed and the boat, Knapp assured people, would skim across the water's surface. Between the two hulls, workers had left some loose bolts and pieces of wood, accounting for some of the great noise. There was no steering mechanism on board, or the crew didn't know how to use it, because the roller boat simply travelled in one direction, stopped, then travelled in a straight line in the opposite direction.

For about an hour that day, however, "Mr Knapp's Wonderful Contrivance" turned through the water, throwing up no wake in front.

"I am delighted with the trial trip," Knapp told reporters. "We have now some experiments to make before we try her for speed."

After the 1897 launch, the boat was towed back to Prescott for some alterations.

Then, late in 1899, Knapp rolled the boat out again.

"Flags floated and whistles blew as it took the water with a great splash," recalled Captain W.J. Stitt, a witness to the event and the son of the carriage maker whose yard Knapp had used to start the first version. "Knapp was there in all his glory and attired to the king's taste."

The inventor and stockholders in his venture boarded the boat as crowds again cheered him on. As soon as the roller boat hit the open water, a strong wind pushed it across the river toward the American side. Then a snowstorm blew up and the boat disappeared from sight. It rolled straight across the river, missed the entrance of the harbour in Ogdensburg, New York, and struck a mud bar. The snow and ice building up made it impossible to tow the boat out. Knapp and his investors, freezing cold and suffering from exposure, were taken off in small rescue boats.

The next day the roller boat was towed back to Prescott.

Knapp overcame several problems in building the roller boat, wrote E.J. Snider forty years later in the *Toronto Telegram*. But it seemed impossible to get the boat to do little more than roll in the "hole" in the water it created by its own displacement. "The roller boat started in a hole and was always rolling uphill. It was as though Mr. Knapp's pencil began to roll in a groove in the desk and stayed there."

But Knapp refused to give up on his idea, and spent three more years after the 1899 mishap tinkering with the engine and the design. He added a shaft and propeller and decided to make the roller boat cigar-shaped. Off he went with his boat to Montréal, where he planned to add a twenty-seven-metre bow on one end, rising one and a half metres above the water, and a fifteen-metre stern on the other. That way, the boat could roll or travel end to end like a traditional boat. Unfortunately for Knapp, the Montréal dry docks kicked him out before he could finish because other, more profitable jobs were coming in.

Stitt, the same captain who witnessed the Prescott launch, was hired in 1903 to tow the roller boat with the tug, *Cardinal,* back down the St. Lawrence, through its small canals, and to Toronto.

With the twenty-seven-metre bow partly built, the roller boat looked like a giant sugar scoop, Stitt recalled. "It was the worst towing job I ever had." His salt-water crew wasn't the best at handling boats in canals, never mind a boat that couldn't stay straight when towed from one end, and the steel plates of the unfinished bow cut the towing lines every time the roller boat moved from side to side. "Three times in the Soulange canal his roller baby got hungry and dove into the nice soft canal banks and scooped a mouth of earth out." Four times between Cornwall and Prescott, the roller boat cut its towing lines and once rolled away and over a shoal. Finally, the roller boat arrived safe and sound in Poison's boat yard in Toronto. Nothing could keep the roller boat from rolling, though. One night, the boat broke loose, drifted into the bay, and ran into the steamer, *Niagara.*

It appears even Knapp had given up by now. He headed back to Prescott, where he had a successful career as a barrister, and died in his fine home, at age eighty-eight, mourned by his family and friends.

The roller boat, which never had an official name, was not so lucky. The owners of the *Niagara* tried to sue the owners of the roller boat for damages, but no one claimed ownership. For years the abandoned roller boat lay on the flats behind the St. Lawrence Market, Stitt recalled, looking like an old, rusty stovepipe. When the Toronto Harbour Commission filled in the land and built new docks, workers blew up the roller boat and covered it with fill. The giant sugar scoop, stovepipe, squirrel in a cage, has rotted away ever since somewhere between the market and Lake Ontario.

When the flood comes, he's laughing

There is no doubt that Tom Sukanen was a large, strong, and determined man. But it's not clear whether he was inspired or insane.

Sukanen fled his native Finland in the late 1800s and arrived in Minnesota, at the age of twenty, where he started farming. He was actually a boat builder by trade, but there wasn't much call for that in Minnesota, so he farmed.

Sukanen, it turned out, was successful as a farmer. But, inexplicably, when he had a nice little farm, a wife, three girls, and a boy, he just packed up and left. At the age of thirty-three, he took some personal possessions but no money and walked away with a vague idea to look up his brother in Saskatchewan, a mere 1,000-kilometre hike away.

He found his brother, who lived near Macrorie, and in 1911 Sukanen settled down on his Saskatchewan home-stead and farmed, again successfully. By 1915 he had paid for his farm and had saved $9,000. He had also gained a reputation as a resourceful guy who could build just about anything.

With his cash and his new farm, he headed south, by foot, back to his Minnesota farm. On arrival, he found the place abandoned and learned that his wife was dead. His children were spread out in foster homes. He did find his son, but was not able to bring him back to Canada.

For about another decade, he lived alone on his Saskatchewan farm, keeping to himself. He did, though, build a little rowboat and travel down the Saskatchewan River to Hudson Bay — another sign of his determination, resource-fulness, and ability.

But when Sukanen started to dream of a bigger boat — a much bigger boat — failure could not be too far off.

He was building this boat, he told the neighbours who asked, to take him home to Finland. Or to keep him afloat during the coming flood. Different people got different answers.

But what was not in doubt was the effort Sukanen put into his dream. He built a steamboat from scratch. He shaped the plate steel into a hull and he built his own pulleys. It took years. Six years to be exact. Not quite fourteen metres in length, the boat was completed in three sections. He had dubbed his boat the *Sontianen*, which means "dung beetle" in Finnish. Odd name for a steamboat, but that was his privilege.

Sukanen intended to follow the same route to the sea that he had taken with his small rowboat. But while he could put his rowboat on a horse-drawn wagon and haul it to the river, the steamboat was a little too heavy for that mode of transport.

So he did what any giant would do. He got himself a winch. A hand winch. And he cranked the boat along the road a few metres at a time. After two years of cranking, Sukanen was three kilometres along.

He had about nineteen more to go.

His failing health might have stopped him. But for this resourceful man who could build anything, that was hardly a challenge. His teeth were becoming loose from bad diet and neglect. His solution? He built pliers to pull his own teeth out. Then he built his own false teeth, out of scrap bits of steel and iron.

What did eventually stop him from getting the boat to the river was an attack on his craft by vandals in 1941. It may have been the target of a hate crime. At the time Finland was being attacked by the Soviet Union, putting it in a position where it had to fight on the same side as Nazi Germany, Italy, and Japan. The difference, of course, was that Finland was forced into the war because it was attacked, not because it was about to invade Russia.

In any event, neighbours who watched him winch his steam-boat along the road called the police and had Sukanen committed to a mental institution. He died a couple of years later.

His boat sat at a friend's farm for decades. In the early 1970s, a crusader had the boat moved to a museum near Moose Jaw. Sukanen's body was also moved to the museum grounds and buried near the boat, which was rebuilt and established as a monument to the determination of a single-minded man. With one bad idea.

Freeze, you damn Nazis

September 1943. The citizens of Genoa, Italy wake up to a chill in the air and a glare on the horizon. They can hear engines approaching, then suddenly, bombers fly off the sea and begin strafing buildings. How they did they get here? There are no landing strips within thousands of kilometres. The answer appears moments later: giant ships — bigger than anything seen on the ocean — some carrying aircraft, some with weird hose-like guns. A German U-boat torpedoes one of the ships and a hole appears in the hull. But within minutes, the hole miraculously seals itself. Smaller ships dart from the fleet and enter Genoa's harbour. Canvas troughs with grapnels at one end are thrown onto the Italian navy ships and hoses pour water into the troughs. The water freezes in seconds and hundreds of Allied soldiers run, or slide, over the newly created ice ramps to the Italian ships. The Italians man their weapons but Allied sailors spray the enemy gunnery portholes with the water, which also freezes instantly and stops resistance cold. Landing barges head to shore and Allied tanks push giant blocks of ice, which are quickly joined to create a six-metre high and nine-metre thick barricade to protect landing soldiers and imprison entire sections of the city. The Axis forces do not give up and a U-boat manages to sink one of the craft. The Axis soldiers cheer and wait for the horrible sight of sailors jumping into the water. But the ship sinks and no one jumps. In fact, none of the other ships go to her aid. It's just an empty decoy ship. Only when the battle is over and Genoa taken do the citizens realize with horror they have been the first targets of the greatest weapon known to the world — the Ice Attack.

Ships made of ice with refrigeration units that can seal any hole. Supercooled water sprayed from hoses to freeze enemy ships and create instant bridges, ice blocks that make instant fortresses.

The plan was... floated... during the Second World War and Canada played a big part.

The only ice ship made was created in Canada. Newfoundland was pegged as the harbour to build the fleet and many of the tests were done in Montréal and Alberta.

The ice ship project was called Habbakuk, after a verse in the Biblical Book of Habakkuk (someone misspelled it for the Canadian project) that read "a work which you will not believe though it be told you." Which many didn't.

An eccentric British genius named Geoffrey Pyke came up with idea and sent a 232-page proposal to Lord Mountbatten in September 1942. Pyke proposed using a mixture of ice and wood pulp to create an incredibly strong material that stayed frozen even at warm temperatures and was unsinkable. In Pyke's mind, the material, later called pykrete, would give the Allied forces the single most important weapon in the war. At the time, Allied convoys were suffering great losses to German U-boats. Bombers couldn't protect the Atlantic convoys because they couldn't fly to the middle of the ocean and back. Meanwhile, Allied commanders were wondering how

National Archives of Canada/PA-171611

Sliding through the water with the grace of an iceberg, it's Canada's floating ice ship, the Habbakuk. *The actual project never got as far as this drawing, but it sure excited Second World War leaders for awhile.*

best to carry men and machines to invade Europe. Pykrete answered all these problems.

Besides describing the attack on Genoa, which could be duplicated all across Europe, Pyke detailed the wonders of ice ships. They could be built big enough, at much less expense, and faster than traditional ships. They could carry aircraft or any material needed for the war effort. Their eleven-metre thick hulls, created by refrigeration units safely inside, could withstand a torpedo hit — the metre-deep crater could be easily filled in by ice. Deep inside the hulls, crews could work and sleep as cozy as Inuit in igloos. Some kind of insulation, such as cork, would cover the hull to protect it from melting or evaporating. Unloading iceberg freighters would be a cinch. Simply carve a hole in the side and presto, cargo could be pushed off onto barges. The holes could then be frozen shut.

As attack ships, the ice warships would be unstoppable. They could ram enemy vessels, or use the canvas troughs to create bridges for boarding parties. The supercooled water that each ship carried could be sprayed on enemy vessels, sealing them shut.

Pyke's theories seized the imagination of Lord Mountbatten. He quickly got British scientists working on the idea, and Prime Minister Winston Churchill enthused. Mountbatten convinced Churchill to take a piece of pykrete into the tub. The surface of the little block of ice and wood melted but the rest survived the bath.

Scientists initially dismissed the supercooled water idea, but found pykrete to be pretty amazing material — able to withstand great pressure and bullets. The results only increased Churchill's enthusiasm. "The advantages of a floating island or islands, even if only used as refuelling depots for aircraft, are so dazzling that they don't need to be discussed. There would be no difficulty in finding a place to put such a 'stepping-stone' in any of the plans of war now under consideration," he wrote in a secret letter to a general on December 4, 1942.

Not only could the ships be used to carry aircraft protecting convoys, they could be used as a base for aircraft bombing the coast of Europe.

Churchill suggested, instead of making the material, scientists simply cut the base of the ship out of ice fields in the Arctic, pour sea water on it to freeze and build it up, then put the necessary equipment on board.

Scientists wisely chose to concentrate on using the less brittle pykrete and not waste time trying to carve ships out of ice fields that could hold 90 percent of their mass under water.

The British Admiralty approved the project early in 1943.

The *Habbakuk* was to be 610 metres long, ninety-one metres wide at the beam, and with a draught of forty-five metres. Her displacement would be 2.2 million tons, twenty-six times that of the *Queen Elizabeth*. Electric motors would refrigerate and move the vessel at a maximum speed of seven knots, consuming 120 tons of diesel per day with tanks big enough for 11,000-kilometre, non-stop cruises. A crew of about 1,500 would operate the ship. In her decks would be room for 200 Spitfires and 100 Mosquito bombers.

And Canada, a land of ice, would build her. The exact method was finalized — thin sheets of pykrete could be built by laying the wood pulp on arctic lakes, freezing it, then skimming it off and building it into large blocks.

The head of Canada's National Research Council, C.J. Mackenzie, was cool to the idea at first, calling it in his diaries, "another of those mad wild schemes.... I am quite sure that if it were suggested in normal circles here we should not have the ghost of a chance of getting it before even a minor official, but I can start with a couple of crazy men in Genland, get Churchill's attention and the attention of the highest people in Canada and even the P.M. here."

Mackenzie's resistance melted, a bit, and research into the properties of ice was begun at the universities of Manitoba, Saskatchewan, and Alberta. Testing of ice took place in Montréal, Banff, and Lake Louise. At Lake Louise, crews cut blocks of ice from the lake and created two- by four-foot beams, twelve metres long, frozen with pine logs or steel and tested for strength. Eventually, Corner Brook, Newfoundland was chosen as the construction site of the full ships. But first, the scale model had to be built in Patricia Lake, Alberta. It seemed like an odd place to build a sea-going aircraft carrier, but at least scientists knew the weather was cold enough.

Work began in the middle of February 1943. A generating station at the nearby Jasper Park Lodge provided power. Workers cleared an area on the frozen surface of the lake and laid wooden flooring and wall studs, then poured lake ice over the floors and into the walls. Steel piping was placed inside the ice to spread cool air throughout and by April, the refrigeration machinery was put into place and was working. The model ship was cut loose from the surrounding ice and floated just fine.

The entire structure was eighteen metres long, nine metres wide, and six metres deep.

The model berg ship was sheathed in timber and an insulated layer of pitch and vermiculite. A roof was built over the ship to protect the machinery and the ice, and some suggest to camouflage the ice ship as a boathouse.

One can imagine a Nazi spy reporting to his superiors.

"No, nothing to report. It's just a nine-metre long boathouse."

Despite the camouflage, it appeared someone figured out what was going on. In the midst of the secret work, an episode of the Superman comic strip came out with — oh my God — iceberg ships! Believe it or not, officials were so worried about this apparent coincidence, they sent the suspect strip to the National Research Council and the University of Manitoba to study. Nothing came of the cartoon. But if the next one had showed ice cannons, Superman would have been in trouble.

There are crates of technical material on the tests and model, but the bottom line is that the ice ship appeared to be feasible. Throughout the summer of 1943, with a one-horsepower engine keeping the refrigeration system going, the ship neither melted nor sank.

The Canadian War Committee agreed in April to build a full ship, with an initial commitment of $1 million, and a total cost equivalent of $100 million in today's dollars. The cost estimates, which he didn't trust anyway, and other tests convinced Mackenzie the project was as crazy as he had at first thought. "The constructional aspects are almost overwhelming," he wrote in his diaries. "The present time schedule certainly cannot be built and it is even possible that the thing can never be built."

He ordered the Patricia Lake ice ship model dismantled in May. The machinery was removed and scientists monitored its durability during the summer. It remained afloat and intact until fall, when it and the wooden boathouse sank. A team of divers found the remains in the 1970s.

But the ice ship idea wouldn't melt away that easily.

A disappointed Churchill tried to get the United States to join the project. At the Quebec conference of Allied leaders in 1943, Churchill arranged to get a block of pykrete to the Château Frontenac. Someone — perhaps Mountbatten or Churchill himself — fired a bullet at the block assuming it would simply lodge itself in the material. Instead, it ricocheted, forcing alarmed military leaders to duck. Churchill then met U.S. President Franklin Roosevelt in a private meeting and had an ice cube dropped into a bowl. Scalding water was poured over the ice cube and the two world leaders, Roosevelt probably wondering what was in Churchill's cigar, watched the expected result. The ice cube melted. Then a cube of pykrete was dropped into another bowl and scalding water poured over it. Nothing happened. "Hasn't melted at all!" Churchill said. With that demonstration and a few designs in front of him, Roosevelt agreed to help build the ship.

A joint Anglo-American-Canadian Habbakuk board was struck and even larger-scale tests were proposed to take place in Canada. But the British Admiralty and the U.S. military weren't as keen as their political bosses. The devoted ice ship designers tried to meet every one of their objections.

The ships were too big to be driven by one or two screws? Fine, the designers said, we'll build rows of propellers on each side of the ship and steer by turning off different sets of propellers.

The ships would be too expensive to build? No they won't, the designers argued. Instead of building ships in a port then launching them, we'll just take giant blocks of pykrete, fuse them together, put them on a wooden raft, and tow them to open water. Then we'll build up a hull, right there in the ocean.

The designers and promoters of the ice ship appeared to be winning as 1943 ended. Plans for creating the first ship were finalized. But over the next year, the demand for the ice ship began to melt. Longer-range aircraft were being built. Iceland and the Portuguese Azores Islands had agreed to be used as air bases, allowing bombers to protect convoys through U-boat alley. The planned invasion of Europe had shifted from the Bay of Biscay, where ships were key attackers, to Normandy, where ships were needed only to drop off troops. In the Pacific, where the United States was eventually going to use the ships, the war was going better than expected.

Besides, said some scientists, the thing wouldn't work anyway. The 1.7 million tons of pykrete needed for one ship couldn't be frozen in one Newfoundland winter. And most of all, the ship's propeller engines would have melted the hull. One has to wonder about using ice ships in the South Pacific Ocean. Or about planes landing on ice. Or how cold it would be inside. Even today, researchers can't agree whether ice ships would have worked. But no one is that hot on the idea.

They're slow and they cost a lot

The British Columbia government had an idea. They wanted to build a faster, lighter, more comfortable ferry for speedy commuter service along the coast and among the islands of British Columbia. If the design was good enough, the West

Coast shipbuilding industry could expand to meet the demands of the orders that would inevitably flow in from around the world. Three ships would be delivered in three years to BC Ferries.

That was the plan. According to the province's auditor general, it was unrealistic to expect even shipyards familiar with the construction of fast ferries to design and build three craft so quickly.

The result was a ferry that was slower than planned, more expensive, and was less comfortable than its designers had anticipated. And the orders have not exactly been flooding in.

When the new ferry began service in 1997, there were great expectations, not least those of BC Ferries, which owns and operates the public ferries in the province. The *Skeena Queen* was the first of the new class of ferry, able to carry more cars and people than the vessel it replaced. The 110-metre long vessel was one of three on order. It is able to carry 600 passengers and up to 110 cars. When it is running.

The hull of the new ferry is considered a success — it looks attractive and, more importantly, leaves only a small wake. The innards are another matter, thanks in part to what turned out to be misplaced concerns about saving money.

Before it was even ready to be put in the water, the ferry was welded together so it could be seen floating on display when dignitaries visited. The boat then had to be cut open so the engines could be installed.

But before the engines were installed, BC Ferries had gone to Transport Canada and asked for, and received, approval to mount the engines using a different method than had originally been contemplated. The newer method, described as "non-traditional" by Bob Lingwood, president of BC Ferries, was a cost-saving measure.

The vibration and noise of the engines caused the first problems. One passenger described them as sounding like a Sherman tank warming up from inside the lounge. In late 1999, because of passenger complaints, the ferry's operational speed was reduced, which meant the scheduled ten trips a day had to be cut to eight.

And, as it turned out, the engines had to be changed much sooner than anyone thought possible. All four of the *Skeena Queen*'s engines have been pulled out and replaced with slower ones. Apparently the engines were being worn out, at least in part due to the "non-traditional" method of mounting them in the hull.

By December 1999, a water leak was found in one engine. A January 2000 inspection showed the engine to be inoperable, so the ferry had to make its way to Vancouver for repairs. On the way, two more engines failed, meaning three of four engines were out of service. The *Skeena Queen* finished its cruise to the dry dock under tow from a tugboat.

Some of the failed engines had already been replaced at least once before. But this time the ferry was out of service for more than half a year. And, while generally speaking, a boat that is dead in the water causes less vibration and noise, and leaves less wake than a moving boat, no matter how well-designed its hull, that is little comfort to BC Ferries or its customers.

Just for fun, here is a partial list of the table of contents for the report on the fast ferry from the province's auditor general, George Morfit, which was delivered in October 1999:

- Fast ferries were not shown to be the best way to meet identified needs
- The risks inherent in the fast ferry project were never adequately identified

- The likelihood that fast aluminum ferries could be built cost-effectively in British Columbia was not demonstrated
- The likelihood of exporting British Columbia-built fast ferries was not demonstrated
- The costs announced were not well-supported
- A realistic budget and firm control on scope changes were never established
- The schedule announced for the project was never announced
- An overriding concern with meeting the unrealistic schedule meant that work was rushed and sometimes done out of sequence
- The designer and design were chosen before BC Ferries operational needs were fully defined
- Construction was started before detailed engineering work was sufficiently complete
- BC Ferries board was pressed into a hurried decision
- BC Ferries board repeatedly tried to obtain more information as the project progressed
- Accountability reporting to the Legislative Assembly and public was inadequate

Did we mention it is a fine-looking machine?

CHAPTER 7

LET'S TAKE A SHORTCUT (CANALS)

During the late 1800s and early 1900s, before roads, cars, and trucks were used to transport goods and people, freight was usually shipped by railway or canal. There was, in some areas, great pressure to build canals as a way to offset the seemingly endless fare increases by the railways. Shipping by ships or barges was cheaper than rail, unless your canal didn't hold water.

One canal turned out to be very costly, especially for Sir Wilfrid Laurier.

As prime minister, Laurier headed a Liberal majority government. By about 1905, however, he could see some decline in his party's popularity. One of his friends, William Mulock, convinced Laurier that to stop that erosion in Mulock's area, the government had to build a canal from Lake Simcoe to Aurora.

Mulock was born in 1844 and grew up in what is today the northern part of York Region in Ontario. He was elected the member of Parliament for North York in 1882 and was a member of Laurier's cabinet, appointed as the postmaster general in 1896, and then as the first minister of labour in 1900.

He resigned from office in 1905, fed up with spending as much time battling internal politics as trying to serve his riding. He was appointed to the bench as a justice of the Supreme Court of Ontario, a position he held until he died in 1944 at the age of one hundred.

Mulock did not leave politics aside with his resignation, however, continuing to be a supporter of Laurier and someone whose counsel Laurier trusted.

Mulock had remained friendly with the businessmen in his old riding and he could see it slowly shifting to the right. In order to save it for the Liberals, Mulock knew in his heart, a canal would have to be built. And he knew where.

In the early 1900s, the Trent-Severn Waterway was under construction, designed to connect Lake Ontario to Georgian Bay through a series of channels stretching from Trenton, through the Kawartha Lakes to Lake Simcoe, and then down the Severn River.

While people had considered a canal in North York before, they had been thinking it would run from Lake

Simcoe straight south to Lake Ontario. The Holland River stretches south from Lake Simcoe, and the Humber and Don Rivers stretch north from Lake Ontario. In between is a rather inconvenient mound of gravel called the Oak Ridges Moraine. The moraine, in spots, is so steep that capstans and ropes were rigged to haul wagons and carts up its sides because horses and oxen couldn't manage on their own.

Most engineers conceded the moraine would have to be cut through in order for a canal to work. This was a doable, if expensive proposition. If the canal were built this way, there would be enough water.

This is not the way that Mulock — who was not an engineer — wanted to do it. Mulock convinced Laurier and his advisers that if they wanted to retain the riding of North York, they would approve a canal running from Lake Simcoe to Aurora, post haste.

Mulock's idea for watering the canal was to take water from the south end, pour it in, and let it run downhill. The hills south of Aurora, which form part of the moraine, are dry. There is not a lot of precipitation. Nevertheless, Laurier authorized an engineer to review the proposal and draw up plans.

The engineer noted there was enough water for the planned canal during the spring but not for the summer and fall. During those times, water would have to come from somewhere else. Mulock suggested it could be stored in reservoirs. Or it could be pumped from Lake Simcoe.

Critics had a field day. Editorial cartoons and papers from Orillia to Ottawa sneered at Mulock for his foolish plan. It was called a "perpetual monument to government folly." It was called "Mulock's Madness." James T. Angus, in his book, *A Respectable Ditch*, described it best: "It was a politician's vision, not an economist's forecast and certainly not an engineer's brainchild."

The Liberals gave the nod to $200,000 in funding for the canal and work began in 1906. They awarded the dredging contract for the first part of the canal — the cheap part from Lake Simcoe to Holland Landing — to the Lake Simcoe Dredging Company. The company was formed by Dr. Phillip Spohn, a Penetanguishene man who worked at the Mental Health Centre, and C.S. Crane, a Newmarket businessman and close friend of Mulock.

The company constructed a barge with a shovel but, unfortunately, neither Crane nor Spohn understood the demands of the dredging system and their machine was not up to the job. They allowed their contract to lapse.

(Oddly, this was not the first time Spohn invested money in a business that didn't do what it was supposed to do. He also was a partner in a glass plant in Penetanguishene that never produced any glass.)

Despite the setbacks, the canal inched south. It was dredged to Holland Landing and then the heavier work could begin.

Meanwhile, back in Ottawa, the political infighting was getting very nasty.

E.J. Walsh, the respected engineer who worked on the Trent-Severn Waterway, had been assigned the job of designing the canal. He had tried to make it as plausible as possible for the politicians who wanted to build it. But when the plan was sent to Ottawa for approval, engineers there with railway sympathies tore it to pieces and redesigned it, increasing the cost of the canal by using more expensive and complicated components. Apparently it was part of a strategy to increase the costs so much that the plan would be killed, damaging the reputations of Walsh and Mulock, a railroad enemy.

For example, the revised plans included building a fifty-metre dock in downtown Aurora. Anyone who ventures into the traffic-congested downtown of Aurora today during rush hour would no doubt be amused at the prospect of a dock and canal helping ease road traffic there.

They also included holding ponds and big pumps to suck water out of Lake Simcoe and pull it up thirty kilometres in a pipe about twenty metres above the water level. Water weighs a lot. The pumps would have had to be enormous, even if the lifting were done in stages.

It was a grand, and purposely expensive, plan.

In the end, though, all the engineers really accomplished was to drive the estimated cost up even more. They had not accounted for the Liberal government, which was intent on building the canal despite the cost.

The system made it to Newmarket and a number of locks were finished. But before the canal could be completed, the Liberals were kicked out of power in the 1911 election. The party, which had been defeated badly in the 1880s when it asked for a mandate to introduce free trade, had inexplicably made that part of its platform again. But free trade was not what people were talking about. People were talking about the spending habits of the government, its corruption, and its nepotism. And the canal from Lake Simcoe to Aurora, one that would cost ridiculous amounts of money to complete and that did not even have any water, was held out as one of the biggest examples of a government gone mad.

Robert Borden, leader of the Conservatives, became prime minister. And one of the first things he did was to cut funding to the canal.

It never did hold any water, but some of the locks remain as a reminder of the grand plan, or will until the piles of concrete that form them are slowly reclaimed by the surrounding countryside.

All we need now is the canal

It's supposed to work this way: Someone builds a canal, then the towns and ports at either end get bigger.

Narcisse Cantin thought it best to try the opposite: Put up a brand new town on a lake, and the canal will have to follow.

The two-metre, 110-kilogram promotional genius almost succeeded and was only a few decades short of becoming a Canadian hero.

Cantin was born in a French Canadian community in 1870 on the shores of Lake Huron near Goderich, Ontario. The eldest son in a shipbuilding family proved his own business smarts at an early age and was already an independent cattle buyer and trader at seventeen. From the community of Hensall, he shipped cattle to Buffalo. He bought his own abattoir to serve the local market. And at nineteen he married and moved to Buffalo to direct his operations.

For the next ten years, Cantin built a successful business and social life. A gregarious and big man, he often sparred with world heavyweight champion John L. Sullivan when the boxer visited Buffalo. For a time, he sold products for a gas company and patented a new kind of gas burner. He also patented a glue, the Instant Crockery Mender, and a new liquid floor polisher. Cantin was always thinking, always solving problems. How, for example, could he get his cattle from Huron County to the rich markets near Buffalo with less damage from the long lake voyage? Aside from the length of the trip, ships collided in the narrow channels, grounded on shoals, and were damaged by weather. By the 1890s, Cantin had his solution. He would build a canal from Lake Huron to Lake Erie, avoiding 240 nautical kilometres of hazardous travel, not to mention Detroit.

The other benefits of the canal would follow — it would be a faster way for people and all kinds of goods to move.

Through the 1890s, Cantin tried to gather investors and government support. Perhaps the price tag, about $25 million, scared people off. Perhaps the lack of a port on the Lake Huron end troubled would-be shareholders in a canal company. Cantin decided to fix that. He'd get attention for his canal. He would, as he put it, build "a drum to beat upon" — nothing less than a town, port, and canal terminus on Lake Huron where only farmland and trees existed.

In 1896, Cantin bought property on the shores of Lake Huron, named it St. Joseph after the patron saint of Canada, surveyed streets, lots, a baseball park, and started building. For the canal that wasn't there yet, Cantin built the three-storey Balmoral Hotel at a rumoured cost of $250,000. He built a lumber mill, two brick and tile mills, a winery, a department store, a factory that built novelties, and of all things, a factory to build pipe organs. Within years, the town of St. Joseph also boasted a blacksmith shop, doctory, post office, butcher, a few dozen houses, and about 300 people. It also had a federal government wharf. Cantin had convinced the minister of public works, a fellow French Canadian, that the port of St. Joseph could bring back many French Canadians now living in Chicago.

The Tory member of Parliament representing the region snorted in derision, and quoted a local newspaper editorial, "St. Joseph needs a harbour as badly as a goose needs side pockets." Cantin got his wharf, at a cost to the federal government of $15,000.

St. Joseph must have looked impressive to investors, especially at night. Cantin took interested business leaders by special trains to Hensall, Ontario, the terminus of the London, Huron, and Bruce Railway. The investors were then transported by fine carriage or later, one of two Stanley Steamer motor cars, to St. Joseph. Some say Cantin whisked the rich financiers through his town in the evening, when he had lights blazing from every window to prove the success and richness of the busy metropolis. He then put his would-be investors up in one of the few open rooms of the hotel, and whisked them back to the train in the morning before they realized they were not in a thriving city, but a small frontier town.

Another tale had Cantin planting silver ore near the town site. He arranged for the "discovery" of the ore while investors were visiting.

Whatever he did, it worked. Some important business leaders did express interest, including Charles Schwab, president of Bethlehem Steel, Lord Shaughnessy, president of the Canadian Pacific Railway, and Oliver Cabana, president of the Liberty Bank in Buffalo. Cantin raised enough money in the United States and Canada to incorporate the St. Joseph and Lake Huron Ship Canal Company in 1901.

According to various reports, the canal would be about eighty kilometres long, from 120 to 215 metres wide, and six metres deep. Only one lock would be needed because there was less than a three-metre difference between St. Joseph on Lake Huron and a point near Port Talbot on Lake Erie. The canal could be built in five years and cost $35 million to $50 million. The 20,000 vessels carrying 70 million tons of freight each year, even at the low rates of 7.5 cents a ton, would soon pay off the cost of construction.

In 1902, Cantin got a bill introduced in the House of Commons that would incorporate the Huron and Erie Canal Company. The bill was defeated.

Cantin kept trying. In 1903, his new St. Joseph Transportation Company presented another bill to Parliament. The bill got as far as two readings in both the House of Commons and Senate, then it too died.

So did a bill in 1904, and another in 1907.

Disgruntled shareholders began to ask why Cantin was spending so much of their money on St. Joseph and not the canal. While he'd been promoting St. Joseph as a resort town, not a shovelful of dirt had been dug on the canal.

In the face of the criticism and dwindling interest, Cantin took a serious second look at his scheme and decided to go even bigger. Why, he figured, build just one canal from Lake Huron to Lake Erie? Why not build a whole series of canals to make the entire St. Lawrence River system navigable? By now he had sold most of his buildings in St. Joseph to a development syndicate and could concentrate on the much bigger canal. He moved to Toronto, and in 1911 created The Great Lakes and Atlantic Canal and Power Company. Businessmen with interests in grain, iron, and coal invested $250,000 in the canal scheme. It wasn't a bad idea. A series of canals, ten metres deep and 120 metres wide, would link Lake Huron to Lake Erie, then Lake Erie to Lake Ontario and finally, Lake Ontario to the Ottawa River and the St. Lawrence River. The cost? No more than $500 million. Unfortunately, the same year the company got its charter, the First World War broke out.

Cantin bided his time and after the war made his pitch for the canal again. He sent out a flurry of press releases and flooded the offices of cabinet ministers with promotional brochures.

"Now that victory is ours and peace is to reign once more and as our country has been stirred up by economic turmoil during the last four years, undertakings which seemed as great tasks and almost impossible before the war are now looked on by our returned soldiers as easy to accomplish," Cantin wrote.

The idea of a canal system that bypassed the rapids of the St. Lawrence had been discussed by both the Canadian and U.S. governments since the 1890s. By 1919, there was widespread interest in the canals and the hydroelectric dams that would go with them. Cantin's company attempted to buy the hydro rights to the rapids between Lake St. Francis and Lake St. Louis near the village of Beauharnois, about twenty-four kilometres upstream from Montréal. The Beauharnois Light Heat and Power Company signed a deal to sell the rights in 1921 but two weeks later, the owner cancelled. "My eyes didn't properly read it," said the power company owner.

Cantin's company sued and at the same time, Cantin paid a go-between to negotiate a new deal with the power company. The go-between, an engineer and investor named R.O. Sweeney, knew a good deal when he saw it and bought the power company himself. The federal government gave Sweeney approval in 1929 to divert the water for hydroelectricity. Opposition politicians discovered evidence Sweeney had bribed some politicians. In the wake of the scandal, the Liberal government fell and both Cantin's and Sweeney's plans collapsed. The Canadian and U.S. governments ended up building the St. Lawrence Seaway, which opened in 1959. Nothing on the Seaway mentions Cantin, one of the original proponents of the idea.

When Cantin died in 1940, friends and family had to take up a collection to get enough money to bury him. The canal from Lake Huron to Lake Erie was never built. And St. Joseph faded away, the buildings sold and knocked down. Subdivisions sit where the port-town was. But St. Joseph hasn't forgot him. There's a plaque in the town that reads, "Narcisse Cantin — Father of the St. Lawrence Seaway."

Speed is everything

Railway fever in the 1800s led to some decisions that today might seem a little, well, ridiculous. Money was flowing like water from government for anything remotely resembling a railway or a link with a railway.

For example, if you look at a map or photo of Wolfe Island, a substantial piece of real estate in the east end of Lake Ontario, you will see it is scored by a straight line through its middle. If you went to investigate it in person, you would see what appears to be a weed-choked ditch. That's a canal. Really.

Wolfe Island has had a colourful history.

The first European to have an interest in it was the son of a Rouen, Normandy haberdasher. René-Robert Cavelier de La Salle, who you might remember from your elementary school education as simply La Salle, received it from his good friend, Louis de Buade, Comte de Frontenac et de Palluau, known simply as Frontenac, godson of King Louis XIII and governor general of New France in the mid-1600s. It came along with old Fort Cataracoui, called Kingston today. La Salle was in debt to everyone at the time and he used Wolfe Island to pay off some of his debt.

For 2,000 years prior to European interest, many Native North Americans had stopped there to fish, hunt, and rest. But by the late 1850s, it was just in the way.

Kingston merchants wanted to participate in the railway boom. What they needed, or so they thought, was speedy transit for boat traffic linking the rail line that ended in Kingston to the rail line that ended in New York State. That speedy transit throughway had to pass right across Wolfe Island.

Hence the canal. It was never really deep enough or useful enough to warrant its existence. Within twenty years of its creation, it was for all intents and purposes gone. Oddly, despite being impassable by all but the smallest traffic, say a person in waders, it wasn't officially closed until the 1930s.

La Salle sucked up to his new pal by renaming the fort, Fort Frontenac.

CHAPTER 8

BUILDINGS

Build it and they will come. It works only in the movies. In real life, sometimes you just keep building and no one bothers to show up.

Always check the deed before you build

You just have to admire some people for their energy. Take Jimmy McQuat, for instance.

Here's a guy in the middle of nowhere in the early 1900s. He's alone and, like most people at that time, struggling just to survive. And in his spare time, he cobbles together, single-handedly, a castle in the bush. Being a Canadian castle, it was made out of wood. But it was a castle, nonetheless. Oh, and it was on land that Jimmy didn't actually own.

But the small details, well, they're for small people, right? Jimmy McQuat wasn't about to let small details get in his way.

McQuat's family came from Scotland in the mid-1800s. Jimmy was the youngest of six sons. He was thirty-one when he left his family behind in the Ottawa Valley and headed west, stopping in Emo to set up a homestead on forty-five hectares. He worked hard and before long, he had two more farms and was looking to get hitched.

He was less successful at finding a bride than he had been at farming so, still single, he sold his properties and went mining for gold. He was even less successful at mining than at marrying — he lost every cent he had.

Landless, homeless, and penniless, McQuat headed deeper into the shield country — a part of Canada that is almost more water than land. He found a remote lake near Atikokan, called White Otter Lake, and built a little cabin. It was 1903.

No one is sure why McQuat built his dream home. McQuat himself told the story of how, when he was a young boy, a friend played a prank and threw a cob of corn at a man. The corn hit the man's ear and the man turned around, saw McQuat, and cursed him — literally.

Jimmy McQuat, the man shouted, you'll never do any good. You'll die in a shack.

McQuat decided he had to prove the man wrong. (Which he did, but not in the best way possible.)

One can only marvel at the sheer effort it must have taken one person to build what became McQuat's castle — cutting down the logs and bringing all of the other materials (for the windows and roof) into the backwoods. Not surprisingly, it took him seventeen years to complete.

McQuat's triumph, however, was marred by one of those minor details that so often hinder great dreams.

It turned out that it was only after he had completed the structure that McQuat applied for ownership of the land on which he'd built it. He was refused. In 1918, before he had a chance to reapply, he drowned in his own fishing nets.

The castle still stands. It is now under the wing of Ignace, a small town near Emo and Kenora.

And check your fiancee, too

Henry Hoet, to get to the point, was obsessed.

The Belgian cabinetmaker had made his way to Cardston, Alberta and he was pining for his girl. She was still in Belgium, thousands of kilometres away. Someday, he would have her here in the New World and they could find a new life.

So he worked. He was an excellent cabinetmaker and was employed in many of the top projects around Cardston. Cardston is famous today for three things: Fay Wray, Mormon roots, and Hoet.

Hoet worked on the Mormon Temple and it was while he was creating the exquisite woodwork there that he got the raw materials he needed.

You see, Hoet needed wood. Special wood. The cabinet-maker was obsessed with the idea that if he could just build a perfect home, his perfect girlfriend would consent to come to North America.

He drew his inspiration from his life experience, his love for his girl, and his current work on the temple. The Mormons were delighted with Hoet's work and allowed him to take the little bits and pieces of waste wood back to his cabin. In 1908, Hoet had purchased the shack, which had belonged to one of the men who helped the founder of the Mormon community after a flood left the property littered with cobblestone and other debris.

The wooden cabin was slowly clad in stone as Hoet used the material brought to the property by the flood. Gathered stones, hauled in a little wagon by his faithful black Lab, were selected for size and colour and then hand-washed before Hoet added them to the house. Once the outside was finished, stonewalled rooms were added, slowly and painstakingly.

The bits of wood he brought home from the work site were hand-sawed and shaped, and used to create wooden ceiling tiles of extravagant design. The hand-assembled tiles were composed of up to sixty or so pieces each. One room had 150 tiles and another 125. Hoet also brought in stained glass from Europe to be turned into lamps and used in doors and furniture.

He lived a reclusive life, speaking little English, and he was known as a hardworking, if eccentric, individual. But his eccentricities were amplified when his girlfriend told him that she would not be coming to Alberta, no matter how fine a home he was building.

Mind you, the home had taken sixteen years to complete.

His dreams dashed, Hoet attacked anything that came near his property, including a cow that started grazing. He took a hoe to it and hacked out a hunk of its flesh. In 1927, Hoet was committed to a mental institution, where he died.

His home was purchased by the Masonic Lodge in 1929 for $1,200. The house, described as a landmark, was appraised at between $20,000 to $25,000. It was back on the market in 1959, and a number of families owned it until Ed and Arlene Flickinger bought it in 1977. They renovated the home and turned it into a restaurant.

Today it is a monument to taste, patience, and unrequited love.

Or maybe just to obsession.

Sam Kee 2, Vancouver 0

Sometimes you *can* beat city hall.

Sometimes you can even give it a wedgie.

Chang Toy was a successful immigrant in Vancouver, British Columbia at the turn of the twentieth century. Despite all the tribulations of trying to get ahead in a province that still believed itself to be very British, Toy not only advanced, he thrived.

A leader in the Chinese immigrant community, Toy was a familiar sight in the city, dressed in his traditional Chinese silk. It was the statement of a man proud of his heritage, especially in a city where most businessmen wore white collars and bowler hats.

In 1912, the City of Vancouver decided to widen Pender Street and, to do so, expropriated a chunk of land from a company called Sam Kee. Sam Kee was owned by Toy and his partner, Shum Moon, another Chinese immigrant, but the company was so strongly associated with the flamboyant Toy that many called Toy by the name Sam Kee.

The land in question was a tiny piece, a small wedge of land pie. The city took a seven-metre strip of the nine-metre wide slice, leaving Toy and Moon with a two-metre wide wedge, probably in the hope or belief that the company would toss in the remaining land as part of the package.

So the city was surprised when Toy actually asked for additional compensation to hand over the leftover land. Obviously deciding that the land was worthless, the city refused to pay any more money and left Sam Kee with his sliver.

If you go to the corner of Carrall and Pender Streets today, you will see what Sam Kee did. There stands what *Ripley's Believe It or Not* calls "the narrowest building in the world" — a two-storey structure twenty-nine and a quarter metres long and one and a half metres deep on the main floor, designed by Brown & Gillam and named the Sam Kee Building, after the company that built it.

The second floor held an apartment that provided space for a family of five, augmented by bay windows that jut out over the sidewalk. Below were public baths that stretched out under the street.

Chang Toy died in 1920. Today, Jack Chow Insurance owns the building, which has become a tourist landmark in Vancouver. The owner of the building recently installed glass sidewalks, giving pedestrians a view of the rooms below the surface. City officials tried to get the sidewalks removed, saying they were unsafe. But the sidewalks proved to be too sturdy to move.

CHAPTER 9

ADVENTURERS

Canada would not have become the country it is today without courageous explorers, devout missionaries, and self-sacrificing heroes overcoming great odds to achieve success. Here are those who overcame great odds to achieve somewhat less.

There's too much water here, throw in some islands

Louis Denys was an accomplished French Canadian sailor and soldier. He also had some success as a pirate raiding English ships (although he reportedly tried to persuade the bureaucrats to underestimate the value of his booty so as to decrease the tax on it that would be owed to the French king).

He was not, however, the most accurate mapmaker in the so-called New World. When he resorted to his imagination in 1744, he created a problem for mapmakers sixty years later.

Denys was one of the first Europeans to explore Lake Superior. He had learned from Jacques Legardeur and local Native people that there were extensive copper deposits in Lake Superior and he convinced some private investors and the French government — who funded his venture through a fur trade lease on Chagouamignon — to finance an expedition to find and exploit the mines.

A forty-ton barque was built on Lake Superior and Denys headed off with a group of German prospectors looking for ore.

They found some, but Denys realized quickly that it would be prohibitively expensive to mine and transport. In the meantime, though, he had some investors at home who were anxious to be repaid. So when he submitted his report, the map he included showed not only a lake at the nose of Lake Superior, but also a number of large islands that he had "discovered" and named after his financiers, perhaps in an attempt to appease them.

Despite the fact that six decades earlier, Jesuits who ventured across Lake Superior in canoes had provided much more accurate information, for some time later, maps — including the one used by officials drawing up the new Canada-U.S. boundary in Paris after the War of 1812 — incorporated Denys' fictional islands. The boundary line ran between two islands, one that didn't exist, and toward a lake that didn't exist. It took some time for both countries to realize the boundary went through several imaginary places.

In business, politics can kill you

He was the man who pioneered office politics. He was pretty good at it, but even four centuries ago, playing both sides against the middle wasn't the brightest of ideas. Especially with bloodthirsty warriors.

Étienne Brûlé was born near Paris, France around 1592. He came to Canada as a teenager with Samuel de Champlain, and died in June 1633 in a cornfield belonging to the Bear clan of the Huron, not far from Toanche, near Penetanguishene in central Ontario. His skull was caved in.

The Huron believed the death of Brûlé, an adopted member of their clan, was the source of the bad luck that almost wiped them out.

It was quite a life and quite a death.

Brûlé arrived in Canada around 1608. Two years later, at the age of sixteen, he asked Champlain's permission to go and live with the Huron. Brûlé left Québec City in June 1610 and made his way to Algonquin territory and possibly to Huronia with Iroquet, an Algonquin chief. He was the first European to see Niagara Falls. He was the first white to travel to the lands of Pennsylvania and to all the Great Lakes except Michigan, and he was also the first European to shoot the rapids at Lachine, near Montréal.

Brûlé returned regularly to Québec and took part in a raid on the Iroquois with Champlain in 1615. In order to attack the Iroquois with a larger force, Champlain wanted the Huron to bring in their allies, the Susquehannahs. Brûlé headed off with twelve of the best Huron braves, travelling south from Huronia. Some historians believe Brûlé took the familiar route of the Coldwater River to the portage, overland to Orillia, down Lake Simcoe to the Holland River to the Humber portage, and then down the Humber to Lake Ontario. The group travelled west along the shore of Lake Ontario to somewhere between the Niagara and Genesee Rivers. From there they made their way to the Native village of Carantouan, the Susquehannah capital.

Unfortunately, Brûlé's timing was off, so while he and the party did manage to get the Huron allies on side, they arrived late for the battle and the Huron and Champlain were whipped.

Brûlé was distracted by discovery.

He had made his way down the Susquehannah River, probably starting at the branch near Ostego, New York and travelled to Chesapeake Bay. On the way back, he was captured by the Seneca and was the first white to be tortured by them. He later convinced them to release him by forecasting the approach of a storm, which he said was a sign from God to spare him. Some discount Brûlé's story and suggest that he may have been released as a gesture of goodwill by the Seneca, an Iroquois clan who wished to cash in on the French trade.

Brûlé returned to Toanche and in 1621-23 took off on another far-flung expedition. This time he went north. Prior to this, the only Europeans to have gone north to the North Channel settled at the copper mines there before returning. Gabriel Sagard, a Récollet friar who lived in Huronia at the time, says in his writings that Brûlé probably made it all the way to the end of Lake Superior, near where Duluth stands now.

"The interpreter Brûlé and a number of Indians assure us that beyond the *mer douce* (Lake Huron) there is another very large lake, which empties into the former by waterfall, nearly two leagues across, which has been called the Gaston Falls (Sault Ste. Marie); this lake, with the fresh water sea, represents about a thirty-day canoe trip, about 400 leagues long," wrote Sagard.

Brûlé was also reported to have been the first to go to the land of the Neutrals by Father Joseph de La Roche Daillon.

Most of the Europeans looked down on Brûlé and others like him for "going native." Brûlé married a young Toanche Bear clan woman. According to Champlain, the marriage did not get in the way of Brûlé's zeal for women and he often philandered about the New World.

In 1629, Quebec was captured by the British. Brûlé then signed on with the Kirke brothers. Sir David Kirke was born in Dieppe, France and moved to the eastern coast of what would later become Canada. Brûlé was not alone. Like a number of well-known scouts and interpreters, after Quebec fell he sided with the British, who paid better and did not push religion on the local tribes.

At the time, Brûlé was on his way back from a mission he was ordered to undertake by Champlain. Freshly returned to North America after being banished by the Jesuits for immorality, Brûlé, in 1629, was not feeling too good about France or the role of the Jesuits in Huronia, where most of his friends and family were. Upon arriving, Brûlé saw three ships in the port of Québec: a French supply ship flying a Union Jack and two buccaneer ships belonging to the Kirke brothers. For Brûlé, it was a wonderful sight. The French would be leaving and he could stay. The Kirkes, recognizing Brûlé's value as an interpreter and trader, hired him on. Champlain was not pleased and as he was forced onto a British ship to be returned to France, he yelled insults at Brûlé. Brûlé knew he would be hanged in France if he ever returned.

For three years, the British clung to the St. Lawrence. When they were finally forced out, Brûlé and the Huron who traded with the English again faced the French.

The chief of the Bear clan, Aenons, was concerned about the return of the French to Huronia because Brûlé was part of his clan. Aenons sent an emissary to Québec to talk with the French, and was told that Brûlé was a traitor, and as such would be hanged or worse. Jean Duval, another man who crossed Champlain, had been drawn and quartered, his head stuck on a pike outside Québec's fortress walls.

It was an image not easily shaken and Aenons didn't want it to happen to him. He also wanted to trade with the French. He was happy they were back to patrol the upper St. Lawrence against raiding bands of Iroquois. The British meant alcohol and ambushes and the Huron were sick of the Brits, booze, and bash-ups.

Aenons held a council meeting in Toanche and discussed the issue. He liked Brûlé — he admired his strength and his vigour. But Brûlé was not a Wendat or a Huron. He was a Frenchman. Aenons' fear was that Brûlé might flee to the south, perhaps in an attempt to put things right with Champlain by brokering a trade partnership with the Seneca and the Five Nations.

On the same day as the council meeting, Brûlé was invited to go deer hunting with two teens from the village. He was found dead, many think at the hands of Aenons. His skull was crushed by a single blow, the style of execution favoured by the Huron for dispatching one of their own.

After his death, the village of Toanche split and the family and friends of Brûlé headed south to establish the village of Wenrio. The southern Huron blamed the northern Huron for Brûlé's death and the Algonquin tribe, who had first brought Brûlé into the Native country, blamed all Huron. There was even talk of war. War came eventually, but not with the Algonquin.

When the Jesuit priest Jean de Brébeuf returned to Huronia in 1634, he didn't know Toanche had split and he arrived in the middle of the night to find an empty village. Following the sound of barking dogs, he made his way to Ihonatiria, where the people from Wenrio had settled. These friends of Brûlé blamed every nasty thing that happened to the Huron on the Toanche peoples. When a disease swept through the area in 1635, the Huron told tales of a woman who spoke like Brûlé emerging from the fires in the longhouses to tell them that this was what they got for killing her brother.

In 1636, during the Feast of the Dead, the Huron moved their villages, and the remains of the dead that had been placed on forest platforms were brought to Ossassane where they were put in a large communal pit. In order to avoid a war among themselves, the Huron decided not to include Brûlé's remains in the ceremony. His bones were left on the tree platform near Toanche, where they eventually returned to the earth.

Four or five years after Brûlé died, the Huron people were worn down to half their number by disease and war. By 1649, they were scattered to the winds, like Brûlé's bones were scattered on the forest floor. Brave and resourceful, Brûlé nevertheless made some bad decisions, leaving him more a footnote in history than one of the main players for both the French and the Huron.

The navigator, drown him, he's just taking up space

Midnight on the barque *Saladin*.

Captain George Fielding of Gaspé paced the deck. The 550-ton ship sailed smoothly, several months out of Valparaiso, Chile, laden with guano, copper, silver, spices, and mail. It was a good ship and he was an experienced captain.

The trouble was, he wasn't the captain of this ship. The real captain lay sleeping peacefully below. There were one too many captains on this ship and Fielding had plans to reduce the number. That night, April 14, 1844, he and a handful of mutineers covered the decks in blood and started one of the dumbest acts of piracy on the high seas. Before they were through, no one who could actually sail a ship was left alive.

A native of Jersey, Fielding was brought up in Gaspé by his father, an ex-soldier. By the time he landed passage on the *Saladin*, Fielding had sailed on fishing vessels off France and trading ships off Newfoundland and Nova Scotia, had married twice, and had a teenage son who travelled with him. Described by a Liverpool newspaper as a "stout, well-built man, with prominent, and rather strongly marked, but by no means unpleasant features," he could speak French, Spanish, Portuguese, and Dutch. He had lately taken command of a ship called the *Vitula* and was bringing guano from South America to the Maritimes. A ruffian by nature and experience, he ran into trouble with the Peruvian government by trying to smuggle guano aboard. Peruvian soldiers boarded his ship, shooting Fielding in the shoulder, and two days later he and his crew arrived in Lima. Fielding was imprisoned but managed to get a message to his son, who was apparently free. His son got Fielding a *puncha*, a large cloak worn by the Native people. The sea captain put on the cloak and slipped by the guards. For several days he hid in a dockyard, covered in wood shavings and other litter. In the middle of the night, he found his way aboard a British schooner, which brought him to Valparaiso. Two other sea captains refused him passage, but Captain McKenzie of the *Saladin* offered to take him and his son back to Halifax for free.

The *Saladin* set sail on February 8, rounded Cape Horn and headed for Nova Scotia. Besides Captain McKenzie, the

155

ship carried the two Fieldings, a cook, a steward, and a crew of nine divided into two watches. By April, the argumentative Fielding had had enough of the stubborn McKenzie. Eyeing the rich cargo, Fielding conspired with four of the crew to take over the ship. Fielding whispered to each man of one watch that if he didn't join, the others would kill him. He eventually persuaded a one-legged sailor named George Jones, a Nova Scotian named John Hazelton, a Londoner named William Trevascus, and a Swede named Charles Anderson to help him take the ship. On the midnight to four o'clock shift of April 14, the mate on watch lay down on a chicken coop, feeling sick. Earlier that day, the carpenter had been working on deck and had left his tools out. The four mutineers seized axes and hammers, struck the mate, and threw him overboard. Next they tried to sneak into the captain's cabin but his dog scared them off. So they called the changing of the watch, and dispatched the first sailor up, James Allen, in the same way they had got rid of the mate. The ship's carpenter was called up, and as he peeped out, he was clobbered on the head with an axe and dragged up and over the side of the ship.

"Man overboard!" one of the mutineers cried. Captain McKenzie rushed up and was attacked. He fought back, but Fielding hit him twice with an axe and tossed him overboard. Two more of the crew were called to the deck, axed, and thrown into the ocean. The cook and another steward came up about six o'clock. Fielding wanted to kill them too, but the mutineers, perhaps sickened by the blood-drenched deck of the ship, stopped him. Sizing up the situation, the cook and steward agreed to join them.

The pirates immediately set to the grog, burned or threw overboard papers and mail, and divided up clothes. They swore on the Bible to remain loyal to one another. They also threw over all the weapons, to eliminate the evidence and the temptation of their colleagues. But Fielding couldn't resist. He approached two of the pirates with a plan to kill the rest. He had apparently hidden two pistols, a carving knife, and a vial of poison. His fellow pirates found out and tied him up. To seal their deal, the other pirates forced the cook and carpenter to throw both Fielding and his son overboard.

With Fielding drowned, the brilliant gang of pirates had successfully tossed over two captains, the only two men who knew how to properly navigate.

The steward, a learned man of nineteen named John Galloway, could read a bit so he tried to navigate their way to the Gulf of St. Lawrence. The plan: to scuttle the ship, take the long boat to shore, and slip away with the money. They cleverly covered the name of the ship with a board and repainted the head. "Every day some portion of the crew was drunk," Galloway noted in his confession.

As they sailed north to Halifax, the crew split up the money and silver, tossed papers and clothing about the cabin, and broke apart some navigation equipment to store their money in the cases.

The *Saladin* reached the coast of Nova Scotia in May and the drunken crew and inexperienced navigator tried to put in at Country Harbour. Instead, they grounded the ship on one of the islands in the bay. Alerted by people on shore, two schooner captains rushed to help the *Saladin*. On board they found the grog-saturated crew, seventy tons of copper, thirteen bars of silver, spice, and about $9,000 divided up and ready for carrying away. The crew was seized. Before their July 1844 trial, the cook and steward/navigator confessed. The four main pirates, Jones, Hazelton, Anderson and Trevascus, were found guilty and sentenced to hang. The cook and steward, Carr and Galloway, were found not guilty of murdering Fielding and his son because they had to do it to save their own lives.

Dubois, is that a French dish?

Canada's history is full of stories of North American and European explorers navigating the vast expanses of the Arctic. Most of them were looking for a way around Canada. Some, like Samuel Hearne, were searching for mines of marvellous metals. Others were seeking out the iceless North Sea. And finally, by the mid-1800s, they were actually going up north looking for each other. Ultimately, and unfortunately, some of them ended up eating each other.

Thankfully, there are no recorded examples of the searchers being eaten by those they searched.

It is ironic that North American and European explorers often expressed fears that Native people of the lands they were exploring and "finding" would be cannibals, given the opportunity and the right wine.

There had, it is true, been some isolated incidents of cannibalism during warfare among non-Arctic Native people (for example, the leader of the Iroquois war party that captured him ate the heart of Jean de Brébeuf, a martyred Jesuit priest, during the raiding of Huronia in 1649). However, by the 1800s there had been thousands of encounters and exchanges between Europeans and Canadian aboriginals with no acts of cannibalism, even during hostilities.

It's not clear why they thought Native people of the Arctic were cannibals. It may have been that "Eskimo," which some Cree guides told European explorers was the name of the Inuit, had the pejorative meaning of "eaters of raw meat." Of course, living above the tree line meant there was not a lot of wood for cooking fires, and the fat from animal blubber, too valuable a commodity to be used for cooking, was saved for lighting and rendering. Perhaps the Europeans were not used to seeing people eating raw, bloody victuals.

On the other hand, some of the Arctic explorers them-selves took rather desperate steps when lost in the barren lands without food supplies.

Not all of them, of course. John Rae, a Scottish doctor before he was twenty and an employee of the Hudson's Bay Company (HBC), spent years roaming the Arctic beginning in his 20s. He was one of the most successful of the Arctic explorers because he followed the customs and methods of the Inuit and Cree. During the mid-1800s, he regularly trekked hundreds of kilometres in the north by himself. While Rae's expeditions may have suffered some fatalities due to accidents, he and the rest of his crew usually returned safely.

Not all explorers were quite so hardy, and not all expedi-tion crews were so lucky.

While he was at Fort Simpson, Rae chewed the fat, as it were, with Pierre Pambrun, an employee of the HBC, who told Rae the tale of Pelly Banks Station. An HBC outpost under Pambrun's charge, Pelly Banks Station burned down in November 1849. The two other men stationed there, Hyacinth Dubois (a French Canadian) and William Foubister (a Scot) managed with Pambrun to rig a shelter from what was left. They survived on tough leather baling cord and marten skins — not for clothes, mind you, but for food.

Pambrun told Rae that he eventually left his two workers with the remains of the supplies and headed off into the bush to a lake some days away. Over a period of two months at the lake, Pambrun ate pounds of rabbit, fish, and partridge as well as a fox, a raven, an owl, and (count 'em) ten squirrels.

While Pambrun could clearly fend for himself in the wilderness, his charges — who may have felt abandoned by their supervisor — apparently could not. When Pambrun returned to Pelly Banks in the spring, only the Scot, Foubister, was alive. Foubister explained that when Dubois died, he had buried the body under some stones but wolves had taken the corpse. Pambrun had his suspicions but bit his tongue, and Foubister explained away the large bones in the fireplace as merely some caribou bones that had been brought in with the firewood.

Pambrun left again and returned within a couple of days. He had managed to kill a squirrel and was going to share it with Foubister. Foubister, meanwhile, was boiling something in a pot on the fire. He claimed it was merely water for tea. Pambrun, however, noticed something floating in the broth that looked more like a human liver than a tea bag and, while he didn't chew him out, so to speak, he did utter a challenge that you don't hear in many workplaces: "Will you confess that you have been eating poor Dubois?"

John Rae got a taste of failed expeditions himself when he set out to find the lost Franklin expedition. Sir John Franklin, in fact, was lost in the Arctic twice — once in 1828 (when he merely resorted to eating his boots to survive) and again in 1844-1845. Lady John Franklin had in part financed the rescue expedition, but when Rae returned with tales of cannibalism among the crew, she and the British government did their best to hush up the scandal. His insistence on bringing to public attention the demise of Franklin and his crew resulted in Rae's achievements being marginalized. Just bringing back the tidbit that the Franklin expedition ended in cannibalism ensured Rae a place in the cellar of history. Eventually, however, the skeletons were found in the closet. There were accounts from Native people who had seen dying members of the expedition with boots used as lunch bags full of boiled human remains.

There were other expeditions that resulted in yet more expeditions to rescue or find them, although in some cases the rescuers were too late.

The Greely Expedition from the United States headed out in 1881 to establish a research station and a fort in the Arctic under the supervision of Lieutenant Adolph Greely. Greely had made a name for himself in the U.S. Army Signal Corps. As a punk lieutenant, he supervised the wiring of the States for telegraph. This was no minor feat, but that it qualified him for an Arctic expedition seems unlikely.

The territory they were bound for is Canadian today. The crew was lost for three years. During the final days before they were found by Lieutenant John Colwell of the United States Army, a number of the survivors resorted to eating the dead. Oddly, two of the dead were bundled up into caskets and returned home. The bodies were later exhumed and revealed obvious signs of cannibalism.

Perhaps Franklin and Greely were reluctant to admit failure — and worse — because both relied heavily on the support and means of so-called modern ways. For example, Franklin's expedition made some of the earliest use of canned meats, had a steam engine for heat and power, and many other of the then-latest scientific marvels. Greely was similarly equipped, and even went so far as to suggest, before his own expedition had to be rescued, that Inuit abilities to survive and work in the north were overrated.

Even today, the belief that cannibalism is being practised by others continues. In July 2001, while the city of Toronto was in the midst of bidding for the Olympics, Toronto mayor Mel Lastman angered many African-Canadians, embarrassed a country, and became a laughingstock when he expressed fears of cannibalism prior to a trip to Africa. "What the hell do I want to go to a place like Mombasa?" he was quoted as saying. "Snakes just scare the hell out of me. I'm sort of scared about going there, but the wife is really nervous. I just see myself in a pot of boiling water with these natives dancing around me."

Perhaps he should be more concerned about a trip to Great Britain, Europe, or America, where the most recent cannibals of Canada came from.

I like a drink with some body to it

John Rowand, a grizzly bear of a man, asked nothing of life. He took. Big Mountain, everyone called him. The chief factor, or boss, of the Hudson's Bay Company's Edmonton House weighed in at 135 kilograms in a relatively short package with an equally short fuse. Born in Montréal, the son of a doctor, he began fur trading at fourteen and soon had only two authorities he would answer to, God and the Company, and not necessarily in that order.

After he became chief factor of Edmonton House in 1823, he built what became known as the Big House, a three-storey mansion complete with a ballroom that could entertain 150 guests and the first glass windows in the west, protected on their voyage from England in barrels of molasses. He loved horses and he raced his own on a track he built. And most important of all, he made money for the Company. People loved and hated him, but they all knew he was boss of the country and the fur trade in the North Saskatchewan district.

Rowand could take on anyone. Once he and missionary Albert Lacombe were resting at a campfire after a day of riding when 200 Blackfoot warriors rode up and surrounded them. Rowand charged at the chief and shouted, "Stop you villains!" Then he went back to his meal. The chief realized who Rowand was, apologized, and called off his warriors.

His death came, appropriately, during an effort to dominate. In 1854, Rowand led the spring brigade of boats laden

Glenbow Archives/NA-1747-1

Fur trade boss John Rowand was as big as life itself. In death, however, he was somewhat reduced.

with fur down the Saskatchewan River. He stopped in Fort Pitt, where his son, the chief trader, was to join him with more pelts on their way to York Factory on Hudson Bay.

At his son's house, he heard a commotion on the docks and raced to see one of his voyageurs fighting with a Fort Pitt man. Fights caused injuries and injuries delayed the brigade, so Rowand roared into the middle of the brawl. He barely got a word out before he clutched his chest and died of a heart attack.

The brigade's departure could not be postponed, so his son and loyal employees buried Rowand at Fort Pitt.

But Rowand had orders for others even after his death. His will stated that his final resting place should be Montréal. His body was dug up in the spring of 1855. A woman was ordered to boil the flesh from his bones in order to make soap, then put the bones in a barrel of rum for preserving.

The barrel was put in a canoe that was supposed to head to Red River, and from there be shipped to Montréal. There are stories the barrel was marked "salt pork" but the crew wasn't fooled. When a storm blew up on Lake Winnipeg, the superstitious crew threw the barrel overboard. The barrel tumbled to shore, where it was discovered later. It was then sent up the traditional route to York Factory on Hudson Bay.

Unfortunately, the ships at York Factory did not sail to Montréal; they sailed to England. So Rowand's remains were put on a ship to England, where Company officials gave the barrel a nice ceremony. Then they forgot to send it back. The barrel was shipped to a Liverpool warehouse where it sat for several years until a worker realized what it was and put in on a ship to Montréal.

Across the Atlantic, for the second time, the barrel travelled. Finally, four years after he died, Rowand arrived in Montréal.

But that wasn't the end of Rowand's troubles. When the barrel was pried open, it was full of water. Four years earlier, it's assumed, the woman who had to boil the body had comforted herself with the rum.

Why won't these damn cows take orders?

Right then, how hard can it be to move cattle?

For someone used to moving men? Can't be that hard. Tally ho!

With that imperial frame of mind, Major James Walker, formerly of the Northwest Mounted Police, began the first large drives that brought ranching and cattle, dead or alive, to Alberta.

The stories of wide-open grasslands rich for cattle grazing — now safe from Indians and free of buffalo — had reached the East in the late 1870s. A Montréal senator named Matthew Cochrane, wealthy from the shoe and leather business, persuaded his government cronies to lease him (and anyone else smart enough to ask) 100,000 acres for twenty-one years at a rate of a penny an acre per year. Cochrane leased 100,000 acres just west of where Calgary stands today. He then looked around for someone who knew the country and knew how to lead men. James Walker seemed to fit the bill, and Cochrane persuaded the Mounties to let their man go.

Late in the summer of 1881, Cochrane arranged to buy several thousand head of cattle from Montana. Because winter was closing in, Walker's crew pushed the thirty cowboys and the herd fast and hard, twenty-five to thirty kilometres a day. The cattle were marched from dawn to dusk, with little time to graze, and were so tired at night they slept rather than ate. They were so crowded together they trampled the grass a few might have been able to munch on the way.

The calves started to die first. Wagons following the drive to pick up errant or weak calves couldn't hold the hundreds falling by the wayside. Many were left to die. Cowboys picked up the rest and sold them to settlers for next to nothing, a cup of tea, a pound of butter. Whiskey traders following the drive

James Walker could move men to battle, and later as Calgary mayor, to vote. He could not, however, get cattle to move. Instead, they simply died by the thousands.

exchanged their liquor for calves, then turned around and sold the calves for profit.

By the time the cattle reached Big Hill, Cochrane's ranch across the Bow River west of Calgary, they were weakened by thirst, hunger, and exhaustion. Then winter came. Hundreds more died.

No matter, Cochrane was rich and Walker was still his man. The next spring, Walker and his cowboys set out to gather and brand the cattle that had made it through the winter. Settlers living in the area agreed to help out, partly to gather up some of their own unbranded animals. Walker didn't bother to worry about the cattle belonging to the settlers. His orders from Cochrane were to brand every unmarked animal he saw. One settler owned a cow and calf that were like family pets and stayed closed to his house all winter. Walker's crew rounded them up. When the settler objected, Walker told him orders were orders. The disgusted settlers and small ranchers quit, but on their way home they took a few side trips. They knew the land better than the hired cowboys did. They knew the secret ravines and hidden coulees where some of Cochrane's cattle had wintered. So they rustled up as many of the maverick cattle as they could, branded them, and recouped their losses. Or in some cases, came out ahead.

Naturally, after the first disastrous drive and questionable spring roundup, Cochrane sent Walker down to Montana again the next year for more cattle. Walker got off to another bad start. He had arranged to buy about 5,000 head in Montana, but his superior, a Dr. McEachern, delayed the deal. By the time it closed, the price had gone up by $25,000. An angry Walker tendered his resignation, agreeing to stay on only until a replacement arrived. Losing money at the beginning of the drive apparently bothered him more than losing cattle at the end.

This drive, however, Walker did manage to bring the cattle from Montana at a slower pace. But a blizzard hit the herd in late September just south of Calgary. Snow buried the trails and huge drifts blocked the animals. The experienced trail boss suggested the cattle be driven into the protection of a nearby valley until the blizzard passed. The cattle could stay for a month, build up their strength, then be pushed to the ranch.

"No," Walker said. "Your contract is to deliver them to Big Hill."

So the trail boss and his cowboys got the strongest steers and drove them through the snowbanks so the rest of the herd could follow.

At Big Hill Ranch, the disgusted trail boss turned to Walker and said, "Here they are. I have carried out my contract. Count 'em now, because half of them will be dead tomorrow."

Walker didn't stick around to see if his trail boss was right. His replacement arrived and he quit. But Cochrane's bad luck continued. The winter storms lasted until mid-October, followed by a thaw that was just as quickly followed by bitter cold. Not only could the cattle not reach the grass through the layer of snow and ice, but with hooves worn to the quick by the long march, they could barely keep upright on the slick hills.

The cattle tried to move away from the area to open grazing lands nearby, but Cochrane wanted them kept on his range. Cowboys worked night and day. Historian Leroy Kelly reported that the people of Calgary could see cattle every day trying to move down to better lands, and cowboys every evening pushing them back up to the deadly range.

The snow stayed until June. By spring, of the 12,000 cattle driven to the ranch, about 4,000 were left. The carcasses of dead cattle thickened the coulees and gullies where they had tried to find protection from the bitter winds. In some places, you could cross or walk the length of a ravine without stepping off a carcass and onto land.

Cochrane gave up and moved the cattle operation further west to the Waterton Lakes area. He ended up putting sheep on the acreage near Big Hill. Walker became a politician, nothing less than the mayor of Calgary. People, it seems, were easier to lead than cattle.

Let's just call the whole province Morice

Two months into their hard journey through bog and forest and wild water, running out of supplies and winter touching the September air, Father Adrien-Gabriel Morice and his Native guides canoed down the Dawson River in the northern interior of British Columbia and into a small lake. The priest noted the date, September 19, 1895, and promptly gave the small body of water the name Lake Thomas to honour one of the guides, a member of the Carrier tribe, Thomas Thautil.

The group continued on and discovered that Lake Thomas was actually a bay that led to a much bigger lake surrounded by cloud-scraping mountains. As soon as his Native guides saw this magnificent lake, wrote Morice's biographer, they insisted it be renamed Lake Morice, after the priest.

The humble priest agreed. It only seemed appropriate.

He was, again in the words of his biographer, the king of the country, a defender of truth and justice, versatile, musical, kind and, if he had any shortcomings, too hard a worker.

The biographer, by the way, was himself.

And he was halfway right. From 1885 to 1903, Morice battled Hudson's Bay Company officials, Native chiefs, provincial government bureaucrats, and even his own holy superiors to become the baron, if not the king, of a huge area in the interior of northern British Columbia. He also became an accomplished cartographer and for his day, an insightful anthropologist.

But try as he might, Morice failed to put himself on the map.

Born in 1859 in France to a wheelwright, Morice seemed destined for some kind of fame. At eleven, according to his own account, he began publishing a handwritten newspaper that he distributed for two years. At fourteen, he entered the seminary and the accounts of heroism and hardship in the New World convinced Morice his future lay in a wilderness mission among the Native people. He left France in 1880 and was posted at first to a few unsatisfactory positions in the more civilized areas of British Columbia. Morice sulked, complained, argued with his colleagues, and performed his duties with such indifference he earned two official warnings from his superiors. One more and he would have been dismissed from the order.

Instead, to everyone's relief, he was posted to the Stuart Lake Mission in 1885.

He was now responsible for the spiritual education and comfort of about 1,600 Native people — Carrier, Babine, and Sekani — living in 165,000 square kilometres, mostly around the lake and the Fraser River. The Native people had long established fur trading business with whites and Morice made his base at the Hudson's Bay Company's Fort St. James. He made his first mission the learning of the Carrier language.

"It was that mastery of the language he ultimately acquired which was to render him the king of the country, especially if we join that linguistic achievement to his great impartiality and his astonishing penetration of the Indian character," wrote Morice about himself.

As king of the country, he had three main rivals: the Hudson's Bay Company bosses, called factors, Native chiefs, and the provincial government's Indian Agent. As soon as he added the Carrier language to his ability to speak French and English fluently, Morice gained an edge over everyone else.

The Hudson's Bay Company usually held the greatest power in similar settlement areas across Canada because it paid for the furs and sold the Native people supplies and white goods. Missionaries were encouraged to "civilize" the Native people, as long as religion encouraged them to work hard and bring in furs.

Morice, however, began to control the Company. Whenever he perceived a slight of some sort, as when a factor didn't call on him soon enough after arriving, Morice threatened to send his Native followers with their furs to nearby Quesnel, where rivals to the Company operated. Not only would they sell their furs in Quesnel, they would buy their goods there as well. Afraid of losing business, one Fort St. James factor paid Morice a donation of $50 a year out of his own pocket to keep the Native trade. It was nothing compared to the business he'd lose if the fur trappers decided to take their business elsewhere.

Now and then, Morice invited rival fur traders to set up shop right outside Fort St. James. Apparently unaware of his manoeuvrings, the Company men were so alarmed they paid off the rivals. And they got the message. They needed Morice.

So did many of the Native people. Morice helped them get work from the Company, advised many of them in legal or personal troubles, and offered assistance in times of illness — pointing out, of course, that shamans could do nothing to help them. As long as Morice was doing a good job keeping the peace, the Indian Agent in charge of the area didn't have to make the long and rough trip into the interior.

His methods of converting Native people followed most of the traditional Oblate methods of the time — whipping, confinement, and ostracism for sinners, the reward of helping the priest for the faithful. For one group particularly attracted to the sinfulness of gambling, shamans, potlatches, Native dances, and songs, Morice created Moricetown. Eight families moved into his chosen land on the Bulkley River, where a church and trading post would be established. The site, however, was too close to the river and flooded, and Moricetown was moved before it was started. Although he ignored it over the years, it eventually took root and is now a hamlet of about 815 people.

His worshippers grew in number for many reasons: simple faith, the fear of white diseases and the lurid Hell described by the Oblates, the desire to succeed in the new order of the world. Native people took Morice's religion in stride, mixing it with their own, using whichever one worked best at the time.

Morice's emotional devotion to the Native people was never suspect, but his methods and hobbies raised eyebrows among his superiors. He never did get around to teaching the Carriers how to speak or read English, a skill the ambitious Native people desired. He didn't do much to teach them farming, either. Morice liked his Native people the way he found them: fur-traders, hunters, and reliant on him.

Morice soon reached dizzying heights of power.

The Company gave him free mail service, yearly donations, a supply of quality ink for his writings, and the culinary delicacies he loved, such as bacon. In winter, Native guides pulled him, wrapped in fur, on toboggans to their villages, then lifted him off and carried him into their houses. At each arrival to a village, he was offered a rifle salute. Morice had "such a tremendous power over the whole North that he literally had its inhabitants at his beck and call," he wrote about himself.

Aside from the occasional difficult trip to a Native village, it was a good life. He had a printing press installed at his mission, paid for by Native donations, and published his thoughts in a monthly eight-page newspaper. In the 1890s, he wrote articles on the Native people for several scholarly journals. He worked for years on an English/Carrier dictionary, using symbols he had created.

And he explored, climbing mountains, traversing dangerous rivers, canoeing white water, trudging through deep forests, all with a lot of help. Morice wasn't much of a walker, never mind a hiker, climber, or snowshoer. He couldn't swim and had to be carried over raging rivers. His Native guides hunted for their food, built the fires, cooked, laid his pine bough beds, carried supplies, built rafts for some of the rivers, paddled canoes in others, and turned around to look for the lost priest when he had fallen and got disoriented.

On a surveying trip in 1899, Morice struggled to the base of a rocky column that led to the peak of a mountain. His Native guides climbed to the top then tied ropes to Morice. Two of them above pulled while one below pushed the priest up. Terrified, gasping, and dizzy, Morice fell on his face. He couldn't stand. He did, however, name the mountain after himself.

The long journeys may have briefly made Morice famous, but some of his followers began to complain. Their priest was never around. Hudson's Bay Company officials were also growing tired of the meddlesome Morice. Another missionary toured Morice's domain in 1903 and reported back to the bishop that Morice's neglected congregation had fallen back into gambling and paganism.

Morice might have parried this latest charge had he been able to keep his ambition in check. He wanted to spend the winter of 1903 in Vancouver to work on a history book. His bishop, Dontenwell, only too happily agreed to Morice's request. Morice got as far as Quesnel when he read a telegram from the bishop intended for someone else, notifying the Native settlement that a new priest was coming.

The new priest soon arrived, and it was none other than the man who made the critical report on Morice earlier that year. Morice refused to continue on to Vancouver, pleading with his bishop by telegram that the replacement priest should be turned around.

Morice tried to persuade the newcomer to give up, but the priest took the boat up the river to Stuart Lake anyway. Morice was torn. He could go to Vancouver and finish the book or go back to the fort and regain control over his mission. He chose the book. The bishop wouldn't let him go back to Stuart Lake and Fort St. James.

"He was doomed never to return to his mission!" his sympathetic biographer wrote. "The half-witted man was left in his place."

Morice fell into a slow decline, still writing books but believing everyone was out to get him. He was transferred to Winnipeg, but decided to edit a French newspaper in Saskatchewan called *Le Patriote de L'Ouest*. Morice worked from sunup to sundown, composing the content and answering complaints about delivery. But the head printer waged a campaign against him and the priest resigned. Soon after, some of his manuscripts burned in a fire in his quarters above the printing shop. He told the employees to be careful with gasoline, but they didn't listen.

Morice headed back to Manitoba, where he became embroiled in a war with yet another colleague, this time sparked by the offender making too much noise in the room above. A war of wills ensued. "Decency forbids us to enter into the details of the shameless abuse, crying injustice . . . which he had to endure," noted Morice's biographer. Morice found more trouble when he joined the anti-Semitic, anti-democratic movement, Action Française. His superiors eventually excused him because it would have been a public scandal to remove the published author from their order and besides, he was crazy.

For the remainder of his years, Morice wrote and waged his war against all slights, above all the slight of anonymity. His maps were published, but when the province of British Columbia put out its official maps, many of Morice's names were changed. Even the grand Lake Morice was renamed. Eventually, Morice did get a different lake, a mountain, and a river's tributary, though he grumbled about not getting the main branch of the river. The changes to his map, he complained to another writer, were made by grumpy, nameless, Anglo-Saxon bureaucrats in Victoria who didn't like a French man spreading his name across the province. Morice made a final case for the names he chose in his biography. It was published in 1930 by Ryerson Press of Toronto and called, *Fifty Years in Western Canada*. The author was named only D.L.S. Morice died eight years later, assured of his own immortality thanks to the extremely laudatory biography.

Fifty-six years later, British Columbia historian David Mulhall undertook an extensive study of Morice for his biography, *Will to Power*. Mulhall dug up a contract referring to Morice as the author of *Fifty Years* and noted that he had previously written under the pseudonym de la Sienne, or D.L.S. The biography of Father Adrien-Gabriel Morice appeared to be written by none other than Father Adrien-Gabriel Morice.

With friends like him, who needs enemas?

Some time after the Second World War, *Reader's Digest* got wind of a hero of fantastic proportions.

George Dupre was well-known in Alberta and many people knew his story. Word had travelled all the way from

Calgary that a man had withstood remarkable torture at the hands of the evil Nazis during the Second World War. This man was a specially-trained spy who had been dropped behind enemy lines to carry out the ruse of being the local village idiot, while in reality he was helping to spirit out downed allied pilots.

After being parachuted into France, where his French Canadian background allowed him to blend in, Dupre behaved as a simpleton. When he was caught by the Germans, the story went, he was taken to local SS headquarters where he was bound and tortured. His head was tilted back, his mouth wedged open, and then boiling water was poured in.

He stuck to his story that he was a simple man.

The Germans then attacked the other end, giving him an acid enema. Still he stuck to his story. Teeth were removed, bones broken, but the hero remained unbowed.

Reader's Digest sent their best writer to interview Dupre. He was invited down to New York City where he stayed with the writer and over a period of weeks, his life story was written down. The writer, a veteran, then went to Alberta and interviewed leading citizens. Clergymen, politicians, and business people all spoke highly of Dupre. The writer was so impressed by the tale that he not only wrote the book, he insisted on sharing half the royalties from it with Dupre.

So the book was published.

One day on the West Coast, a veteran picked up the book and read the story. He recognized his old friend, but not the story.

Reader's Digest was contacted and a photo showing Dupre and his old companion was forwarded. The date the photo was taken was the same time Dupre was supposed to have been saving aviators downed behind enemy lines.

Dupre came clean. He wasn't a spy.

He still thought his story was a good one, showing the importance both of being determined and of a good colonic.

Reader's Digest wrote a three-page retraction in its next magazine. The publisher decided to make some lemonade from this lemon of a story, and advised bookstores to move the tome from the non-fiction to the fiction section.

As long as we still have the truffles, I think we can make it

Members of the expedition could only watch helplessly as two of their special half-track trucks, their lifeblood, crashed thirty metres down a bluff and into the river below. What could they do now? The trucks were supposed to carry them through the rough British Columbia wilderness. They plodded on, then disaster struck again. Another truck was lost in the rapids of the same river. They did not lose hope, however. They still had each other, and of course, their champagne, truffles, caviar, silverware, silk pajamas, portable toilets, beds, bathtubs, French shoes, quilted pants, servants, and one mistress. And the filming of the trucks' demise — which took several days to arrange — was going to look great on a movie screen.

Nothing was as it seemed during the Bedaux Sub-Arctic Expedition across the uncharted wilderness of British Columbia in 1934 by French-born American adventurer Charles Bedaux. The real name of the expedition surfaced through the years that followed — the Champagne Safari — and to this day no one is sure how much of the safari ended in true failure or in planned disaster.

Born to poverty in France in 1886, Bedaux spent his teen years working in the bars of Paris and then New York. At nineteen, he immigrated to the United States with one dollar in his pocket and only a few words of English at his command.

These things worked great in the showroom. In 1934, Charles Bedaux took Citroen half-track trucks, an entourage that included his wife and mistress, and luxury food on an expedition through northern Alberta and British Columbia. The food was good, at least.

Somehow Bedaux managed to get himself a job at a St. Louis chemical plant, where he expanded upon previous studies of time management and invented a method of measuring workers' output. Industrialists in the United States, Germany, France, and Italy bought into Bedaux's ideas and soon he was rich. Always looking for adventure and a way to prove himself, Bedaux traversed the Sahara Desert by automobile in 1930 and hunted through northern British Columbia in 1926 and 1932.

"I am just a nut who likes to do things first," he once said.

He also liked the publicity. When he decided to be the first to take a fleet of vehicles through northern British Columbia, he hired a New York publicist to shape his image. Newspapers in New York began printing stories about Bedaux's scientific and geological expedition from Edmonton, Alberta, to Telegraph Creek, British Columbia — a distance of about

1,760 kilometres through mountains and muskeg, over raging rivers, and along dangerous precipices. By truck. And in style.

In June 1934, Bedaux and his team arrived in Jasper, Alberta, for a strict fitness regime, consisting of many fine banquets. He landed in Edmonton in July, heading a parade of five cream-coloured, nickel-plated Citroen half-track vehicles imported from France, jammed with twenty tons of gear. With Bedaux were other members of the purely scientific expedition — his wife, his mistress, his wife's maid, a gamekeeper, a Citroen tractor expert, a mining engineer, two government land surveyors, a radio operator, and a Hollywood camera operator. "On the running board of the leading car was the mascot, a little black and white terrier," wrote the *Edmonton Journal* on July 4, 1934. More than 500 people watched the members of the expedition parade down Jasper Avenue to the Governor's House, where they were sent off with official best wishes in their attempt to conquer the wilderness by man and machinery.

"The tractors themselves are marvelous at surmounting obstacles," the *Journal* exulted. The Citroens were equipped with rollers on the front to go over boulders, and rear wheels that could be taken off and replaced with tracks. Rafts would be built to take the trucks over rivers, and winches could pull them up steep gorges. Just to make sure the expedition was successful, an advance party of six men and fifty packhorses had already broken a rough trail to Fort St. John, British Columbia, dropping off supplies of gasoline along the way.

That didn't seem to help. The rain began to fall on the outskirts of Edmonton and rarely stopped throughout the entire expedition. The ground turned to gumbo, a slick muck that clogged the vehicles' transmissions. At an average speed of about seven kilometres an hour, Bedaux's expedition pushed on to Grande Prairie, Alberta, across the border, and by July 17 to the farming village of Fort St. John, British Columbia. Bedaux stayed there for five days, getting the tractors repaired and, just in case they weren't up to the task, hiring more than one hundred packhorses and cowboys. Bedaux also made sure his camera operator, Floyd Crosby, filmed an emotional farewell to the town, in which the expedition's leader handed several people $10 bills.

As the expedition rumbled into British Columbia, the rain, muck, and troubled Citroens threatened to tarnish Bedaux's hard-earned image, so on July 28, he fired the radio operator. The press could be managed through careful releases taken by couriers, but a wireless radio operator could send real information out to the world each day. The radio had to be abandoned because of the weight, Bedaux explained to reporters later.

Soon Bedaux had to push on without his half-tracks. The constant repairs made them a liability, so Bedaux arranged to have them destroyed. Some historians suspect the Citroens were a publicity stunt all along. It took four days for Bedaux to negotiate a 200-metre bluff on the Halfway River, about 150 kilometres from Fort St. John. On August 11, two half-tracks were pushed to the top of the bluff while Crosby rolled his camera. The bluff collapsed and the half-tracks crashed into the river below, their two drivers leaping out at the last moment for the cameras. On August 13, another car was sent down the river on a raft. It was supposed to crash into a cliff that was rigged with dynamite to collapse. The raft missed the dynamite and got stuck on a sandbar. Bedaux just left the other two vehicles at a ranch.

Newspapers dutifully reported the press releases issued over the next few days, detailing how the team was reluctantly facing the loss of the vehicles, and then how the half-tracks finally failed. One story described the near death of nine team members when one vehicle crashed. Rumours filtered through the New York publicist that one wrangler had died.

The forty-three men and women of the expedition pushed ahead on horseback, but many of the 130 horses fared no better than the vehicles. Dozens got hoof rot and had to be destroyed. The expedition caught up with the advance party, bogged down in the mountain passes by heavy snow. About 500 kilometres from Telegraph Creek and the Pacific Ocean, still a fifteen-day march away, Bedaux realized his dream of making a luxury safari across northern British Columbia had ended. The expedition had already cost close to $200,000. The final figure would be about $250,000. Finally, on September 28, he turned the enterprise around.

Bedaux continued to sell the expedition as a heroic battle against all odds and newspapers continued to buy that story. Communities on his path back gave him a hero's welcome and in one, the wranglers and the rivermen with the party engaged in a game of baseball for everyone's entertainment. Along the way, the expedition also came across its dead horses, abandoned supplies, and damaged vehicles. No matter. "The stocky grey-eyed leader seemed not one whit downcast by the failure," the *Edmonton Journal* wrote of Bedaux as he journeyed back to Alberta.

Bedaux disclosed he had discovered a new route for a highway linking Canada to Alaska. It's not clear how he did that, considering he dumped forty-five kilograms of the surveyor's equipment as soon as the going got tough. (The champagne and caviar, of course, he kept.)

"The story of our expedition is almost a tragic one and, realizing the dangers through which we have passed, we are thankful that no worse tragedy, such as the loss of life befell us," Bedaux told the *Journal*. He blamed the expedition's failure on three things: the weather, the inability of the trucks to go through the gumbo, and the hoof rot among the horses.

There were rumours the loss of the Citroen half-tracks was nothing more than a movie stunt. Bedaux denied the rumours and deflected questions with a promise to build a lodge near Hazelton, British Columbia where the loyal surviving horses might live and he and his wife, perhaps his mistress as well, would "retire from the strenuous life we lead."

Some historians still consider Bedaux's expedition a somewhat valuable, if elaborate exploration. It did provide some information about the interior, and the Alaska Highway was built close to his route. There is even a mountain named after Bedaux in British Columbia. Some writers think Bedaux was a nothing more than a successful publicity hound. Many think he was merely crazy and destined to fail. His later career tends to support all the theories.

Three years after the expedition, Bedaux managed to get Britain's most romantic couple, the Prince of Wales and the woman he abdicated the throne for, Wallis Simpson, embroiled with the Nazis. He arranged their official trip to Nazi Germany, which outraged many Britons. Bedaux himself stayed in France during the war, working with the Nazis and the Fascist government in Italy. In 1943, Bedaux ended up working on the trans-Sahara pipeline project that was to provide oil for the Nazi war machine. He was captured by advancing U.S. forces. Still an American citizen, Bedaux was flown to Miami and put behind bars. Complaining of insomnia, he convinced his guards to give him sleeping pills, which he hoarded. On February 19, 1943, a day after he learned he would be tried for treason, Bedaux took an overdose of pills and died. There was a suicide note. "I cannot defend my good name without endangering those I love," Bedaux wrote, a tireless self-promoter to the end.

CHAPTER 10

HERE'S A GOOD SPOT TO LIVE (SETTLING)

Here's the traditional pattern for settling in Canada:

Wait until winter. Pick the worst spot. Remember the dead fondly. Try somewhere else.

None other than Samuel de Champlain and his rich backer, French nobleman Pierre Du Gua de Monts, made the first attempt at truly settling Canada in 1604.

Even before they set sight on the island they would call home for one disastrous winter, their reasons for choosing it were suspect.

On his first trip to New France in 1603, Champlain explored the St. Lawrence River and seemed captivated by the possibilities of colonization along its shores. On his way back to France, though, he stopped at the trading post at Île Percée off the Gaspé coast and met a trader named Jean Sarcel de Prévert of Brittany. Prévert filled Champlain's head with stories of huge amounts of copper to be found along the coasts of what are now New Brunswick and Nova Scotia. Perhaps Prévert, a rival trader, simply wanted to keep Champlain and his financial backers out the St. Lawrence, which led south into his territory. Perhaps he just liked a good joke.

In any case, the next year, instead of exploring the St. Lawrence River, Champlain and de Monts headed straight for the outer edge of the new land. De Monts had been given the fur trading rights for an area roughly from present-day Philadelphia to the St. Lawrence. In return, he was to colonize the New World for France. Three of his ships were sent across the ocean to head down the St. Lawrence and trade for furs. Two ships, with 120 workers, Champlain, and de Monts himself aboard, headed for the coast.

The ships arrived at what are now Green Bay and LaHave River in Nova Scotia on May 8, 1604. Like campers circling a provincial park looking for the perfect site for the weekend, Champlain and de Monts worked their way down around the southern tip of Nova Scotia and the inside shore of the Bay of

Fundy trying to spot the ideal place for a settlement. They rejected several would-be harbours because of the tides and rocks, noted the potential of the future site of Port-Royal in the Annapolis Basin, and passed on.

It was early summer and there was no rush.

The ships turned south and explored what is now New Brunswick, eventually heading into and up the Passamaquoddy Bay to where two rivers met like a cross. De Monts promptly named the island nearby Ste. Croix.

"This place we considered the best we had seen," Champlain noted in his journals.

The island offered a sheltered harbour, some areas of clay and sand for making bricks, other areas of sandy soil that looked good for growing crops, and a forest of firs, birches maples, and oaks for building. Being an island, it was also easily defended from any Indian attack that might occur. The river was rich in alewives and bass and when the tides ebbed, great amounts of shellfish could be gathered.

Champlain was serious about colonization. He laid out a plan for a village on the flatter, north end of the island that included the usual buildings and, of course, a public square with a tree in the middle of it. The ships had brought sawn lumber for de Mont's house and a storehouse, and stone for chimneys. De Mont's house also featured ornate woodwork, glass windows, and heraldic banners brought from France. His house, the storehouse, an assembly house, and the dwellings of Champlain and other nobles were linked by a palisade that created an inner fort within the settlement.

Outside of the palisade, in the suburbs, the 120 workers cut down trees and, as best they could in a short time, built residences for themselves, a blacksmith shop, a carpenter's house, an oven and cookhouse, barracks for soldiers, and a hand-mill for grinding wheat. A well was dug and construction of a water mill started. Gardens were laid out and wheat sown. Just in case anyone attacked, cannons were placed at the north and south ends of the island. It seemed a perfect arrangement. Some of the men left for France, leaving seventy-nine others with a small barque, food and drink safe in the storehouse, and fresh drinking water rushing past the island.

The first signs of trouble surfaced that fall. Wheat sown on the island had come up well, but was quickly scorched from a lack of rain. Instead of rain, the settlement got snow.

"Winter came upon us sooner than expected," Champlain wrote in his journals. The first snow fell October 6 and ice appeared in the river in December. Bitter winds swept down the river and onto the island. The colonists had cut so many trees they had little protection from the wind. The wintry blasts raced through the poorly constructed buildings, forcing the men to huddle around the fire and freezing the cider in the casks of the storeroom. Men were given the cider in pound blocks. The only liquid that did not freeze — the wine — had to be rationed out. The river, their source of fresh water and fish, froze up with "great cakes of ice carried by the ebb and flow of the tides," Champlain wrote. The men were trapped. They cut down more trees to feed the fires that kept them somewhat warm in their drafty quarters. That exposed the settlement even more to the harsh winds. They started drinking melted snow. On top of all that, they had to keep guard day and night against an attack by a band of Micmac Indians.

Living mainly on salted meat, huddled together in cramped, cold quarters, doing very little, the men got scurvy. It was Champlain's first experience with the disease and he described the decay of the men at great and gory length. A Jesuit priest who spent two winters with Champlain only a few years later noted that the only men who did well that winter on Ste. Croix were "a jolly company of hunters," who caught rabbit, skated on the ponds, and even threw snowballs at each other rather than laze about in bed or huddle around the fire talking about Paris and its good cooks.

The Native people camped along the river at the foot of the island, and for awhile seemed to be doing quite well in comparison. They built what looked like large racquets for their feet, clothed themselves with fur, and hunted moose and other game. Instead of doing the same, the colonists stood guard at the cannons, including Champlain himself, fearful of an attack. Winter went on forever. In March, the colonists overcame their fear and traded some bread with the Native people in return for game. It was too late for many of the colonists. Of the seventy-nine men on the island, thirty-five died and twenty barely survived.

Exhausted and afraid, the colonists waited for a French ship to arrive with supplies in April. It did not. Neither did a ship come in May. The colonists decided to make a run for Gaspé, where they might find a ship heading back to France. Finally, on June 15, the French supply ship arrived. With blasts from their cannons and trumpets, the weary settlers welcomed their saviours. The ragged bunch moved across the Bay of Fundy to the bay at Port-Royal, the place they had earlier bypassed. That became Canada's first successful settlement.

Champlain had learned the lesson of colonizing Canada. "On arriving in summer everything is very pleasant on account of the woods, the beautiful landscapes, and the fine fishing for the many kinds of fish we found there," he wrote in his journals. The problem with Canada, though, he concluded: "There are six months of winter in that country."

If it's not the mosquitoes, rain, drought, snakes, or wolves, it's the Americans

Except for the mosquitoes, malaria, swamps, a foreman who wouldn't do what he was told, and an enemy threatening at the doorstep, Baldoon, Ontario was the perfect place to start a new town.

And so Lord Selkirk, in 1805, brought fifteen Scottish families to the New World. The 102 pioneers persevered and made a home from the wilderness. But were books written about them? Were there television series celebrating their homespun happiness? Are there heritage plaques to mark the first houses? Not in this pioneer fairy tale.

Once upon time, there were poor Scottish Highlanders who lived in war and peace in the beauty of northern Scotland, safe in their clans if not in their houses. Oh, a few marauding warriors from rival clans might cut off the head of the odd in-law now and then and put it on a pike, but at least you knew where you stood, lad. Ah, but life changes. In a contest for the throne of Britain, Bonnie Prince Charlie came along and promised a Scottish king. In 1746, his supporters chose the worst possible place to fight the English, the mucky moor of Culloden, and were destroyed. The clan chieftains lost their power and apparently their interest in the crofters, who squatted on the chieftain's land in return for killing who- ever the chieftain wanted. The war over, the chieftains cleared their loyal men off the land to lease the acres for English sheep. These Highland Clearances displaced and impover- ished thousands.

Along came Thomas Douglas, fifth Earl of Selkirk, Baron Daer and Shortcleugh, born in Scotland in 1771. He grew into the age of the Scottish Enlightenment, a heady mixture of social justice and common sense. As a young man, Douglas travelled through Scotland and considered the poverty of Highland crofters. The solution, he figured around 1792, was immigration to the New World.

It took a few years for Douglas, eventually the fifth Earl of Selkirk, or Lord Selkirk, to persuade the government to give him approval to try his settlements. Selkirk first eyed St. Mary's, the future site of Sault Ste. Marie, as the ideal spot to start a settlement. But reports of a poor climate and the opposition of the North West Company to settlers in its fur trading area convinced Selkirk to try elsewhere. The British government pushed for a settlement in Prince Edward Island. As a compromise, Selkirk agreed to one settlement there and one in Upper Canada, now Ontario. In 1803, Selkirk accompanied 800 settlers going to Prince Edward Island and took advantage of the voyage to tour other parts of Canada. While in York, now Toronto, and poring over maps of what is now Southwestern Ontario, Selkirk settled on a piece of land on the shore of Lake St. Clair, about halfway between what became Windsor and Sarnia.

It was, he wrote, "the most eligible situation for such a settlement."

The parcel he called Baldoon, and Selkirk began hiring workers to prepare ox stable, mess room, and storehouse. Selkirk visited the site in June 1804 and viewed the work already done. He also tramped up and down the land and canoed along the many waterways. Separated by water from the Yankees, Baldoon could remain distinctly British. The area was key to the British military control of Upper Canada, there was room to grow, plenty of rivers for travel, and the soil was known to be rich. Few forests had to be cleared for the sheep, 1,000 of them already bought to form the economic basis of the new community.

Selkirk envisioned a settlement where up to 15,000 sheep, one hundred cattle, twenty dairy cows, and both feed and export crops would provide a good life. For now, he took 1,200 acres for himself and 200 acres for each of the families recruited in Scotland. The latter would get fifty acres apiece fronting the eastern bank of the Chenail Écarté, a natural waterway running off Lake St. Clair. On his own 1,200 acres he would build the Home Farm, the administrative centre of the community.

The fifteen families had been gathered up from the excessively rainy county of Argyll, which experienced crop failures in 1790 and 1791. The price of anything the poor folk there could grow or gather, even kelp, had dropped so low by then that, in some communities, up to one hundred people a year survived on public charity. The families signed contracts that required them to work out their debt to Selkirk before striking off on their own.

An experienced farmer himself, Selkirk arranged for the building of a barn and fourteen houses. By the time his settlers arrived in Quebec in 1804, crops had already been planted by workers, five pairs of work oxen were on the way, and beef, ewes, and Indian corn were on order to help the settlers survive the first winter.

The fifteen families and Selkirk crossed paths and met briefly at Fort Erie, then Selkirk headed east to the Maritimes and Scotland and the settlers west to Baldoon. The settlers arrived September 5, 1804 to a flat, fertile, and relatively treeless land.

That was the good news.

The bad news was it rained almost every day for a month and a half, and Selkirk had no idea how the lowlands of the Great Lakes could flood. Creeks overflowed their banks, the two houses already built were flooded, and the rains made it impossible to build new ones. Mosquitoes rose in clouds and brought malaria. The woods became knee-deep in water. And the decay in the swamps stunk.

Selkirk had hired a manager for the settlement, Alexander McDonnell, a York politician who visited the area in September 1804.

"The settlers with the exception of four or five are all sick," an alarmed McDonnell wrote to Selkirk. "I found everything in the greatest disorder, nothing to be heard but discontent, nothing to be seen but distress."

By November 1804, sixteen of the settlers had died, likely of malaria.

McDonnell wrote again. The crops of peas, barley, and oats had been stacked, but the rain had destroyed them all. Flooded waterways made it impossible to reach the fields of hay or move the sheep to new pastures. Baldoon "can never be a healthy place," McDonnell wrote.

So take the settlers out of there to higher ground, Selkirk ordered.

Well, maybe it's not that bad, McDonnell wrote back the next spring. He decided everyone should stay. Surely this summer couldn't be as wet as last, he figured.

He was right. The second summer at Baldoon there was a drought. The crops failed from dryness. Many of the sheep became ill and died. Rattlesnakes and wolves preyed on the flock. The horses were almost driven mad by flies. A twister touched down in August and tore the roof off a house. Despite the drier weather, the mosquitoes still made their appearance, as did the fever.

In August 1805, McDonnell wrote to Selkirk. Of the heads of the fifteen families, seven were dead and two were close to death. Give it up, he told Selkirk, and he moved the settlers briefly to a new location but brought them back in the fall.

Getting the news by mail, much after the fact in the fall of 1805, Selkirk realized the settlers needed to find a new home until the marshes around Baldoon could be drained. He petitioned the Lieutenant Governor of Upper Canada to let the families settle in neighbouring Shawnee Township and drain the marshes. The government refused, because the land was set aside for the Native peoples.

Selkirk then ordered McDonnell to abandon Baldoon for awhile and set up farms on the Thames River. McDonnell didn't tell the settlers until the spring of 1806. They voted on the matter and decided to stay. Or so McDonnell said. His letters bounce between despair and hope. In March 1805 the settlers were "totally incapable of any exertion." A month later, "all the settlers [were] in perfect health."

That summer was better than the previous two, but Selkirk was still pushing to get the settlers out of the swamps of Baldoon and into Shawnee Township. Selkirk ordered McDonnell to move the families into the township, hoping a new Lieutenant Governor of Upper Canada would be more agreeable to the settlement.

McDonnell told the settlers nothing. They stayed in Baldoon while McDonnell, a member of the Assembly of Upper Canada, spent the winter comfortably in York.

The next spring, 1807, found the settlers in such good shape, McDonnell wrote, he didn't bring up the matter of removal. Besides, they seemed to like being near a local distillery.

For the next three years, Selkirk and McDonnell squabbled over the management of the settlement. McDonnell's bookkeeping was so bad, Selkirk had the books audited and ordered McDonnell to come to England to explain himself. The manager had paid little attention to Baldoon, living most of the time in York. It wasn't until he failed to get a job as Receiver of the Province in 1809 that he decided he'd better keep the job in Baldoon.

In his absence, he had appointed a farmer named John McDonald to manage the farm. A complainer and layabout, McDonald lasted only two years, long enough to infect the settlement with his malaise. At least two shepherds left because of him. The rest of the settlers struggled on, through the usual pioneer mishaps — sick animals, floods, accidents. There were good moments, such as the battle between a boatload of settlers and some Yankees over a catch of fish caught in American waters. Aside from the joy of knocking heads, the Baldoon men got to keep the fish.

Then a new calamity appeared: the U.S. Army. Selkirk's vaunted strategic spot with its proximity to the United States put it in the path of marauding militia. Sure enough, in July 1812 with the Americans occupying nearby Sandwich, a militia unit pillaged the settlement, taking 1,000 sheep, 200 bushels of wheat, nails, guns, hoes, pitchforks — fifty-two items by Selkirk's own count. The British got some of the sheep back when they took Detroit, but the Americans took Baldoon again in 1814.

By then Selkirk had had enough of Baldoon. He leased his own farm, the so-called Home Farm that was to be the model for and centre of the settlement, to another farmer. Then he sold it outright in 1818. He died two years later in France. In 1822, finally, the government opened up the land nearby for settlement. As fast as they could, all the Highlanders left Baldoon.

How do you say, "Land of very bad ideas?"

It's all in the marketing.

The stark benches of land running between the Thompson River and the low hills about seventy kilometres west of Kamloops, British Columbia had been given the name Walhassen by the Shuswap Indians.

The word meant, "land of round rocks."

The Native people were being charitable.

They could have named the area "land of horribly hot summers," or "land of bitter winds in winter," or "land where hardly anything grows."

Yet even "land of round rocks" would not do for the British Columbia Development Association in 1910. Hoping to capitalize on the land boom that had seized the rich Okanagan Valley and other parts of the province, the giant developing company had bought two ranches along the Thompson River two years earlier. The ranchers who sold were only too happy to part with their mostly useless rangeland, their buildings, livestock, and additional land leases for $229,000.

Looking for a romantic name to call the place, the Development Association settled on Walhassen, but changed the spelling to Walhachin.

The company slightly altered the meaning in brochures it sent out to Britain. The Shuswap word no longer meant "land of round rocks" but "an abundance of food products of the earth."

Who wouldn't want to settle there?

The targets of the brochures were the ne'er-do-well sons of British aristocrats and the upper middle class, known in Canada, Australia, and South Africa as the remittance men. For any number of reasons — because they caused a family scandal or wasted family riches — they were sent to the colonies to live and, with some luck, prosper and straighten out. Or simply stop bothering the family. From the 1880s to the First World War, stern and disappointed parents sent hundreds of their sons and daughters away to make a new start. They survived on regular family allowances, the remittances.

Ah, the Walhachin hotel. Let's slip inside, sip a few nightcaps, and try to figure out why we settled in the middle of a bone-dry, windy river bench where nothing grows.

Some drifted away to jobs in Winnipeg or Calgary; some tried their luck as cowboys.

And some landed in new towns with romantic names that promised a heady mix of British gentility and Wild West fortune. Towns with names like Walhachin, British Columbia and Cannington Manor, Saskatchewan.

The still well-connected but no longer wealthy Edward Pierce and his sons, fleeing misfortune in Britain, came to Canada in 1882. As the kind of stock Prime Minister John A. Macdonald wanted for the Prairies — British, not at all like those Slavic and Asian people cropping up everywhere — Pierce and his four sons could each get 160 acres of free land. The five chose land in southeastern Saskatchewan, hired workmen to build a house, and wrote letters to English newspapers extolling the beauty and potential of the Prairies. As soon as seven families signed up, Edward's son Duncan began creating his new city, called Cannington Manor. A fine church, with glass windows and a hand-carved cross on the bell tower of course, went up. In order to bring in more money and settlers, Pierce set himself up as an educator of young Britons hoping to learn how to farm the Canadian way.

It worked. Dozens of young men were shipped to Cannington Manor to learn how to farm. And learn they did. They improved their tennis games, their cricket skills, their hunting, their painting, their glee club singing, and of course, if they could be improved at all, their social graces. In short, the young Britons had no more desire to get their hands dirty than Pierce did.

As Canadian neighbours looked on in amusement and Canadian workers collected hard cash for helping out, the Cannington Manor residents haphazardly ran the town's various enterprises — a store and pork packing house — into the soft prairie ground. Pierce died in 1888, but his vision was taken over by brothers William and Ernest Beckton. They had just come into a small fortune from shares in a mine and in the house of a now dead relative. They decided Cannington Manor would be just perfect for a horse-breeding ranch. In style, of course. The estate house, built of stone dragged from a creek over a kilometre away, contained twenty-two rooms, including a ballroom, bachelors quarters, and billiard room. The ranch, known as The Didsbury, also included a stone racing stable with mahogany-sided interior, kennels for purebred dogs, sheds for carriages and cockfighting, and a bunkhouse. The Becktons did nothing by halves. They built a racetrack with a grandstand and lost thousands betting on their own horses, even though some came from the finest stock in North America. They hosted polo matches and shipped foxhounds from Iowa for the annual hunt and dinner/dance. No matter that the hunt took place during harvest. The crops were there mostly for scenery.

Naturally, the Becktons' fortune began to dry up. When it did, reality surfaced. The Prairies weren't the English countryside and they never would be. In 1900, Canadian Pacific Railway laid its tracks sixteen kilometres away, dooming the community to second-rate status. Back to England, or to the Klondike Gold Rush, or to established Canadian cities, the Brits escaped. Nearby farmers and real settlers stripped Cannington Manor of anything useful, tilled the soil, and where the gentry once played polo, planted wheat.

About the same time Cannington Manor was fading, the dreamers of Walhachin in British Columbia were grasping their destiny. Or at least the fine offer of a ten-acre lot, planted with fruit trees for $3,500 and a four-room house for $1,100, payable in four easy installments at 6 percent interest. By 1914, 150 descendants of Britain's finest families had bought lots in Walhachin. Few of them actually wanted to work the land, so 110 workers were eventually hired. They built the residents a hotel, with a games room, an English garden, beverage rooms, and a formal dining room where evening dress was always required.

But even the best Canadian workers couldn't grow fruit trees in a near-desert that got less than twenty centimetres of rain a year. Summer highs reached 36°C and winter lows sank close to -40°C. The benches of the fruit farms were too high above the Thompson River to draw water from that source for irrigation. So the settlers and the agricultural branch of the Development Association operating the town had a flume built from Deadman's Creek, thirty-five kilometres through rough terrain, to the fruit farms. The flume was built quickly to save the dying fruit trees, and as inexpensively as possible.

In April 1910, six months and $100,000 later, Walhachin had an irrigation system. The only problem: the flume did so good a job irrigating the land along the way there wasn't much left for the farms. Water leaked through thin wood that was not lined with cement or gravel. The leaking water seeped into and rotted trestles that in some places were simply dug into the dirt or resting on a stone. If the flume was allowed to carry the full amount of water, the entire structure began to shake. Fifteen centimetres of water was allowed to flow down the flume to the thirsty farms. To make things worse, the settlers planted vegetables in the rows between the trees and the vegetables sucked up the nutrients the fruit trees needed.

Still, life had to go on. And just as they had in Cannington Manor, the remittance men and their families enjoyed a reasonably good life of dancing, drinking, playing sports, including golf on a course they had built, and ensuring good British society flourished.

With money coming from their families, the settlers opened stores, restaurants, and other businesses. Like the flume, though, the town was resting on poor supports and rotting from within. Apparently recognizing that Walhachin would not turn a profit, the Development Association pulled out in 1912. When the First World War broke out in 1914, forty-three men and many women rushed back to Britain to help defend the Empire, or to get as far from British Columbia as possible.

A new and rich settler, Charles Paget, twenty-eight and the Sixth Marquis of Anglesey, had bought out the company's shares and taken over the town. With an estate boasting a cement swimming pool, the Marquis allowed life to flow on as merrily as it had before. Of course he had huge debts. Just as the war ended, a rainstorm, of all things, destroyed the irrigation flume. The Marquis could not persuade the British Columbia government to take over the settlement and its debts. The fifty remaining residents moved away and by 1922, all of them were gone. In 1947, the Marquis finally got rid of the land. The same land the Development Association bought in 1907 for $229,000, the Marquis sold for $40,000. A rancher bought the property. It was pretty good for grazing.

French fried, British beefs

Between the French and the English, it's a wonder Prince Edward Island ever got settled.

If it weren't for a bit of war, a bit of rebellion, and a bit of politics, the charming, agricultural, crescent-shaped isle in the Gulf of St. Lawrence would have remained a rocky forest with a few sad tenants trying to scrape out a living.

The French messed things up first.

Explorer Jacques Cartier was the first European to sail by the island, landing a couple of times in June 1534. Traders and fishermen likely used the island's coves in the years that followed, but settlement didn't really begin until the early 1700s.

After losing Nova Scotia, New Brunswick, and Newfoundland to the English in 1713, the French encouraged its settlers, known as Acadians, to head to Cape Breton Island, known then as Île Royale. Most Acadians refused, content to remain in Nova Scotia and continue farming on rich land rather than moving to the fog-bound rock of Île Royale.

The French then decided to encourage settlement on Île St. Jean, the present day Prince Edward Island. Just to make sure the island was suitable, French officials took a good look around. The land, they declared, was just as good for agriculture as Île Royale.

That was hardly an advertisement. But about 250 colonists set out for the island in April 1720, arriving four months later in Port La Joie, close to present day Charlottetown.

Small settlements grew along the coast. One, Trois Rivières, was founded by Jean Pierre de Roma, a stubborn yet hard-working director of the Company of the East. In 1731, King Louis XV gave the company an area of land drained by three rivers, the Cardigan, Brudenell, and Montague. Roma brought 300 people to the colony in 1732 and they immediately cleared the land, built a harbour, erected houses, and planted vegetable gardens. But the colony turned no quick profit for the company, and the directors gave up after only two years. Roma bought the land, but his luck turned sour. A fire in 1736 destroyed a year's crops and a plague of mice destroyed another crop two years later. Roma struggled on, borrowing money to keep the colony afloat, surviving even the wreck of a cargo vessel. Things finally looked up by 1745. Then the British attacked, set the homes on fire, and burned the crops.

The rest of the island wasn't doing much better. For dozens of years, the settlement struggled, growing from about 300 people in 1728 to about 430 in 1735. Not much happened on the island for a long time, aside from the planting and harvesting of crops, fishing, and cutting down trees to build cabins. As they did in Île Royale and the Old Country, the Acadian and French settlers planted their favourite crops, wheat and peas, with some cabbages and turnip thrown in. In 1741, some farmers tried growing tobacco. No one bothered to try growing potatoes.

After the British took Louisbourg and Île Royale in 1745, the island across the Northumberland Strait began to look inviting to Acadians. Hundreds of them migrated to Prince Edward Island. By 1752, 2,223 people lived on the island. Based on the detailed census of that year, a typical long-time settler might have some oxen, cows, pigs, and fowl and several acres of cleared land for wheat and peas. Overall on the island, about 700 acres was sown for wheat, 180 acres for peas, and 130 for oats. There is no mention of potatoes.

Despite the increase in population over the years, the colony managed barely to survive. It wasn't all really the colonists' fault. The French neglected the colony in favour of the far more important fortress at Louisbourg on Île Royale. Perhaps because of the large forests, the island was seen as barely suitable for agriculture and many crops were planted on tidal flats. Some of the best farmland was ignored. Île St. Jean was supposed to help feed Louisbourg, but hundreds on the island relied on help each year from Louisbourg to survive.

Through the continuing war between France and Britain, Île St. Jean managed to remain French. In the 1750s, when the British ordered Acadians on the mainland to fight all future wars against the French, Île St. Jean suddenly looked attractive. Hundreds moved there. In 1755, the British told mainland Acadians they had to sign an oath of loyalty and began deporting the disloyal. Two thousand Acadians fled to Île St. Jean but there was little refuge there. The crops had not been good. And no one had planted potatoes. After the fall of Louisbourg to the English in 1758, the Acadians on the island, too, were deported. A few hundred remained, even after Île St. Jean officially became Prince Edward Island in 1763.

In 2001, by the way, Prince Edward Island farmers harvested about 108,000 acres of potatoes, one-third of all of Canada's potatoes or about 7.7 million kilograms. "If you could visualize the perfect place for growing potatoes, it would be Prince Edward Island," notes the province's potato board. "The Island's rich sandy soil, clean air and water, and its long cold winters that naturally cleanse the soil, provide the perfect environment for growing high quality potatoes."

So what happened to the French? Why didn't they grow a few potatoes? Potatoes weren't part of their traditional diet, says historian Andrew Hill Clark.

"It was a great misfortune for the Acadians that they did not have the potato among their domesticated crops," writes Clark.

Potatoes saved later British settlements in times of hardship. "With codfish, the potato was to be a famine defence," Clark notes. "There are few instances in the history of pioneer settlement where cultural ignorance of, or indifference to, an uniquely suitable plant (which easily could have been introduced) did so much to hamper the development of satisfactory practices of land use."

If nothing else, there would have been more Acadians to defend the island against the English. Or form a greater base for the future. Or at least enjoy the time they had.

The British knew enough to plant potatoes. But they made a mess of planting people on the island. Once they had it in their hands, the Brits divided Prince Edward Island into sixty-seven lots of about 8,000 hectares each, then held a lottery in 1767 that gave the entire island away. Only the rich were allowed to play and most of them grabbed lots only in an attempt to speculate, hoping to resell the land later for a profit. They were obliged by the terms of the lottery to pay a yearly fee, called a quit rent, settle the land, build roads, and pay the salaries of legal and government officials who oversaw the island's development. Few paid the rent or brought in settlers. One who did, James Montgomery, faced the kind of luck that made the island seemed cursed. He arranged for a group of fifty Scots to settle at Stanhope Cove in 1770 to create a 40,000-hectare flax farm. The Scots could work the land for four years, then be free of their contract. So they cleared the land and built a mill. In the second year, a fire destroyed the mill. It was rebuilt. The same day it was done, it burned down again. The third time it went up, its dam was destroyed by a flood. Then the contracts expired and the Scots decided to go elsewhere.

None of the settlers on the island could ever own the land. After cutting down trees, moving rocks, building houses, planting seeds, harvesting crops, and civilizing the wilderness, all they could aspire to be were tenants. For decades tenants complained to the government in England, but the landlords were wealthy and had the right connections. Nothing was done.

In the 1830s, advocates for tenant rights proposed a special court that would expose landlords who had failed to pay rents or settle the lots. Their land would then be sold or given to the tenants. England ignored the idea. After a long struggle, Prince Edward Island was given responsible government in 1851. The islanders were responsible for everything but the landlord's lots. Finally, in 1853 the assembly passed legislation allowing the government to buy lots if the landlord was willing to sell. But the island government had no money to buy more than a few estates, so angry tenants turned to violence. A Tenant League was formed in 1864 and 11,000 tenants refused to pay rents. Confrontations between tax collecting sheriffs and stubborn tenants escalated. The governor had to bring in British troops to quell the clashes between farmers and rent collectors. Eventually, even the government realized the landlords' property had to be bought and turned over to the families that had worked the land for generations. In exchange for $800,000 to buy the lots and $3 million to cover a railway debt, the island joined Confederation in 1873. Two years later, the provincial government passed legislation allowing it to buy the landlords' property and turn it over to the tenants. By 1895, all the land had been bought.

The climax in the battle for Prince Edward Island, though, had taken place thirty years earlier. On St. Patrick's Day, 1865, about 500 members of the Tenant League marched through Charlottetown in a peaceful protest. A deputy sheriff named James Curtis decided it would be a good time to arrest a tenant he recognized, Samuel Fletcher. A strong supporter of the League, Fletcher had refused to pay his rent in two years. When Curtis tried to make the arrest, Fletcher hit him in the face. As other tenants joined in the melee, Fletcher fled.

Furious government leaders set about organizing what must pass as the most useless posse in the history of law enforcement. On Friday, April 7, Sheriff John Morris stood in front of the bank in Charlottetown and called out the names of 200 men to join his posse. Apparently, Morris picked many Tenant League supporters in order to punish them with a quick march through the spring muck.

"The select Two Hundred, with unpardonable ingratitude for the honour thus conferred, were immensely disgusted and indignant at the summons," wrote the *Charlottetown Examiner*, a pro-tenant newspaper, with tongue in cheek.

The men complained to the lieutenant governor, but the higher authority ruled the sheriff had the right to call a posse. About 150 of them actually showed up and headed, as the *Examiner* wrote, "to the scene of war. Some were in wagons — the most uncouth and rickety concerns that could be searched up for the occasion — some on horseback, broken-winded, dilapidated nags, which, if the season favoured, the crows would have admired — and a considerable number preferred to propel themselves by 'Shanks Mare.'"

Some of those walking, on their Shanks Mares, made better time than the others and stopped to rest at a tavern. The rest of the posse didn't discover them until the trip back home where the quick-marchers were still in the tavern waiting for their comrades.

The main body of the posse camped overnight, then approached Fletcher's farm the next morning. On the way, many in the posse floated Tenant League banners, sang Tenant League anthems, and blew the tenants' traditional tin trumpets, normally used to warn fellow tenants the landlord was coming. Farmers watching the posse go by also blew on their horns. This was hardly a sneak attack. Sheriff Morris might as well have led a parade to Fletcher's farm.

It appeared Fletcher was ready. On the way to his farm, the posse came across a small fort at a blacksmith's shop, bristling with cannons and men armed with rifles. The posse approached slowly, then realized the cannons and fort were made up of old stovepipes, and the men were straw scarecrows.

That scare behind it, the posse moved on. Soon it arrived at Fletcher's farm. And there he was, the stubborn fool, leaning against his gatepost waiting. The posse members moved forward cautiously, then breathed sighs of relief. It was another straw man, dressed, according to the *Examiner*, "in garments not of the finest and newest texture, nor of the latest fashion." Fletcher had fled again. (He never was caught and apparently lived on the island for another year before heading to Massachusetts where he died in 1870.)

The two-day march wasn't a total loss. Inside Fletcher's house, the posse found an elderly woman and some small children who offered the attacking force some buttermilk. The posse returned to Charlottetown Saturday evening. "Two ugly tumbers in the mud," the *Examiner* reporter, "were the only casualties that marred the glory of the enterprise."

CHAPTER 11

FARMING

For much of its history, Canada was an agriculture-based nation. No thanks to these farmers.

A sand trap

Cue the theme music for a horror movie, perhaps *Jaws*. Show the happy scene of beachgoers that begins the movie about a giant white shark preying on a small community.

But don't film the water. In this horror movie, it's the beach that swallows everything in its path. Call this movie, *Sand* or *The Dunes That Ate the County*.

The dunes, called the Sandbanks, form part of the shore on the northeastern side of Lake Ontario in Prince Edward County. Built up over thousands of years, the triangular bar of dunes runs about eight kilometres long, from a tip less than a hundred metres wide in the northwest to an almost one-and-a-half-kilometre wide base in the southeast. The dunes, which give both the area and the provincial park located there their names, slope gently up from Lake Ontario to an inner lake, West Lake. On the Lake Ontario side, the dunes reach about three metres in height, but as they near the West Lake side, they tower up to twenty-five metres high.

For hundreds of years, the sand banks stayed mostly where they were, held by water on two sides, and trees and brush at either end. A modification in taxes in the United States changed all that. After the Civil War, the U.S. government raised the tax on whiskey from 25 cents to $2 a gallon, and with their typical, can-do attitude, Americans simply switched to beer. As beer sales rose, so did demand for barley. Luckily for farmers in Prince Edward County, American brewers believed Canadian barley produced better beer.

And so began what people in the county called the Barley Days, three decades beginning in 1860 of unprecedented prosperity. It's estimated about 15 million bushels of barley were exported from the county in those thirty years, rising from about 300,000 bushels in 1861 to more than 800,000 in 1888. From dawn to dusk, schooners loaded barley at a place called West Port for shipping to Oswego, New York or Montréal. Small boats collected barley from the edge of farms themselves, before taking them to the schooners.

Barley meant money. The price rose to $1 a bushel in 1890, and those hundreds of thousands of bushels sold each year translated into fine homes, nice farms, even vacations abroad for farmers and merchants. And the more land you had in barley, the more money you made. In 1861, about 11 percent of the cultivated land in the county was planted with barley; by 1881, barley was grown on over 30 percent of the cultivated land.

Farmers near the Sandbanks area of the county took full advantage of the boom. They cleared land for hops and barley. They felled and sold the tall white pines growing near the dunes for ship masts. So many of the eighteen-metre high trunks were taken out a road was built and called the Mast Road. Pines and cedars around the dunes were cut for building ships, houses, and farm buildings. Cedars on the dunes were used for firewood and fence posts. More land was cleared for cattle — even the dunes themselves, where cattle grazed on the grasses in the hollows and on slopes. And all the time, the westerly winds of Lake Ontario kept blowing.

The barley boom went bust in 1890 when the United States, at the urging of its own farmers, passed the McKinley Tariff on crops and other material from Canada. The high tariffs and the move of the brewery business to the Midwest, where barley was easily grown and bought, dropped the price of Prince Edward County barley from $1 a bushel to 50 cents a bushel in a day.

That was just the beginning of the bad news for farmers and other landowners near the Sandbanks.

With protective cover gone, the dunes were more exposed to the westerly winds off Lake Ontario. With the trees and brush that used to keep the sand in check cleared, the dunes began to move. And well. The sand dunes travelled 450 metres between 1852 and 1912, up to twelve metres a year, burying cedar, pine and spruce groves, covering eighty-five acres of agricultural land, and sweeping over roads and buildings. Dunes eighteen metres high covered the tallest trees. The road between two towns, West Point and Bloomfield, had to be moved five times and in 1912 was still getting covered with sand.

Parts of southern end of West Lake, the body of water between the dunes and Lake Ontario, were filled with sand. One large sand bank behind the Evergreen House, a hotel near the dunes, drifted in so quickly, the hotel had to be abandoned. Nothing could stop the sand.

Even the West Lake Brick Products Company, set up in 1915 to mine the dunes for brickmaking, was inundated with sand. When it closed in 1922, perhaps because of the sand itself, the creeping dunes took over the entire property.

Farmers tried fighting back in the early 1900s, planting willows to stop the sand. They took their complaints to the provincial government and in 1921, the province began planting trees to reforest the area. It was tricky work, because sand could easily overwhelm the saplings. Crews had to erect fences of wire and brush, and lathe two-and-a-half-metre high planks. Snow, and the sand overriding it, often buried the catch fences each winter, and the planks would have to be pulled up and recovered with wire and brush.

It took two attempts, one from 1921 to 1931 and one in the 1950s, to stop the sand. In 1929 alone, 116,115 trees were planted, mainly poplar and willow. The planting worked, but only for land to the southeast of the banks. The dunes were still encroaching on large sections of land to the south, and the province started a new program in 1957, using a combination of trees and snow fences. Pine and spruce joined poplar trees in protecting the land. From the 1920s on, more than three million trees were planted.

Everyone gave up on using the sand dunes for anything but fun. The province even created a park, Sandbanks Provincial Park. And the sand went back where it started, just waiting for someone else to make a mistake.

Milking the taxpayers

The cows, at least, got to see new parts of the country. But for taxpayers involved in the attempt to bring a dairy to Yellowknife, Northwest Territories, the only thing that really got milked was them.

The dairy, opened under the name Agriborealis Ltd. in 1986, was supposed to produce milk that was less expensive than milk shipped in from the south. It was also supposed to feed the development of other agricultural production plants.

People knew there were risks. "Everyone who evaluated the project objectively recognized that it was a high risk venture," concluded Justice J.Z. Vertes in a judgment years later. But the dairy had the inside track with the territorial government. Several of its investors were civil servants and the company's president and major investor was a financial manager in the territorial government. The money flowed — a grant of $166,000 from the federal and territorial governments, and a loan of $119,000 from the territorial government to start.

The loan arrangements were puzzling. No one seemed to sign a guarantee for the loan and no one seemed to worry about how the money went out. At the trial, the straight talking Vertes noted, "funds were disbursed although no witness at the trial could explain just what did happen." Only one payment was made on the loan. "No one," concluded Vertes, "could tell me, what, if any, arrangements had been made for making the monthly payments."

No matter, the dairy got up and running. Sort of. There were technical problems from the start, according to Don Portz. He was brought in as general manager in May 1987 and quickly realized how badly things were going. A dairy processing expert had warned the government that the dairy's equipment was antiquated. The equipment was used anyway, and some of the milk was contaminated. Water from a nearby lake was going to be used, but the lake sediment turned out to contain fifteen times the legal limit of arsenic. The dairy had to spend $200 a day to truck enough water from Yellowknife, which sent costs soaring. The northern climate caused lower evaporation levels which in turned caused the composter to fail.

But the territorial government wanted the dairy to work. So it gave another $300,000 to the plant in March 1987. Four months later, the dairy was put into receivership. That might have been the end of any other business that didn't seem to work, but not the Yellowknife dairy. Instead, it got a new name, Tuaro Dairy, and a new bank, the city of Yellowknife. The major investor who had once been working with the territorial government had moved to a job as the city's finance director. For the next ten years, the dairy struggled to make it, failing to pay back hundreds of thousands of dollars owed in back taxes and leasing deals. Still, the city kept pouring in money. Don Portz appeared before city council in 1995 to warn them about the dairy's shortcomings — the water quality, manure runoff, equipment failures. Most councillors ignored him. Two years later, though, they'd had enough. The city's finance director, still an investor in the dairy, resigned his post.

Even after he left, Yellowknife continued to bail out the dairy. There were still problems with contamination and by the summer of 1997, the dairy's owner had to sell milk off the back of a truck because the stores in the city wouldn't carry it. Finally, in October 1997, the dairy was shut down.

But its legacy lingered like a bad smell — manure to be exact. A neighbour complained to the city that manure was running off the dairy farm and into a nearby lake. The city ignored him, saying the manure was frozen. But territorial inspectors took a look, saw the manure running into the water, and forced the city to plug up holes in a dyke and pump manure out.

Don Portz, the general manager who tried in 1987 to turn things around, later sued the territorial government. He had left a $56,000 a year job to take the position, and he had personally guaranteed a loan of $25,000 from the territory. When that first investment went under, the government demanded its $25,000 back from Portz. Portz countersued, claiming he was misled into giving up a good job to take over a dairy everyone but him knew was failing. In 1996, Justice Vertes dismissed both claims. The entire episode was a mess, he concluded. "The parties have been in litigation for over six years in this attempt to recover $25,000," he noted, then added the most apt description of the dairy. "I think it is also accurate to describe this venture as one giant pit into which government officials kept pouring the public's money."

Newfoundland, fruit basket to the world

This time would be different.

This time Newfoundland would get the factory, the jobs, the profits, and the acclaim of being on the cutting edge of technology.

Everyone had learned their lessons from the crazy Joey Smallwood days, when the Liberal premier lost millions trying to set up more than a dozen companies that had no business in Newfoundland. This time, the money would go into one surefire operation. What could be more natural for a rocky, windswept, cold, and non-arable island in the Atlantic Ocean than a hydroponics plant? Fresh vegetables all year round! Newfoundland, the fruit basket to the world. Step right up!

In 1986, Conservative Premier Brian Peckford did just that.

Only thirty-five years earlier, the province had handed over most of the millions it received for joining Confederation to a series of mainly German-owned companies promising to make everything from chocolates to leather gloves. Most of the companies failed.

It's hard to believe there wasn't something Smallwood hadn't tried, but Charmar Holdings Limited, a good old Newfoundland company, approached the government with a proposal to grow fruits and vegetables in a giant greenhouse. Charmar had obtained the exclusive rights to a system operated by Philip Sprung. The Sprung greenhouse, already working in Calgary, used a computerized light and nutrient system to grow fruits and vegetables. Government officials did their homework; they asked Sprung if it worked. Sprung told them his system could produce nine million tons of cucumbers and tomatoes a year. Peckford and government officials visited Sprung's Calgary facility. Civil servants visited the facility, too. A crop and agricultural specialist concluded the thing wouldn't work in Newfoundland. There wasn't enough light, especially in winter months, to grow the vegetables. Nothing he saw convinced him a greenhouse in Newfoundland could produce the yields promised.

No problems, said Sprung, I'll just put up artificial lighting.

That was good enough for the government. On May 8, 1987, only a month after the agricultural specialist raised doubts about the plan, the cabinet approved the proposal to build a $14.5 million plant. The government would contribute $11.4 million in grants, loans, and sales tax rebates and a $1million parcel of serviced land in Mount Pearl, just outside of St. John's. The Sprung Group of Companies would contribute about $4 million in cash and a loan guarantee, and arrange to lease then buy $3 million in lights.

"For once Newfoundland will be first in new technology and not just in unemployment rates," Peckford told reporters.

With Newfoundland's huge hydroelectric capabilities, Peckford could envision a string of hydroponic greenhouses across the province. "There isn't anything we've found that we can't grow," promised Sprung.

Move over, Florida and California, an enthusiastic Canadian Press reporter wrote. Newfoundland could be exporting oranges and grapefruits within a couple of years.

The hydroponic greenhouse would employ 150 people producing forty-five-centimetre cucumbers every six days, year round. A province with the lowest percentage of first-, second-, and third-class farmland in Canada would soon be growing 3.2 million kilograms of vegetables a year, almost twice what Newfoundlanders consumed in tomatoes and cucumbers when all of their vegetables had to be imported.

Some naysayers were worried about Sprung's Calgary operation, which was due to close because gases from nearby ground pollution were killing the plants. The Calgary site was really just a test facility, Sprung replied. When the federal government refused to invest, Peckford attributed their reluctance to pressure from the powerful greenhouse lobby.

Construction began in 1987 and the plant was completed in April 1988. The growing lights weren't operational until October. Problems cropped up faster than the cucumbers. A later assessment showed that carbon dioxide was hurting the plants, nutrients and water weren't properly monitored, algae was spreading in the growing fluid, and the plants weren't pruned to ensure proper growth.

In the face of poor yields, the province made a new $825,000 loan guarantee in the summer. Briefly, things improved. For one week in November, production of cucumbers reached 75,000. But those numbers fell in December and by mid-month, all the cucumbers were dead. No one was sure why. There was suspicion someone had contaminated the growing solution with herbicides, but tests on the plants proved inconclusive. The government lent another $1.3 million to the plant to get the operation going again. But by January 1989, Peckford gave up. The plant was put into receivership.

Then began a series of financial transactions that would land anyone else in the poorhouse. In June, the province bought the plant from the receiver for $3 million. That money was used against a $7 million loan the province owed the Royal Bank for lending the money to build the plant in the first place. Then the province sold the plant it had just bought for $3 million to the consortium for $1. That's not a misprint, that's $1.

It's as if an ordinary person borrowed $7 from the bank to help a friend buy a house. When the friend skipped town, the bank took the house over. The first person then took $3 out of his pocket to buy the house from the bank. Still owing another $4, the person sold the house to someone else for a penny.

But it was okay, because the new owners of the plant were going to make it work and pay the province up to $10 million a year, if the company made a profit.

A year later, the consortium bailed out, selling the plant for $700,000 to a Montréal company. The government got a share of the proceeds and was finally out of the hydroponics business.

A Royal Commission into the Sprung deal concluded the government did just about everything wrong — from not checking to see if the plant would work, to not checking to see who was spending how much on what. The province's final bill: $22 million. Cucumbers produced in the two years Sprung ran the plant, according to the former agriculture minister: about 800,000. The cost per cucumber: $27.50. The price of a cucumber in grocery stores as of 2002: about 50 cents.

CHAPTER 12

MISSED OPPORTUNITIES

Sometimes, when opportunity knocks, no one is listening.

Sure, George Brown was a Father of Confederation. He even has a college named after him. But the one-time leader of the Liberal party had more than Sir John A. Macdonald working against him. He also had to contend with his own bad judgment about investments.

In the mid-1800s, George Brown met this Scottish guy who seemed fairly bright. He had lots of ideas and he had come to Canada looking for a place to develop them. One of his inventions was a strange-sounding plan to connect wires, carbon, and other materials to create a communications device. Brown decided to make an investment in that idea and staked Alexander Graham Bell to $25 a month — not an exorbitant amount, but a respectable sum in those days. The deal was for six months and Brown was to get a half interest in all British and foreign rights in the invention, later known as the telephone.

Bell asked Brown to register the new invention at the patent office in London. Brown dutifully packed the specifications of the invention and headed off to England. But apparently, during the voyage, he started having second thoughts. He worried that he might become a laughingstock trying to get a patent registered for this goofy idea, as he explained to Bell later.

Once in Merry Olde, Brown prevaricated. He kept sending back messages saying that he was in the process of registering. He delayed almost to the point that other inventors, with devices similar to Bell's, might have received that crucial first patent registration that would have given them the exclusive rights to the invention, effectively shutting Bell — and Brown — out of the telephone business. Fortunately, he ultimately registered Bell's patent first, but only just before other competitors.

Oh, and that six-month contract for funding Bell? Brown made only one payment and defaulted on the rest. Apparently the whole experience left Bell with such a sour taste for Canadian investment that he never again sought out Canadian backing on a project.

As for Brown, he continued on as a businessman of modest proportions, which means by Canadian standards, he was wildly successful. However, Brown met an untimely end. He was killed by an angry ex-employee.

Forget that oil, we've got asphalt

Charles Nelson Tripp is the man who tossed out the world's biggest lottery ticket, threw in his hand with a royal flush, and dropped the genie bottle into a pile of thick, black muck. Oil, as it turned out.

"Gum beds," deposits of oil and dried up petroleum called bitumen, had been noticed by Native Canadians in the far reaches of southwestern Ontario for years. White surveyors in 1832 and 1833 apparently never bothered to ask about the landscape because they missed the beds and concluded swampy and heavily forested Enniskillen Township was poorly suited for settlement. Seventeen years later, government surveyors came across the beds and realized there was bitumen in the swamps.

About the same time, Tripp, twenty-seven, had already displayed his inquisitive and practical intellect, designing a new stove front for the factory where he worked, and leasing lead and copper veins in Hastings and Prince Edward Counties. The love of minerals ran in his veins. They could feed the world and make him rich. His brother, Henry, twenty-two, lived in Woodstock and may have run into one of the government surveyors, who was another Woodstock resident. In any case, Henry soon found out about the oil fields and told his brother. The elder Tripp wasted no time, and in 1850 headed into the forests and swamps of Enniskillen.

It was true — the land bubbled with thick, black goo.

Tripp sent some of it to a chemist in New York and a gas company manager in Hamilton, Ontario. This stuff is good for paints, plastics, and cements, said the chemist. If you boil the asphalt even more, said the gas company manager, you'll get lighting oil.

Sure, sure — oil, lights, whatever, Tripp figured. He didn't need that. He had his own form of gold. He had asphalt.

By 1853, Tripp had bought a 200-acre parcel of land and two years later, owned 1,350 acres. It was the beginning of an empire: the asphalt empire.

He and his crew dug up the hard bitumen or scooped up the muck near the surface. Then they boiled it in a big cauldron. The goo that was left was poured into molds of asphalt. When the surface beds were depleted, Tripp dug deeper into the heavy oil. As he boiled the oil, he likely produced naphtha and kerosene, a newly discovered substance becoming popular for lighting. Then he dumped it in nearby creeks.

There's no doubt Tripp knew the value of the oil for burning. In 1854, he formed the International Mining and Manufacturing Company, which owned two large asphalt beds and six oil and salt springs in Enniskillen, as well as lead and copper veins elsewhere. His petition for a charter did mention the possible production of oil naphtha and "burning fluids," but it was clear his mind was set on asphalt as the key to riches.

For awhile, it seemed as if Tripp was on the right track. No less a man than the geologist for the province on Ontario, William E. Logan, asked Tripp to send him some asphalt exhibits to be displayed at the Paris International Exhibition of 1855. The government would pay for the shipment and display of the asphalt.

Logan's display of fifty-one minerals from Canada was a hit. "Among all the countries whose productions attract attention in this building," reported *The Globe*, "none stand so prominent."

Logan was awarded the Grand Medal of Honour for his display from Canada and Tripp, though he did not attend, was given an honourable mention for his asphalt. Better than that, the city of Paris ordered enough asphalt to pave its main streets. Paris had been using asphalt since 1838, and now Canada seemed to offer a cheap and ready supply.

Tripp set about trying to fill the massive order. As hard as he worked, it looked like the Paris order was turning out to be too much of a good thing. One shipment went out in the winter of 1856, when Tripp had to have the asphalt taken by sleigh to Port Sarnia then loaded on boats.

He had little experience in running a company large enough to produce and ship the asphalt. His expenses topped his income and soon his banks and suppliers were pressuring him for money. By the end of 1855, the Bank of Upper Canada had gone to court to get £500, and eight people had writs against him for another £1,094 in goods and services. He tried to find new investors but failed. Tripp's financial woes continued in 1856, with creditors now looking for more than £1,500.

In the meantime, Tripp hooked up with a man named James Williams. Originally from the United States, Williams had built a successful carriage business in the booming town of Hamilton, Ontario. It looked to Williams, however, like the carriage business was going to hit some hard times, or at least stop growing. The Great Western Railway was going to start building its own carts instead of buying them. Tripp owed Williams some money for a wagon, and he kept talking about these asphalt beds he owned in southwestern Ontario.

Williams didn't care about asphalt. He cared about oil. He and a group of other Hamilton investors bought 400 acres of land from Tripp, perhaps to settle Tripp's debt. Then he hired or persuaded Tripp to help him look for oil on the land. Ever the enthusiastic miner, Tripp might have done it partly just for fun.

The two men tramped about Enniskillen for two years. The story of their first discovery is clouded in legend. Some say they were digging merely for drinking water, desperate to find some while working on an asphalt swamp, and got lucky. Others say Williams knew there had to be oil flowing beneath the goo on the surface. Whatever the reason, early in the summer of 1858, the two men dug a hole fifteen metres into the ground. Oil and the smell of sulphur, like rotten eggs, oozed up. Williams and Tripp had discovered the first oil well in North America.

The discovery sparked an oil boom in southwestern Ontario that lasted forty years, made many men many millions of dollars, created two towns, and led to the creation of the Imperial Oil Company of Canada. By 1860, 1,600 men were digging in the land around the new town of Oil Springs. A year later, the first of the wild wells — the kind that send oil shooting hundreds of metres into the air — was discovered. Oil rained from the sky, filled creeks with one-metre thick layers of goo, and slicked the streets. More than 10,000 men and the accompanying prostitutes, wives, merchants, cooks, tavern-keepers, and speculators poured into Oil Springs. At one point, the town boasted twelve general stores and nine hotels. Kerosene lamps lit the streets. Everyone wanted kerosene, which provided a much brighter light than coal. Five hundred teams a day left the town for Chicago filled with oil.

By the mid-1860s, the oil was tapped. But in 1866, a new gusher was discovered in the nearby, six-shack town of

Petrolia. Within months, the little no-account settlement had 2,300 people, four churches, stores, and a hotel. Oil barons built palatial homes. Eventually, the oil boom died in Petrolia too, and the refinery business moved to Sarnia.

Williams, the first to discover the oil, began by producing about five to a hundred barrels a day. He charged seventy cents a gallon for illuminating oil, sixty cents a gallon for machinery oil, and sixteen to twenty-five cents a gallon for crude. He bought out his partners and became a millionaire. At forty-nine, he was elected to the Ontario legislature. He died in 1890 at age seventy-two after a rich and satisfying life, his wife and family at his side. The oilmen who owed their riches to him paid him tribute and mourned his passing.

As for Tripp, the asphalt king, he fled Enniskillen before the boom started, creditors at his back. He returned in the summer of 1866 and sold one of his lots. His brother had continued to pay the taxes on the property. In an interview with a Canadian reporter, Tripp billed himself as a multimillionaire silver miner on the verge of even more riches. Some say, by then, the only thing Tripp mined well was a bottle. His wife he had long since deserted him. After a brief visit to the site of his would-be empire, he headed back to the United States. Only three weeks later, he died in a room at the St. James Hotel in New Orleans, alone. He was forty-three. His loyal brother claimed the body and had it buried in Schenectady. Tripp's obituary mentions his explorations in oil, copper, lead, zinc, and iron. It says nothing about asphalt. Instead it refers to Tripp by a title the Canadian reporter had bestowed upon him only weeks before Tripp's death. Despite the irony, the title has stuck to Tripp like, well, asphalt. In death, if not in life, Tripp became forever known as, "The Original Oil Man of Canada."

Great idea, bad company

Thomas Ahearn, the man who would come to be known as "the Canadian Edison," made one of his early forays into inventing by placing Ottawa's first long-distance telephone call, in 1877, using some homemade cigar boxes, magnets, wire, some existing telegraph lines, and — without permission — Alexander Graham Bell's patented technique for telephone communication.

He managed to avoid litigation and went on to a successful career. He established the Ottawa Electric Company and the Ottawa Electric Railway (responsible for introducing electric light and the electric streetcar to Ottawa). He was appointed chairman of the forerunner of the National Capital Commission, and later to the Privy Council; and, in 1927, he made the first transatlantic telephone call to Britain — presumably, since the call was placed with Prime Minister Mackenzie King and Justice Minister Ernest Lapointe, with permission this time.

Those of us who eat hot meals can also thank him for the electric stove. In 1892, his invention was used to cook the food for a banquet held at the Windsor Hotel in Ottawa. *The Ottawa Journal* heralded the event as the "first meal cooked by electricity" and described it as "cooking by the agency of chained lightning."

But Ahearn sold his patent rights for his "food heaters" to the American Heating Corporation in exchange for stock in the company. Unlike Westinghouse or General Electric, you've probably never heard of the American Heating Corporation — it went bankrupt shortly after obtaining Ahearn's patent and before Ahearn could make any money from it.

Not even the best inventors can be smart cookies all the time.

You give me the million-dollar idea and I'll give you a big drink

It looked like magic.

The wind had died and the ships sat becalmed near the harbour of Saint John, New Brunswick on a summer day in 1834.

Except for one, the schooner *Royal George*, captained by Silas Kelley. The *Royal George* hadn't stopped. It was making its way into port. How on earth was it moving?

Inventor John Patch is how. He had attached his latest novelty, the screw propeller, to the *Royal George*. As the other ships lay still, Patch and Captain Kelley turned a crank that turned gears that turned the propeller that pushed the *Royal George* on.

It wasn't the first or last time Patch astonished spectators with his screw propeller, one of the single greatest inventions in sailing. The screw propeller is what pushes motor boats today. Patch, however, never made a cent from his invention.

Born in 1781 in Nova Scotia, Patch became a fisher and sailor. He appears to have thought of the screw propeller in the 1820s, perhaps by watching sailors propel small boats with a single oar turned, screw-like, over the stern. For years Patch tinkered with the idea, although scientists he contacted told him the propeller would never work.

He persisted. In the winter of 1832, he got some space in a small shed in Kelly's Cove and built his propeller. Two brothers, Robert and Nathan Butler, later testified they helped him build the gears and crank that would attach to it. Patch fastened the wooden screw propeller to a small boat and, under cover of night, tried it out in Yarmouth Harbour in the summer of 1833.

It worked. Later that summer, Patch tried the propeller in daylight and citizens were surprised to see the little boat

John Patch invented the propeller that makes boats and ships go. He should have gotten rich. Instead he died in poverty, all because he didn't know a bad deal when he saw one.

skim up and down the harbour without a sail, oar, or paddlewheel in sight.

After the success of the *Royal George* voyage, Patch was encouraged to head to England to patent his invention. He decided to try Washington instead, and headed to the United States in 1834.

But something happened on the way to fame and fortune. In one version of the story, Patch met two unscrupulous opportunists while sailing from Yarmouth to Boston. The three men got drinking and before long, Patch had signed over the rights to his invention for a bottle of liquor and a barrel of flour. In another version, a patent lawyer talked him out of registering the patent then sold the idea to the English. In yet a third version, Patch got to Washington where officials told him the propeller was useless and he was wasting his money.

Whatever happened, Patch never got his patent.

Meanwhile, other inventors in other parts of the world were also tinkering with the idea of a screw propeller. Ten years after Patch's ill-fated voyage to Boston, the British Navy began using the propellers to move ships. Patch believed for the rest of his life that someone in Washington had sold his information to the British. Other men made the money and got the honour from patenting various versions of the propeller.

Patch returned to Yarmouth and a life of poverty. He was so destitute that by 1858, a petition signed by one hundred citizens of Yarmouth asked the Nova Scotia legislature to help the man. The Butler brothers, who had worked with Patch to build the crank and gears for his propeller, sent a letter in support of the petition.

Patch, "afflicted with lameness, seventy-seven years of age, and being unable to earn a livelihood, is now an inmate of the Poorhouse of this town," the petition read. "Although other men may make their fortunes by his invention and the commercial world be benefitted by it, he would simply ask for the necessary means to enable him to support himself comfortably and respectably."

The legislature decided to give money to a man to rebuild a house destroyed by fire. Patch, the politicians concluded, deserved nothing. He died three years later in the poorhouse.

CHAPTER 13

OH, WE'RE SUPPOSED TO MAKE MONEY

If you really want to succeed in business in Canada, come up with an idea that's so unusual it must be good and pitch it to a bunch of politicians trying to buy votes with jobs. And make sure no one watches the bank account.

If at first you don't succeed, try, try, try, try... you get the picture

No one, but no one in Canada, did failure better than Joey Smallwood. If there were a patron saint of Canadian blunders, it would be Saint Joey of the Perpetual Handout, the long-serving and first premier of Newfoundland.

Other provinces and other levels of government have dumped millions of tax dollars into sinkholes with no bottoms. Other carpetbaggers have arrived in capital cities to fleece the unwary rubes running the place. Other companies with questionable business plans have been propped up with government money only to fail. But in the early 1950s, Smallwood created no fewer than fifteen factories making typically Newfoundland products like gazelle-skin gloves and chocolates.

No less a carpetbagger than a pill popping, Nazi sympathizer handled the money. No more valuable a resource than the $45.5 million Newfoundland received for joining Canada was drained.

And no province could afford the failures less.

For that reason, however, Smallwood has to be given some credit for trying. After Newfoundland joined Confederation in 1949, the federal government started paying Newfoundlanders old age pensions and unemployment insurance. Smallwood's Liberal government added its own set of welfare benefits — for destitute women, for example. Yet thousands of people continued to leave for jobs in the rest of Canada. To make matters worse, Newfoundland companies were no longer protected by tariffs and had to compete.

Like Santa Claus, the first chance to create industry and jobs came on Christmas Eve, 1949. Four men showed up at Canada House and told Smallwood they were Icelandic herring fishermen. With Newfoundland money, they could create a herring fishery in the province. All they needed were the boats. Smallwood thought this was an excellent idea and gave them a contract. They came back the next spring with four aged purse seiners. Over the next nine months they caught six barrels of herring. Then they disappeared, as did $412,000 in government money. They left the boats, which were sold three years later for $55,000. The man who bought them borrowed the money from the government that was selling them.

Still, Smallwood had a slogan in his head, the central idea that would drive his government for the next decade. "Develop or perish!" he called out. He just needed the right man to help.

Federal government officials — and for this the rest of Canada probably owes Newfoundland an apology — directed Smallwood to a part-time civil servant in Ottawa named Alfred Valdmanis. Dr. Valdmanis, as he liked to be called.

Valdmanis told Smallwood his life story. Born in 1908 in Latvia, a province of Russia, he was a child genius, reading and writing by four. His father, a university professor, was killed by Russians when Valdmanis was young. He attended an elite school and earned three degrees by twenty-four. He could speak seven languages. At twenty-nine, he was appointed Minister of Economics, Finance and Trade in Latvia and president of the Latvian Iron and Steel Industry. War destroyed his country and his future. The Russians imprisoned him. The Germans did the same because Valdmanis led his country's resistance movement. His life was spared by Hermann Goering, a fellow Grand Commander of the Swedish Order of Stella Polaris, the top Swedish honour. After the war, he made his way to Montréal then Ottawa, where Smallwood found him, obviously underutilized and underappreciated, as a consultant to the Department of Immigration and Department of Trade and Commerce.

The real story? His father was a schoolteacher. Valdmanis may have earned two degrees. He was finance minister in Latvia for nine months. He offered no resistance to either the Russians or the Germans during the war. Instead, he collaborated with both, Latvian refugees told authorities later. He was accused in 1943 of persecuting Jews in Latvia. His Swedish honour was a third-rate decoration. He did, however, speak many languages, knew a lot about fine wine, and professed to have contacts among German industrialists.

Smallwood didn't look past the image. Years later when he wrote his autobiography, *I Chose Canada*, Smallwood concluded Valdmanis was "brilliant and knowledgeable."

Soon Valdmanis was making $25,000 a year, three times what a cabinet minister was, as Director General of Economic Development. About one-third of Newfoundland's $45.5 million from Canada was supposed to go to operating the public service while two-thirds, $25 million, could be used for building the new province. The federal government had buildings such as schools and hospitals in mind, as well as developing the province's resources.

Smallwood and Valdmanis wanted something else — companies, big companies, companies of all kinds, with owners from all over the world. The first three companies they set up made some sense. A cement plant in Corner Brook would use nearby limestone and shale and sell at least some of the cement in Newfoundland. A gypsum plant in the same community would use local gypsum to create plasterboard for the building industry. A hardwood and plywood plant near St. John's would turn imported and local wood into veneer, flooring, doors, and plywood.

Still, cement, gypsum, and hardwood weren't enough. So off Smallwood and Valdmanis flew to Germany, where they were entertained by cabinet ministers and industrialists.

Back in Newfoundland in October 1950, Smallwood told reporters five new industries with 4,000 jobs would be established almost immediately. "Our target is 10,000 new jobs for Newfoundlanders in the next two or three years. I talked with many industrialists and financial magnates who are most anxious to establish a stake for themselves on this side of the water."

No doubt they were. Aside from the facts Germany was in ruins and the Russians were knocking on the door, Valdmanis and Smallwood had figured out a new way to start up factories. The government paid the full cost of setting up the first three, about $6 million, in the hope of selling them later. But the province could attract more industries if it didn't have to pay the full cost of building them. What if, instead, the province put up half the money in guaranteed loans and the industrialists put up the other half? Of course, the other half didn't have to be money. It could be equipment, or managing, or even know-how. In other words, anybody with a good idea and a factory or two in his past could come to Newfoundland, offer his services, and get millions from the government to set up a factory.

When Smallwood and Valdmanis went to Europe a second time in the fall of 1951, more than a dozen entrepreneurs signed up. On their return, Smallwood promised fifteen more industries bringing another 5,000 jobs within two years of startup.

In the next three years, Smallwood and Valdmanis — and the rubber-stamping cabinet — created more than a dozen new industries for Newfoundland.

"Newfoundland has entered upon an era of development that will make this province, in the next few years, one of the most prosperous parts of North America," Smallwood promised in his October 1951 Speech from the Throne.

His expectations were a little high, given that Newfoundland's market was small, the national and international markets were an expensive ship and rail ride away, and imported raw materials were expensive to bring in.

It might have helped if anyone, including many of the factory owners, knew what they were doing.

Here are some of the highlights:

Newfoundland Tanneries, 1952: Cost: $600,000. Goals: 150 initial jobs, 150 hides tanned a day. Accomplishments: In four years, twenty-one people were hired, putting out one hundred hides a day. Unable to meet orders. Complaints of poor quality leather. Lost money each year of operation. Deficit of about $120,000 by 1957. Closed in 1957.

Newfoundland Hardwoods, 1952. Cost: $2 million, $700,000 over original estimate. Goals: 250 jobs in creation of plywood and veneers. Accomplishments: By 1957, losing $1,000 a day. Unable to compete on plywood with foreign companies that had less expensive raw resources. Closed in the 1980s.

North Star Cement Co., 1952. Cost: about $3.5 million. Goals: 200 jobs, 100,000 to 150,000 tons of cement and $1 million in profit a year. Accomplishments: Losses of about $325,000 in first year of operation, and $433,000 in the third. Started as a government owned company. Buyers were difficult to find. Eventually North Star bought it, with a $4.3 million loan… from the province of course.

Atlantic Gypsum, 1952. Cost: $3 million. Goals: 300 jobs. Accomplishments: By 1957, was employing 186. The government tried to sell it but it was rejected by one would-be buyer as too slow a mill, with too small a market. Relied on mainland for 90 percent of its sales, increased competition by 1954 led to huge price drops. Closed.

Canadian Machinery and Industry Construction Ltd., 1952: Cost: $2.5 million. Goals: 500 jobs initially, 5,000 eventually, in creating of heavy machinery for mainland market. Expected to get large defence contracts from federal governments. Accomplishments: Ended up building bumpers for St. John's buses and school desks. By 1957, employed about 200 men. Ran up debt of about $500,000. Sold to private sector. Closed in the 1980s.

United Cotton Mills, 1953. Cost: $2 million. Goals: Importing raw material from Turkey, Iran, the United States, and Haiti and making clothing. Accomplishments: Six years later, fewer than one hundred people working at plant. Synthetic materials become popular in clothing industry. Transportation costs underestimated by German owners. Sold to private sector in 1960s, closed in 1986.

Hanning Electric Company, 1953. Cost: $325,000. Goals: One hundred people building 50,000 automobile batteries a year. Accomplishments: Within six months, seventeen people on the payroll. Newfoundlanders buying 12,000 batteries a year, but only 3,312 of them from this company in 1956. Closed in 1958.

Superior Rubber Company, 1953. Cost: $1 million. Goals: 400 workers making rubber clothes and boots. Accomplishments: Local Catholic population threatened to boycott and picket plant if rumours it was producing condoms for South America were true. The futuristic plant was built so poorly, the architect quit so his name wouldn't be attached to design. By 1954, producing only sixty boots a day and needed another $400,000. By 1955, complaints about soles becoming unglued after two weeks of wear. Grand total sales in one month: $203. About a $630,000 deficit by 1955. All German employees fired. Closed in 1956.

Atlantic Gloves Limited, 1954. Goals: To create high quality gloves from leather at nearby tannery. Accomplishments: Gloves sold for one-third of cost in 1956. Deficit of $200,000 in 1960. Closed in 1960.

Gold Sail Leather Goods, 1954. Goals: To build handbags and wallets from leather provided by nearby tannery. Accomplishments: According to consultant's report in 1957, company sold handbags Newfoundlanders couldn't afford and didn't want. Closed in 1960.

Adler Chocolate Factory, 1956. Estimated cost: $550,000. Goals: To sell English-style chocolate to Newfoundlanders and mainlanders. Accomplishments: Closed 1960.

Eckhardt Knitting Mills Ltd., 1955. Estimated cost: $387,000. Goals: 300 jobs. Accomplishments: Created out of style clothing unpopular with buyers. Needed continued government bailouts. Closed in the 1960s.

Smallwood told Newfoundlanders repeatedly that the industries were working out just fine. Even he couldn't ignore the reality forever and in 1957, the government hired a Boston firm to assess the companies. The consultant's report recommended three plants be closed and two be merged, and generally concluded the industrialization plan was a disaster.

Smallwood, of course, didn't release the entire report to the voting public. Bit by bit he issued statements that showed most of the companies were doing well. He quoted only the best parts of the report. The battery plant got a good reference, he told the public in November 1957. The report actually said the battery plant would never sell as many batteries as it was making, but couldn't afford to make any less.

By the time most of the plants had closed and reality sank in, Smallwood had moved on to much larger and in some cases, more successful projects, such as the Churchill Falls hydroelectric development.

Valdmanis was long gone too. He had warned Smallwood in 1952 that the industrialization program wasn't working, but Smallwood ignored the advice. With disaster looming, Valdmanis resigned as director general of economic development in 1953 to head another of his brainchildren, the Newfoundland and Labrador Corporation. The corporation was supposed to work with private partners to develop the province's raw resources. It fizzled out only months after Valdmanis took over, although it was in trouble long before that.

Valdmanis moved to Montréal, to be close to investors, he said. His past finally caught up to him, though. Tipped off by a Latvian immigrant living in Newfoundland, Smallwood learned Valdmanis was taking bribes from the European companies investing in the province. The money was going to Smallwood's Liberal party, Valdmanis told the investors. Overall, he was believed to have made at least $470,000 on two deals. The Royal Canadian Mounted Police (RCMP) arrested Valdmanis in April 1954 and threw him in jail. The former *uberfuhrer* of Newfoundland's economy revealed to guards that he was addicted to tranquilizers. A doctor at his trial testified Valdmanis suffered from mental illness because of his experience in prison camps. Valdmanis pleaded guilty to $200,000 fraud on September 15, 1954 and was sentenced to four years in prison. Most of the money was never recovered, though Valdmanis suggested he had to pay it out in blackmail. He served two years. The man who spent millions barely survived as a businessman. He was killed in a car crash in August 1970. Smallwood made no public comment at the time.

Although the deals swallowed about $30 million in unpaid loans and interest — almost all the money the province received for joining Confederation and the equivalent of $150 million today — Smallwood argued in his autobiography that his and Valdmanis's industrial plan was not a total loss, because several factories stayed open and they all provided jobs for awhile. In one sense, the deal did work out well. Newfoundlanders got to watch their politicians merrily throw away almost all the money the government had. They could finally feel truly Canadian.

This isn't going to work

Shortly after the Second World War, a deal was struck between Canada and the USSR.

Hearken back to the days just before the Cold War was in full heat or frost, and good old Canadians were looking for ways to help strengthen the bonds of commerce with their old allies from the war.

Russia had the best — what, herd? — of sable in the world. Lots of luxuriant sable, the most beautiful fur on earth, attached to those wretched, little weasel-like beasts.

Canada had some pretty nice mink fur, also attached to wretched, little weasel-like beasts. Raising the animals for fur was quite an industry in both countries, but neither had the other's breed.

So, Canada and the USSR worked out a deal for a swap.

A date was arrived at and a number of male and female pairs were crated up in each country and shipped. The Soviets received beautiful mink breeding pairs with nice thick fur. The Canadians received beautiful sable breeding pairs with nice thick fur.

Imagine the Canadians' surprise when they learned the females were neutered prior to shipment.

M stands for "Montréal" and "missing money"

Something about Montréal produces the best failures in Canada.

In fact, Mirabel Airport and the Montréal Olympics are synonymous with the term, "white elephant." They failed in so many different ways, only a short outline can be provided here. Besides, too much detail is depressing.

Mirabel International Airport was proposed in the 1960s as the hub of all air travel in Eastern Canada and a booming Montréal, its six runways and six terminals capable of handling 50 million passengers a year. Montréal's city airport, Dorval, would soon be overwhelmed by traffic and could not be expanded into the surrounding urban area without raising objections over noise and pollution. The plans for Mirabel were announced in 1969 and the federal government expropriated 88,000 acres of top-grade farmland, two-thirds the size of Montréal. The budget was set at $100 million.

That was the price of progress. Progress, however, flew right over Mirabel and landed in Dorval. Situated sixty kilometres north of Montréal, Mirabel proved unpopular with air passengers. Why fly to Mirabel then make your way to Montréal, when you could simply fly into Montréal? In the 1970s, Transport Canada gave air carriers the right to land in Toronto. That meant transport aircraft from Europe could bypass Montréal and fly directly to Toronto. Then the election of the Parti Québécois in 1976 drove businesses and individuals out of Montréal, stalling the projected boom.

And it turned out Dorval could handle any increases in traffic. In 1997, the agency running both airports opened up Dorval for regular international passenger service. Mirabel was left with charter and freight flights, losing about 60 percent of its passenger flights. Because freight is also carried on passenger flights, Mirabel also lost 40 percent of its freight business. The cuts translated into about 600 jobs lost, with another 1,200 transferred to Dorval.

After all the millions that were spent and the hundreds displaced, Mirabel today handles not 50 million, but one million passengers a year. And the bleeding never seems to stop. In summer 2002, the airport authority was ordered by the courts to pay $17.9 million to the owner of a hotel near Mirabel, who claimed losses of $70 million because most of the passenger flights had been transferred to Dorval five years before. Thanks to losses of $20 million a year, the rest of the passenger flights were going to be transferred, the airport announced in 2002. Mirabel was to be left with cargo traffic only.

Four sinkholes are better than one

Pick a spot in Manitoba, say… there, The Pas.

Now pick any old stranger who comes along, say… that man, there. Dr. Kasser, he calls himself.

Now pull out your wallet and start counting. $10 million? No. $20 million? Keep counting.

Then give the money to the stranger, put him in The Pas, and see what happens.

Those are the basic principles behind Manitoba's northern development strategy in the 1960s, which culminated in the creation of four industries that barely made a living for years, an RCMP takeover of a plant, a provincial commission, and international lawsuits.

The roots of Churchill Forest Industries go back to a 1958 report called the Economic Survey of Northern Manitoba by U.S. consulting firm, Arthur D. Little. That report determined that northern Manitoba's untapped timber could be turned into a valuable pulp and paper, plywood, hardboard, and newsprint industry. A couple of years later, another report by the same consultant suggested several ways to overcome the many barriers to such an industry, such as the great distance from the market and the fact there were no towns in the area where workers could live. The solution was government help. Money for a townsite and low stumpage rates, the fees charged for cutting the trees, could overcome all the problems.

The report ended up in the Manitoba treasury, where an alert bureaucrat read it then outlined all the ways a pulp and paper industry would not work in northern Manitoba.

The ruling Conservative party didn't listen. In two years, an election was coming. Jobs equaled votes. The industry would soon pay for itself and then some. Besides, the north had to be developed, everybody knew that.

Yet the politicians were cautious. The politicians were wise. They developed an objective test to determine if the proposal was valid. If someone decided to invest, the project just had to be worthwhile. Private investors don't make mistakes. And so the newly created Manitoba Development Agency looked for an investor. First it tried to get an Italian firm to build the project. The Italian firm studied the plan and said no. So the government changed tactics. Private enterprise just needed some help.

Here's what the province came up with. A pulp mill at The Pas would cost about $37 million to build. The province would provide 60 percent of the funding at 6.5 percent interest. The government would also pay $180 per employee for the townsite development, build a transmission line to the mill, and waive business and realty taxes. Even with these inducements, companies in the United Kingdom, France, Italy, and Japan declined to get involved. Finally, in 1965, the Swiss firm, Monoca A.G., expressed interest in the plan. A few other companies started asking questions about the project, but Monoca was there first.

The deal signed was complex but amounted to Monoca setting up Churchill Forest Industries to oversee the construction and management of the chemical pulp plant. The government provided the money to build the plant, cheap electricity, trained woodcutters, and a better port at Churchill. The $100 million project would provide jobs for 2,000 people, the Conservative government announced in February 1966, and four months later it won re-election.

For the next few years, as the project stumbled along, the Manitoba government dipped further into its account to help out Churchill Forest Industries. The trouble was, cabinet approved the deal without really knowing what it was getting into. The politicians figured the Manitoba Development Fund knew what was going on, and the Manitoba Development Fund figured the government knew. Under Swiss law, the directors of Monoca did not have to be revealed. Manitoba respected that law, and its contract didn't require Monoca to reveal either its owners or connections to other companies.

The deal's weaknesses did not go unnoticed; the media and opposition in Manitoba pressured the government for answers. Into the troubled woods strode a figure heroic in the world of international finance — Alexander Kasser. Though he played nothing more than a shell game, he did it on boardroom tables across the world. He set up companies on paper that appeared to be separate from each other, used tenuous connections with real firms to create credibility for his shadow companies, traded that credibility for multimillion-dollar deals, then had his shadow companies award each other contracts and purchase orders — at nice profits.

Kasser was connected to Monoca through a partner company, Technopulp. By the time he finished negotiating with the Manitoba government in 1968, the project doubled in size in some areas and tripled in others. Churchill Forest Industries would operate a 600-ton per day pulp mill, while three other companies would operate a 600-ton per day paper mill, a pulp and paper machinery plant, and a 100-million board feet sawmill. Each of the four separate companies would be eligible for federal grants totalling $12 million, more than one large company could get on its own. The Manitoba government would have to increase its investment to $40 million.

The good news, Industry and Commerce Deputy Minister Rex Grose reported, was that the risk was spread among four companies. The bad news, he did not know, was that Kasser would finagle a way to get financial interest in each one. He controlled the company building and operating the sawmill, the firm building the pulp and paper machinery plant, and the company building and operating the paper mill. In other words, he controlled everything. And the government was financing it all.

Feasibility studies went out the window, because Manitoba bureaucrats and politicians figured surely the four companies and all the subcontractors knew what they were doing.

They knew what they were doing, all right. A provincial Commission of Inquiry later determined Kasser and his associates were paid $26.3 million in excessive fees. As for the $10 million spent on a machinery plant in the middle of the woods, that was just absurd, the commission said. It's not clear if Kasser ever intended to operate the companies.

Thanks in part to the growing financial scandal, the New Democratic Party won the 1969 election. Then *Financial Post* reporter Philip Mathias reported that the cost of the project had reached $142.6 million. A provincial auditor's report concluded loans had been flying out of government hands to Churchill Forest Industries with few controls. Usually, a lender doles out money in increments, as different machines for a plant are delivered. The province handed over the entire loans as the machinery was being made. Now and then, the province tried to get more information about the finances, but the four companies refused to hand over the paperwork. Swiss law and all, you know. Consulting firm Arthur D. Little, which had started the process almost fifteen years earlier, said things were fine. But government officials and advisers got a different view when they visited the building site late in 1970 and found things weren't moving along as quickly as promised.

In the face of growing pressure to act, a handful of RCMP officers on government orders took over the plant on January 8, 1971. Kasser and his associates left the country the same day.

Eventually, the pulp, paper, and sawmills were put into operation. The pulp and paper machinery plant never got off the ground. The final bill was $154.7 million, to build a complex worth $73 million. It cost the Manitoba government another $4 million to prosecute Kasser and his associates. Kasser was found not guilty. Three associates were found guilty. They were ordered to pay costs to help the Manitoba government recover its losses. The amount Manitoba recovered: $100,000.

In the old days, $28.5 million bought you something

Remember this figure: $28.5 million.

It seemed like a lot of money to spend, especially if you were a taxpayer in Nova Scotia in the 1960s.

By the time politicians, engineers, and a stubborn scientist with a secret were finished, though, that $28.5 million seemed like a dream of the good old days.

The money was supposed to build a heavy water plant at Glace Bay, Nova Scotia. Canada's CANDU nuclear reactors use heavy water — where the two hydrogen atoms in H_2O are replaced by two heavier deuterium atoms — to control the nuclear reaction in uranium. Demand for power — and heavy water — grew in the 1960s. The two new nuclear plants at Chalk River and Douglas Point in Ontario were going to need tons of heavy water.

The federal government's Atomic Energy of Canada Ltd. (AECL) had asked for proposals to build a heavy water plant. Of four contenders, the AECL and the federal departments of Finance and Industry, and Trade and Commerce preferred a proposal from a firm in Victoria, British Columbia, called Western Deuterium Company. It promised to provide its own financing and three energy sources, all cheaper than Cape Breton coal, to make heavy water out of fresh water.

Not as preferred was a proposal by a company called Deuterium of Canada Ltd. (DCL) to build a plant in Nova Scotia. DCL was headed by U.S. scientist John Spevack who had worked on the atomic bomb project in the 1940s and during the next decade patented new processes for producing heavy water. DCL intended to make heavy water in Nova Scotia from ocean salt water, which had never been done before. DCL was controlled by Americans. And the plant would need to consume large amounts of coal for fuel, costing the federal government $1 million a year in subsidies to the coal mines.

The AECL recommended Western Deuterium get the contract.

The federal government, of course, chose DCL.

Why? Politics. With jobs scarce in the Cape Breton region, Nova Scotia politicians hounded the new Liberal government in Ottawa to choose Glace Bay. And to ease federal concerns, the province of Nova Scotia took control of the majority of DCL shares. On December 2, 1963, Nova Scotia was awarded the heavy water plant.

Western newspapers and politicians complained, but Nova Scotia celebrated the great deal it had secured. Through the province's Industrial Estates Ltd., taxpayers would become the majority shareholder of DCL, putting up $12 million for those shares only after DCL raised the other $18 million for the plant. The nuclear plant would form the foundation for an industrial complex in Cape Breton and consume hundreds of thousands of tons of Cape Breton coal.

Just to make sure the plant would work, engineering firm Burns and Roe was hired to check out the proposal. It sure will, came the answer. Confident in the plan, the province signed the final contract with DCL. So confident was the province, it agreed to a change in the contract that required it to raise its $18 million investment before DCL raised its $12 million investment. Under the new contract, company president Spevack would be paid $25,000 a year, although he didn't have to work full-time.

It was only a matter of months before the price on the plant began to rise. Burns and Roe had been hired to oversee the design, engineering, and construction. Early estimates that the design work would cost $1.5 million were soon changed to $2.5 million. Early estimates of the plant's cost were changed, too. An engineering report put the total price tag at $32.8 million.

The province began to get leery. Aside from the cost increases, DCL was having trouble raising its $18 million share. So the province began looking for other investors. But the price of the plant rose so fast it made would-be investors' heads spin. Three deals fell apart in 1965 and 1966 because Spevack refused to tell the potential investors how his secret heavy water technology worked. No one (except perhaps the provincial government) wanted to spend millions on something before finding out what the something was.

With no new investors in sight, the province loaned DCL another $15 million, the first $12 million contribution having already been spent. And the costs kept rising. The engineers had never built a heavy water plant, and the first mechanical drawings had to be changed 2,500 times in 1965 and 1966. Equipment was slow to arrive. Labour relations fell apart, partly because of bad managers, and partly because new unions were springing up to represent the skilled construction workers and the unions fought one another for members.

Then there was the ocean. Sometime before the plant opened in 1968, the equipment was tested and sea water flowed into the heat exchangers. The water didn't flow fast enough and there was some corrosion. Even worse, either someone forgot to flush out the system or there was a technical error, because salt water sat in the pipes for three months. When poisonous hydrogen sulphide was put into the system to start up the plant, it went into the pipes, through the leaks, and into the air. Fortunately, the gas blew out over the bay and no one was hurt, but the cost of fixing the corroded parts of the system was estimated at $15 million.

Fed up with all the problems, the province of Nova Scotia made what politicians considered a rational choice — in 1966, it bought out DCL so it could own the plant outright. The costs kept rising. By 1969, it had cost $100 million and it was estimated that it would take another $30 million to make the plant work.

In a valiant effort to increase the pain but spread it among a greater number of taxpayers, the federal government, in the 1970s, decided to help out and contributed $41.4 million for buying heavy water from the plant. Shortly after, Prime

Minister Pierre Trudeau announced the federal government would lease the plant from Nova Scotia and pay the $95 million rebuilding costs. Some historians think Trudeau was trying to bolster the Liberals' chances in the 1972 federal election.

For the next four years, the rebuilding took place in fits and starts. The idea of using sea water was scrapped, so a freshwater reservoir had to be built. Labour problems continued, with four strikes in two years. The plant started up in 1976 then closed a year later for more rebuilding. The rehabilitation of the plant cost not $95 million, the 1971 estimate, but $225 million. Finally, the federal government took the plant off the province's hands for another $66 million.

After all that, demand for heavy water fell. By 1985, the newly elected federal Conservatives had had enough. On May 23, the federal government announced Glace Bay's heavy water plant was closing. Rough mathematics — and why should we be any different than politicians — put the cost for Nova Scotia taxpayers at $130 million and the cost to federal taxpayers at about $291 million.

Remember that $28.5 million? We might just as well laugh as cry.

Blowing money

George Copeland was a lumber baron. He owned lots of land in Simcoe County. In fact, the Copeland Forest, southeast of Midland and Penetanguishene, was once part of the Copeland family empire.

But this story isn't about forests. Or lumber yards. It's not even about wood. It's about glass. Well, perhaps glass and brass. The kind of brass it takes to bluff townspeople out of money and dreams.

In 1879, Copeland sold two acres of land he owned in Penetanguishene to a group of trustees of the Penetanguishene Glass Factory. They were Phillip Spohn, a doctor, James Wynne, a wine merchant, and the Reverend Theo Laboureau, a priest.

One Richard Davis, who had convinced the trustees to invest in the glass factory, was to take over the operation. Davis was from England and said he was a glass-maker. No one ever actually saw him make any glass.

The Chatham Street location for the factory did create a sample of glass in 1880. One local paper, *The Orillia Times and County of Simcoe Expositor*, said in its January 28 edition of that year, "We have been shown several specimens of the glass manufactured in Penetanguishene, and to all appearances, it is faultless." The paper breathlessly extolled the virtues of the product and predicted the facility would no doubt be profitable. Most newspapers are a little more critical about business today.

By February, a building that would have covered a good chunk of a Canadian football field was erected and 250 employees were hired. The workforce was predicted to double by June.

By April, Davis had consented to come to Penetanguishene to take over the operation, but he didn't feel the need to spend all of his time there. He bounded about towns in Ontario, including St. Thomas and Sarnia, promising glass factories and raising money and disappearing, only to pop up somewhere else.

By August, the factory in Penetanguishene was still languishing. In the late summer of 1880, the *Barrie Northern Advance* reported it "unlikely" the factory would ever open. It turned out they were right. The factory never produced any glass.

By 1881, Davis had left Penetanguishene for good. Some

Penetanguishene citizens were longing for an indoor ice rink and eyed the seventy-five metre long building with a certain lust only skaters can understand. But the trustees later sold the land to Peter Baldwin and it eventually ended up back in Copeland's hands.

No one ever knew whether Davis was actually a glass-blower, or just a guy who was good at blowing smoke.

CHAPTER 14

WARS AND THE MILITARY

Canadian soldiers have fought valiantly at home and overseas. Sometimes in spite of the government.

At one point during its construction, King Louis of France mused that with all the money he had spent on Louisbourg, he expected to be able to see its walls from France.

Construction of the French fort was started in 1713 and when it was finished, it was the biggest fort in North America. Strategically located on Île Royale (Cape Breton), Nova Scotia, its presence was meant to deter English incursion into the Gulf of St. Lawrence and up to Quebec.

While its location was strategic, it was not a pleasant place. It was cold, storm-wracked, and low. There was a swamp on one side and the area had such a short growing season most food had to be brought in by ship. Other than that, it was great.

The French poured tons of money and resources into building the fort and once complete, they garrisoned it with 5,000 men. It was such an awesome fortress that the English avoided attacking it altogether. And so the French slowly extracted forces from the defence of the fort, making it, naturally, more and more vulnerable.

When King George's War erupted in 1744, the French in North America acted like the proverbial thorn in the side of the English by attacking shipping with forces based in Louisbourg and Quebec. The British retaliated by capturing the fort in 1745. Led by merchant and militia officer William Pepperrill, an amateur army crossed the swamp that led to the fort's most unprotected side and started firing at it until the garrison surrendered. It was returned to France in 1748.

The British captured it again in 1758 under Jeffery Amherst, but this time it took more than an amateur army. Along with 27,000 soldiers and sailors, upwards of 150 vessels, and more than 1,800 guns, Amherst had Brigadier

General James Wolfe, the governor of Nova Scotia, Charles Lawrence, and an ancestor of Sir Winston Churchill.

The French, under Augustine de Boschenry de Drucour, had only 3,500 soldiers, 4,000 sailors and militia, and eleven ships. Despite the odds against him, the fort allowed Drucour to hold out long enough to prevent the English from attacking Quebec during the same season.

While it was formidable to attackers, Louisbourg was truly only effective when it was staffed with sufficient troops. In 1760, Amherst ordered Louisbourg destroyed on the basis that it was no longer expedient to maintain it at such an expense.

Typical of Louisbourg's unusual history, the reconstruction of the fort in the twentieth century was based on the plans prepared by John Henry Bastide, the British army engineer who oversaw its destruction.

Perhaps we should have tried something smaller

If you have a chance to travel to Hudson Bay (and who wouldn't take the opportunity to treat themselves to the bugs and the mud of spring, or the ice and the cold of winter), do not under any circumstances miss the chance to visit Fort Prince of Wales.

The British built it at the mouth of the Churchill River starting in 1733. It was finished thirty-eight years later in 1771. It was surrendered to the French only eleven years after that in 1782.

If you see it, you'll understand why — this most northerly fort in the British Empire is an astonishingly massive, modern-looking, concrete structure out in the middle of the wilderness.

Consider how difficult it would be to build it today. Then consider how difficult it was to build — and staff — some 250-odd years ago.

In fact, it took three attempts to build it. The first version was built in 1689 but was destroyed by fire before it was finished. A second fort was built eight kilometres upstream, but proved to be too far upriver to provide an effective defence. The third and final one was built by the Hudson's Bay Company and Great Britain to help them retain control of the area. The French had what the British considered to be a nasty habit of sneaking into the Hudson Bay area and taking over forts.

It was, however, a bit roomy.

Samuel Hearne had been awarded command of Fort Prince of Wales in recognition of his two-year hike in the wilderness in search of copper (although he actually brought back only a few ounces). In August 1782, the Comte de La Pérouse arrived. Uninvited, needless to say, but there, we've said it.

Hearne surrendered the fort to the French. Given the size of it, perhaps that should be a surprise. But, as with so many other forts, it was expensive to keep it sufficiently manned and the walls were too long to be defended by the number of men available. La Pérouse demanded surrender and, because his men outnumbered Hearne's, he got it.

The Comte then tried to destroy the fort, but it was too massive. The French later abandoned it, and the British then took it over again. They used it as a trading post, but not a fort. It was just too big.

Now we both lose

The traditional view of Canadian settlers is of a group of people who may have been independent pioneers, but who helped each other out to survive in a hostile environment.

Not so the Canadian version of the Hatfields and McCoys — Charles de Saint-Étienne de La Tour and Charles de Menou d'Aulnay — who made their environments even more hostile.

Both men brought colonizing settlers from France to the Acadia area. As was the method of French settlement at the time, each group of settlers was sponsored by private investors who expected to receive some of the proceeds from the settlers' ventures — a form of capitalistic exploration.

This approach often forced individuals to act in the best interests of their investors, who usually favoured the elimination of competition. This was not necessarily a productive goal when the competition was one of your countrymen. The time, resources, and energy that Menou and La Tour spent fighting each other might have been put to better use preventing England from establishing footholds in New France.

It would appear that while La Tour arrived first and managed some remarkable accomplishments, Menou prevailed. That is, until Menou died in a boating accident, at which point La Tour married Menou's widow. La Tour was a widower, his wife having died while a captive of Menou.

There is no question that both men were true to France, despite their hatred of each other. When the English from the upper New England states raided and captured a fort held by La Tour, Menou was ordered to assist in the retaking of it. La Tour refused to work with Menou. But Menou, following orders, captured it on his own.

That's not to say La Tour was not a patriot of France. Before Menou arrived, he had fought off an attack led by his own father, who had sided with the English.

La Tour's father, Claude, had been captured by the English in 1628. In 1629, when the English captured Quebec, Charles' Fort Lomeron was the sole French possession in New France. Claude, not liking France's odds in the New World, decided to throw his lot in with the English. The English king granted Claude a huge tract of land in Nova Scotia for switching loyalties. Claude returned the favour by marrying an English lady-in-waiting. He boarded a ship and headed west to talk to his son.

Claude believed that Charles would join him. France had all but ignored her holdings in the New World except to demand taxes, which had made life both dangerous and expensive for his son. So, in 1630 when Claude and his new wife and two English men-of-war pulled into the harbour at Cap de Sable, where Charles held Fort Lomeron, Claude was confident that he could convince his son to accept the English terms.

But Charles remained true to his country and refused to turn his back on his king. Claude decided he had no choice but to treat his son as an enemy. An assault force of English soldiers and sailors from the two men-of-war led by Pop La Tour attacked Lomeron. The assault raged for two days. There has been nothing like it since in the New World.

Charles prevailed and Claude retreated to Port Royal to consider his fortunes. Eventually, he asked his son to forgive him and for permission to return to Lomeron and rejoin the French presence. After some discussion, Charles agreed.

Things were relatively calm with La Tour for some time. In 1632, the French king appointed Isaac de Razilly as governor of Acadia, with the exception of the La Tour holdings. Razilly and La Tour had different business interests but managed to work together to the benefit of both.

In 1635 Razilly died. His successor preferred to run things from France through the person of one Charles de Menou d'Aulnay. He and La Tour did not work together. In fact, they fought each other fiercely for more than a decade.

At one point, shortly after Menou had recaptured La Tour's fort without La Tour's help, Menou used a blockade to prevent supplies from France from arriving at La Tour's outposts.

Once England and France were at peace, La Tour had no qualms about trading with New England businessmen in order to get the things he needed. Menou reported to the king that La Tour was refusing to deal with France and was siding with the English. This sort of behaviour on the part of Menou somehow increased his profile at the French court and diminished La Tour's.

The climax came when Menou attacked La Tour's fort, called, oddly enough, Fort La Tour, while La Tour was in Boston. Françoise-Marie de La Tour, Claude's wife, was home at the time of the attack and led its defence.

With Menou's promise of rights of pillage, his men attacked relentlessly and suffered severe losses. The lady La Tour continued to battle. She let it be known to Menou that unless he promised safe quarter for all survivors, she would fight to the last. Menou promised.

Once inside, he took back his promise, binding her with rope around her neck and forcing her to watch the slow strangulation of almost all of her defenders. She died two days later.

La Tour, penniless and heartbroken over the loss of his brave wife, moved to Quebec where he stayed for four years until Menou died in a canoe accident. By that time, Menou was also living in poverty.

La Tour did return to France to clear his name at the French court and, ultimately, Menou was posthumously criticized for his actions in New France and Acadia. La Tour returned to Acadia and Cap de Sable. He met with Menou's widow, Jeanne d'Aulnay nee Motin, and made peace. Eventually they married. And, other than the time in July

1654 when La Tour was captured by an English expedition sent over by Oliver Cromwell (yes, that Oliver Cromwell and yes, England and France were at peace, so it's not clear why the "man of the people" took this action) and held prisoner until 1656, La Tour lived happily ever after at Cap de Sable.

He died in 1666, a survivor of France's "capitalism run amok" method of financing exploration and settlement, and perhaps the New World's first hostile takeover bid.

Fine then, I quit

Great Britain was not so great to many of its soldiers.

Robert MacDouall started the War of 1812 as a captain and aide-de-camp to a British general. By 1814, he had risen to the rank of lieutenant colonel. MacDouall was, by all accounts, an intelligent and motivated leader. His men performed miracles for him and the local Native people respected and admired him.

In 1814, MacDouall was given the small task of marching 300 men and supplies from Kingston, Ontario to York (where Toronto is today), then up Yonge Street to Lake Simcoe, across Lake Simcoe to where Barrie is today, on to a small depot on an Indian portage in the middle of a swamp — the largest surviving swamp in southern Ontario — where he and his men were to build thirty or so large, open boats and make their way across Georgian Bay to resupply and man Fort Michilimackinac. This in the days when Yonge Street was at best a rough goat's path and at worst a stump-infested swamp.

Oh, and they started this mission in the teeth of winter. By the time they got to Georgian Bay in their open batteaux, they faced April storms and ice. Not a man was lost. By comparison, a lesser commander had men die on him in a short march from Barrie to Penetanguishene in the summer. Even marching can kill.

But MacDouall got all his men to Michilimackinac.

Months after MacDouall and his men arrived in Michilimackinac, the Americans arrived to attack. They failed to take the fort by force and so decided to starve the fort into surrender. They left their ships, the *Tigress* and the *Scorpion*, behind to patrol the lake and Georgian Bay, and took their two larger boats to Lake Erie, where they hoped to intercept the supply vessel, the *Nancy*, at a small depot at Wasaga Beach.

MacDouall, second-guessing the Americans, had already dispatched a man to race down to the *Nancy* and warn the sailors and soldiers. The British tried to hide the supply ship but its masts were spotted by the Americans. After a fierce gun battle, the British blew up the *Nancy* to deny capture by the Americans.

The British had a second store of supplies up the Nottawasaga River. After the battle, they retrieved it and two batteaux and made their way up to Michilimackinac. On their arrival, MacDouall and the men from the *Nancy*, in a daring night raid, managed to capture the two ships the Americans had left behind.

The war was over for MacDouall and his prisoners. But the Treaty of Ghent returned the area to the status quo, which meant MacDouall's fort had to be given to the Americans. He moved his men to another island, further east, and started a new fort on Drummond Island, in the throat of Georgian Bay.

While MacDouall was a star during the war, he was neglected afterwards. His foresight and courage had denied the upper Great Lakes to the Americans, and while they seized the lower Great Lakes, his actions helped keep the war to a draw. But on Drummond, the inaction and neglect made it hard to keep discipline. He began losing men to disease because the army did not provide enough fresh fruit and in the winter of 1816, with five men dead from scurvy, MacDouall quit and walked away.

Oh, yeah? Well, my army can beat your army

After the War of 1812, the British (who were in charge of the northern part of North America) and the Americans (who were in charge of most of the southern part) decided they had to devise a way of properly defining the border between the two countries.

It was a long border and it took a lot of time. Sometimes the boundaries were drawn with only a tiny bit of knowledge of the terrain, so the border areas were not always clearly defined.

In the case of San Juan Island, a small island between Vancouver Island and Washington State, both sides laid claim to it. The Hudson's Bay Company had a nice little stock farm on the island and the governor in Victoria, British Columbia tried to encourage settlement by offering free land and other incentives. No one really wanted to go, since it was small and the ferry service, being non-existent, was not what it is today.

The Americans, however, liked it and by 1858 there were a couple of dozen of them living on the island they considered home. So much so that one day, when a pig belonging to the Hudson's Bay Company farm wandered over to an American settler's property and helped itself to some potatoes in the settler's garden, the American apparently felt justified in shooting the pig and eating it.

The Hudson's Bay Company complained to the British magistrate who ordered the American arrested. The American threatened the authorities with deadly force. Then, perhaps sensing just how important this moment could be in the history of world politics, he called directly upon the assistance of General William Harney. This was prior to the American Civil War, during a time when Americans were clearing the west of troublesome warriors and consequently had many trained American soldiers on the coast.

Harney, who was nicknamed "Goliath," sent troopers of the Ninth United States Infantry over to the island to protect the Americans from any further attacks by swine or pushy legal authorities. The next thing you know, four British warships and Royal Marines dropped by from Victoria. Then more American troops and volunteers arrived to bolster the outnumbered Yanks.

Finally, the American president, James Buchanan, sent General Winfield Scott, the supreme deluxe commander of American land forces and highest officer in the American army, to cool things down. But that was not before a British warship, HMS *Ganges*, and its eighty-four guns arrived. Ultimately about 5,000 troops and sailors from both countries were on or floating about the island, all 145 square kilometres of it, staring each other down.

In the end, the British lost the island, but it took years and the German Kaiser Wilhelm I, who had been asked to intervene, to settle the dispute.

Ow, that hurts!

The federal Liberal party kicked the Tories out of power in the 1990s because of a number of factors. There was a swelling dislike for Brian Mulroney, who appeared arrogant and detached. There was a string of ministerial disgraces. There was bad tuna.

And there was the promise to purchase a group of EH-101 helicopters, which had one role — as sub-hunters —

and seemed out of touch with the reality of the end of the cold war.

There was a great need for helicopters, but the cost of the EH-101, coupled with its partial task as a sub-hunter, seemed to annoy voters. Jean Chrétien and his Liberals promised to rip up the contract to buy the helicopters, and they did.

Another helicopter was needed. A smaller, lighter, utility chopper. A multi-tasking chopper that could do many things well.

The Liberals didn't buy that chopper, either. Instead, they purchased the Griffon — a fine, off-the-shelf, civilian helicopter.

According to the 1998 Auditor General of Canada, the Griffon was not up to the task. Perhaps the most spectacular problem arose when the craft was used for personnel transport. In this case, it was replacing the aging Huey, made famous by the Americans during the war in Vietnam. The Griffon could carry people, no problem. But few civilian choppers have people swinging below them on long ropes so they can slide to the ground in rough terrain.

Soldiers want to hit the ground in an alert state. They have to be ready for anything — from enemy fire to ensuring they are not landing on another soldier's bayonet. So it is a bit of an issue if the descending soldier is zapped by a huge charge of static electricity, which is what happened when the unmodified helicopter rotors created a charge as they spun, only to have that charge travel down through the soldiers to the earth.

"Operational tests that could have been carried out on the Griffon to assess the aircraft's suitability for military use were not done before acquisition. As a result, the department is now discovering that the aircraft's capabilities are being stretched to the limits, particularly when the Griffon is used in applications that push its envelope, such as search and rescue operations.

Problems not yet resolved include engine overtorques and electrostatic shocks to personnel who ground the aircraft as it hovers," concluded the Auditor General's report.

The Griffon also did not meet the military need for a chopper that could carry its new howitzer at least one hundred kilometres. The gun was supposed to weigh 1,400 kilograms and turned out to be heavier, which wasn't the chopper's fault. The bottom line was the chopper was woefully short of lift and could only carry the gun about twenty-five kilometres. The report also said the military's own tests showed the chopper could not realistically meet the requirements to provide supplies to soldiers in the field at the level they requested.

Really, there was nothing wrong with the Griffon. It was a great helicopter for civilian use, but it was grabbed off the shelf and plugged into a role for which it was not intended. In one of a never-ending list of Canadian government cost-cutting schemes when it comes to the military, it just wasn't the right tool for the job.

The government could have just as easily gone out and purchased a bunch of used American Motors Gremlins for troop transport. And we could be writing about how inadequate the protection of the passengers is when the windows are unrolled, and how easily bogged down the carrier becomes when it tries to travel cross-country.

A one-man failure machine

Sir Samuel Hughes is possibly the most dangerous failure this country ever produced.

No one before or since has put so many Canadians at risk for no reason other than an unwavering belief, no matter what the evidence, that he was right.

And he was so often wrong.

Hughes was a politician, soldier, bigot, and perhaps worst of all, a small town newspaper editor. But his most dangerous role was as the man in charge of the militia during the First World War. As such, he was responsible for training, equipping, and preparing Canadian forces to go overseas to fight.

Oddly, Hughes got his first taste of war fighting alongside the English in the Boer War. Oddly, because members of his family were among the tens of thousands of Irish who fled to Canada in the mid-1800s to escape from the potato famine and the diseases that were scything the population. Neither the British landowners in Ireland, nor the English who had imported milk and butter from Irish cattle throughout the potato famine, had lifted a finger to help the dying country.

Hughes was born in Ontario and his family farmed near the small community of Solina, near Darlington, Ontario. Hughes grew up to be a fit and energetic young man, said to be handsome and an accomplished athlete. By the age of sixteen, Hughes was already teaching school. He wrote textbooks and became a school inspector. He was also a superpatriot. He loved Canada and Canadians almost blindly.

Well, some Canadians.

By the time he was thirty-two, Hughes owned a newspaper in Lindsay called *The Victoria Warder*. He used the paper as a bully pulpit, hacking away at the foundations of French Canada. The Orange country surrounding Lindsay meant there was fertile ground for the kind of poisonous nonsense Hughes wrote and printed, and that made his paper a success.

In 1899, when Hughes was serving as a member of Parliament, the Boer War broke out. His speech about Canada taking a lead in providing troops was key in promoting the militia and the role it would play.

He was somewhat less successful at defining the role he would play. Although he had absolutely no military experience, he was determined that he should be a field commander. His request was refused and he eventually left for South Africa as a lieutenant.

The Boers were mostly Dutch-descended settlers who had resisted English rule. They had lived in South Africa for so long, they considered themselves one of the local "tribes" and were remarkably well-adapted to life in that part of the world. In the mid-1830s and 1840s, to avoid English rule yet again, they moved to and established the Orange Free State and the Transvaal. Then, in 1886, they found gold. The resulting flood of English prospectors, miners, and speculators soon meant that the English outnumbered the Boers. To protect themselves, the Boers denied the foreigners citizenship and the vote, and imposed heavy taxes. The English turned to Queen Victoria for help, who responded by sending in the British Expeditionary Force.

English Canada leapt to help. Hughes, despite his Irish heritage, leapt with them.

A young nation, more than willing to prove itself in war, English Canada had all the immortal daring of a teenage boy with a fast car and a driver's licence.

(French Canadians, who saw too many similarities between themselves and the Boers — both people with their own language trying to maintain their culture under the heavy influence of Victorian England — were not as supportive. As Henri Bourassa remarked during the debates about the war: "The doctrine is new to me that under the British Flag and under the Canadian Flag, we should go and broaden people's minds with dum-dum bullets.")

The British government believed the war would be a short-lived and rather brutish one for the Boers. On paper, the Boers, a small loosely organized militia, should not have been able to withstand the might of the British Army. But even Hughes admired the fighting qualities of the Boers, who were not defeated until 1902.

While in South Africa, Hughes sent back (uncorroborated) dispatches detailing the glory that was his as he led victorious routs against the Boers. And while Hughes hated career soldiers, referring to them as "parasites," his fierce patriotism led him to believe that the Canadian volunteer citizen soldiers were the best fighting men in the world — far superior even to the highly trained British soldiers. And he was not shy about saying so.

As it happened, Canada did deliver the first Commonwealth victory of the Boer War at Paardeburg. And the Canadians did fight well, no doubt reinforcing Hughes' views, but it seems more likely that this was in spite of, not because of, their lack of training.

Hughes, on the other hand, did not do as well and was sent home for being a blunt and outspoken critic of the British commanders. Nonetheless, despite being removed from the theatre of war, he arrived home a hero.

Installed as the military critic for the opposition Conservatives, Hughes was then named by Liberal Prime Minister Wilfred Laurier to a special committee that was to examine the possibility of opening a rifle plant in Canada. Laurier had been unsuccessful in convincing the British company that made the Lee-Enfield rifle to create a Canadian plant, and was hoping that a Canadian munitions and weapons industry could be established.

Sir Charles Ross, a Scot, said he would build a rifle factory in Canada and make a rifle that was better than the Lee-Enfield. Hughes fell in love with what was known as the Ross rifle and became its staunchest supporter, despite glaring problems with it.

In 1911, Robert Borden was elected prime minister, defeating Laurier in a battle that the Liberals said was over free trade, but that most of the populace and the opposition Conservatives said was over corruption and rampant government spending. Borden promptly made Hughes Minister of Militia and Defence. Then, in 1914, the First World War broke out.

Hughes accepted his increased responsibility with all the patriotism, pride, energy, and sheer bullheadedness that he had previously exhibited. Not only did he ensure that Canadian soldiers would have to contend with the Ross rifle, Oliver Gear, and the MacAdam shovel, but he also put his own remarkable — and sometimes inexplicable — stamp on staffing, organizing, training, and mobilizing the army he was in charge of.

He did, without doubt, mobilize Canadian troops at an astonishing speed when Canada entered the war. And he honestly believed in the superiority of his Canadian soldiers and wanted only the best for them.

But Hughes had his own way of doing things. Instead of using the existing training bases, he insisted on having a new one built at Valcartier, Quebec which meant the camp had to be constructed before the troops — the vast majority of whom had little or no experience — could begin training to go overseas.

Hughes had never trusted career soldiers, so when he was assembling his commanders, a number of top army officers were ignored or sacked in favour of Hughes' cronies, like the Valcartier real estate agent, William McBain, who was made a lieutenant colonel with full pay — and no military experience.

For reasons one can merely guess (although it may have had something to do with Hughes' unshakeable belief that traditional soldiers were far inferior to Canadian farm boys or factory workers with just a little training and the right weapons), the Royal Canadian Regiment, the only professional unit in the Canadian Order of Battle, was not used to train the raw recruits and bolster the fighting force. Instead, Hughes shipped the regiment off to Bermuda. No word on whether the Kaiser ever had designs on Bermuda. The unit did eventually make it to France — almost two years later.

Historian Jack Granatstein told journalist Patrick Watson, in an interview for Watson's piece on Hughes in the series *The Canadians: Biographies of a Nation*, there was already a mobilization plan for the troops in place, but Hughes threw it out. "He miraculously created a camp [Valcartier] that didn't have to be created, mixed up historic regiments ... it was, I think, totally disorganized chaos."

In any event, troops were quickly processed through Valcartier with a minimum of training, equipped with their questionable gear, packed on ships, and sent off to Britain and then France. Hughes himself spent some time around Valcartier — publicly screaming at some officers and praising others, demoting, promoting, and even demonstrating the proper way to charge with a bayonet. This was not without its humour since the bayonet on the Ross rifle had a habit of falling off. However, while this may have been amusing at Valcartier, it was not so amusing on the Somme.

While in England, Hughes kept appointing top people with overlapping responsibilities, causing numerous delays and problems. He also, for no apparent reason, told complete lies to the press and his troops about an assassination attempt on him and about meeting a spy on a boat while travelling across the Atlantic.

Hughes was knighted in 1915, but by 1916, Prime Minister Borden was forced to ask for Hughes' resignation. While Borden had been a longtime defender of the renegade minister, Hughes — unaccustomed as he was to worrying about the consequences of his actions — was creating too many problems for Borden by acting outside his ministerial authority.

(Hughes was not quite as loyal, once "praising" the prime minister by saying, "Mr. Borden is a most lovely fellow, as gentle-hearted as a girl.")

Hughes remained in Parliament as a backbencher and died in 1921.

Following is the best of what Hughes had to offer.

Did anyone see my bayonet?

The Ross rifle was big, heavy, expensive, and unreliable. And the bayonet kept falling off.

Regardless, it was the rifle chosen for the Canadian Army in the First World War.

Sam Hughes was its biggest supporter and insisted that the Ross rifle be provided to Canadian troops. Sir Charles Ross, who named the weapon after himself, set up a rifle factory in Quebec, after the British Lee-Enfield company refused to build a plant in Canada.

The Ross rifle was almost half a kilogram heavier and a third of a metre longer than the Lee-Enfield. It was also more costly, jammed more easily, and could not take the muddy conditions of combat.

In perfect conditions with perfect ammunition, it was a very accurate weapon and was retained by Canadian forces as a sniper rifle well after the First World War. The Lee-Enfield's ability to deal with junk ammunition made it less than accurate at long distances, but hey, with thousands and thousands of rounds being expended along the front every hour, volume makes up for accuracy.

The Ross was accurate but unreliable.

John Boyd/National Archives of Canada/PA-061466

Why are the soldiers in this June 2, 1915 photograph so happy? Probably because they're turning in their Ross rifles at Barriefield Camp in Kingston, Ontario. Heavy and prone to jamming, the Ross rifle was the last thing you wanted to carry through the trenches.

In war it became outright fatal — for the people using it.

The bolt that had to be pulled to eject a spent shell quickly became red hot with repeated firings — like the kind you have, say, in fierce combat — making it impossible to touch. Many Canadian soldiers died trying to loosen the bolt by using their boots on it.

The British-made ammunition was not machined to high enough standards for the Ross and repeatedly jammed in the Canadian guns. This meant the gun could not fire. A gun that can't fire can still be used as a club, but that is a rather rudimentary method of combat that is not, as they say, ideal. The Lee-Enfield was more forgiving of the rough and ready ammo.

Canadian troops quickly learned the Ross rifle's shortcomings, and soldiers in the hundreds dumped it as quickly as possible once they had liberated a Lee-Enfield from a dead or wounded British soldier. The Canadian field commander in Europe eventually convinced the Canadian government to let the soldiers officially switch to the Lee-Enfield so they would-n't have to resort to pillaging dead Tommies for them, but it was a decision Hughes bitterly disagreed with.

The dirt keeps falling out

For soldiers who spent days digging trenches and foxholes overseas during the war, shovels were undoubtedly an integral part of their equipment.

Samuel Hughes, Minister of Militia and Defence and a sometime inventor, capitalized on his secretary's idea that shovels issued to soldiers could do double duty as shields. This was something the Swiss had toyed with in the past. Hughes registered a patent for this new and improved shovel in the name of his personal secretary, Ena MacAdam, and the Department of Militia and Defence bought thousands of the MacAdam shovels for use by Canadian forces in the First World War.

The idea was that soldiers could use the shovel to provide some cover from enemy fire (no doubt while they were sitting up, since the Oliver Gear they wore prevented them from lying on their stomachs). Unfortunately bullets went right through the shovels, making them useless as shields. And, equally unfortunately, the hole on the left side of the shovel blade, designed to hold the soldier's rifle to enable him to shoot at the enemy, made them useless as shovels.

The MacAdam shovel was also heavier than the British-made shovel. Weighing two and a half kilograms, it was just a lovely addition to the soldier's kit, along with the heavy Ross rifle.

Nevertheless, the Department of Militia and Defence pur-chased fifty tons of the beauties only to sell them for scrap later. As the National Archives of Canada so understatedly

National Archives of Canada/PA-202396

Hey, look at this great idea! A shovel with a hole in it so you can prop your rifle up! Samuel Hughes, Minister of Militia and Defence during the First World War, didn't worry about the dirt falling out. The shovel did make for great scrap metal.

says about the MacAdam shovel, "Caution kept it from being used on the Front."

My tunic's shrunk and my boots have dissolved

Sir Sam Hughes did not profit from First World War munitions sales. But his friends did. And often at the cost of the soldiers who had to use the shoddy gear they manufactured.

Instead of making the best available equipment for Canadian soldiers fighting under the already horrendous conditions of the Great War, they came up with:

- tunics that were too tight and tended to fall apart after only a little wear,
- combat boots that dissolved in the mud, for soldiers who were destined to live in the mud for years, and
- the Oliver Gear, which turned out to be a spectacularly multi-faceted failure. The Oliver Gear was recommended to Hughes by a doctor in Halifax, despite being hated by soldiers in the Boer War. It consisted of complex webbing for hanging gear from soldiers. It was designed with the ammo pouch on the soldier's chest or stomach, depending on the size of the soldier and the looseness of the gear, which stretched when wet, effectively denying him the ability to crawl, and thus presenting a wonderful target to the Germans. It also cracked to pieces after it was dried out from being sodden in the trenches, a common occurrence. And, to top it off, the bullet pouches and the water bottle pocket were too small to be of much use.

I just love a good castle in wartime

One of Sir Samuel Hughes' shining moments was the day in 1914 that the Canadian army training base at Valcartier, Quebec opened — the largest training camp in Canada.

The base itself was composed of land expropriated from farmers and a piece of land purchased from William McBain, a land agent, or kind of glorified real estate agent.

For his trouble, McBain was made a lieutenant colonel with full pay.

It took more than 400 workers less than three weeks to transform the forests, hills, and valleys into roads, streets, offices, and quarters with electricity, water, and sewers. But no ordinary quarters would suffice for Hughes — he got, no kidding, his very own castle to stay in while he was there supervising his troops. Probably something to do with building morale — his, if not theirs.

It's true that there were already other bases for training soldiers in Canada, like Camp Petawawa. But Hughes apparently wanted his own brand new base to train and mobilize Canadian troops quickly before they were sent overseas during the First World War. And, perhaps coincidentally, Hughes had friends who owned the only rail link into Valcartier. Taxpayers were only too happy to help Hughes and his friends fight the war, and line their pockets.

CHAPTER 15

POLITICS

Some parts of Canadian history are too depressing to make light of, such as our recent prime ministers. So we instead offer a short quiz on the biggest prime ministerial flops in Canadian history.

A Canadian failure quiz

Q.: In 1972, what Conservative leader came within two seats of being prime minister, then fumbled the 1974 election thanks in part to a football play?

A.: Robert Stanfield. Stanfield's Conservatives won 107 seats in the 1972 election, two shy of Pierre Trudeau's Liberals. The New Democratic Party won thirty-one and the Social Credit eleven. Trudeau's minority government fell over its budget two years later. During the ensuing campaign, on May 30, 1974, Stanfield went to catch a football in front of newspaper photographers. He dropped the ball. The photograph of Stanfield looking pained as the ball hit the ground cemented an image of the leader as clumsy, especially compared to the more glamourous though more annoying Trudeau. Stanfield also made the mistake of promising to implement wage and price controls to fight inflation. Trudeau was too smart to tell voters the truth, and he won an easy majority with 141 seats to the Conservatives' ninety-five. A year later, Trudeau implemented wage and price controls.

Q.: Which prime-minister-for-a-day brought in a budget in 1979 that annoyed everyone, then forgot to count the seats in the House of Commons, thus losing his job?

A.: Joe Clark, the shortest serving elected prime minister in Canadian history. Known as Joe Who?, he seemed to come out of nowhere, or Alberta as it is known to non-Central Canadians, to win the 1976 Conservative leadership. He beat Trudeau's Liberals in the June 4, 1979 election, but couldn't beat the onslaught of jokes about his clumsiness and aw-shucks appearance. After a long summer holiday, he proceeded to alienate oil-rich Arab nations by promising to move the Canadian Embassy from Tel Aviv to Jerusalem, then had to apologize. His finance minister, John Crosbie, brought in a budget with an eighteen-cent-per-gallon oil surtax in the fall. The Liberals and NDP rallied all their members of Parliament (MPs) back to Ottawa, including one on a gurney from the hospital and two in Brussels meeting with NATO officials. External Affairs Minister Flora MacDonald, at the same NATO meeting, was called too late and missed her plane. Clark lost the vote by 139 to 136, with six abstentions. Clark lost the February 18, 1980 election to Pierre Trudeau, who came out of retirement to lead the Liberals to victory.

Q.: Which deposed prime minister got a 67 percent approval rating from his party after a disastrous showing in an election, then decided that wasn't good enough and launched a leadership race, which he then lost?

A.: Joe Clark. The race in 1983 gave Brian Mulroney his second chance to win the party's leadership. Mulroney became prime minister. Perhaps because Clark is a decent man, Canadians forgave him for letting Mulroney happen.

Q.:   Which Liberal prime-minister-for-a-day, just after call-
        ing a snap election, announced seventeen patronage
        appointments for retiring MPs?

A.:   John Turner. In power for eighty days from June 30 to
        September 17, 1984, the handsome, silver-haired,
        blue-eyed Bay Street lawyer and leader-in-waiting took
        over after Prime Minister Pierre Trudeau resigned.
        Turner looked like a shoo-in when he called the elec-
        tion. But he was a stiff on television, especially during
        the key debate when Conservative leader Brian
        Mulroney challenged him on the patronage appoint-
        ments. "I had no option," Turner said. "You had an
        option. You could have said this was wrong. Instead,
        you said yes to the old system and the old attitudes.
        You could have done better." The Conservatives won
        the election with 211 seats, the most ever.

Q.:   Which prime-minister-for-an-eternity tried twice to
        convince Canadians that his vision of Quebec's role in
        Canada was the correct one, only to lose both times
        and make Canadians inside and outside of Quebec
        furious?

A.:   Brian Mulroney. Somehow he led the Conservatives for
        nine years although his approval ratings once fell to 8
        percent and he is recognized as one of the most disliked
        prime ministers in modern history. (He may yet place
        second to Jean Chrétien.) The Goods and Services Tax
        (GST), the Free Trade Agreement, Mulroney's
        smarminess, and his family's display of wealth eventual-

ly turned off voters, but he didn't help much with his attempts to get the ten provinces to reach a constitutional agreement.

Pierre Trudeau had managed to get Canada its own constitution in 1982, but couldn't get Quebec to sign it. Mulroney did. First he and the ten premiers met at Meech Lake and thought up the imaginatively named Meech Lake Accord, which gave Quebec "distinct society" status. Nobody was sure what that meant, but English Canadians didn't like it, and Native Canadians wondered why they didn't get the same thing. The accord had to be ratified by all the provinces by June 22, 1990. Manitoba Native MLA Elijah Harper held up debate in the legislature long enough that the accord did not meet its make-or-break deadline. Newfoundland Premier Clyde Wells announced the vote would not go ahead in his legislature, either. The Meech Lake Accord died.

With a disappointed Quebec threatening to hold a referendum on independence in 1992, Mulroney and the premiers tried again, meeting in Charlottetown, Prince Edward Island. They came up with the imaginatively named Charlottetown Accord. This deal gave Quebec its "distinct society" status, Native people some kind self-government, and all the provinces more power. The accord would be sent to a vote of the people on October 26. At first everyone agreed to vote yes. Then Canadians thought about who had made up the accord and voted no. Four months later, Mulroney announced he was resigning as leader of the Conservatives.

Q.: Which attractive, energetic, and quick-tempered prime-minister-for-a-day decided to take over the most hated party in modern Canadian history (until the turn of the millennium federal Liberals), then tried to win an election by making fun of the way her opponent talked while consistently putting her own foot in her mouth?

A.: Kim Campbell, who became the country's first female prime minister by taking the Conservative leadership when Prime Minister Brian Mulroney resigned. Deep-thinking party members in Quebec ran television commercials making fun of Jean Chrétien's unusual way of speaking out of the side of his mouth, a twist brought on by a childhood illness. To ensure her success, Campbell also said an election was no time to talk about the economy or health care, and that Canadians were too stupid to understand the failed Charlottetown Accord. On election day, October 25, 1993, the Conservatives won two seats.

Q.: What attractive, energetic, and geographically and geologically impaired party-leader-for-a-day made so many mistakes he almost took his whole party down the river with him?

A.: Stockwell Day, chosen leader of the Canadian Alliance Party in the summer of 2000. The new party had a rough start. A committee of Reform Party supporters spent a year considering names for a new party that would unite the right in Canada. A year of work boiled the choices down to five. Then a party convention spent two hours debating until supporters chose the Canadian Conservative Reform Alliance Party. Or CCRAP. The name was quickly changed to Canadian Alliance, or as it became known, the Alliance Party.

Alliance members threw out the old Reform leader, Preston Manning, in favour of Stockwell Day. In the October 2000 federal election campaign against Prime Minister Jean Chrétien, Day tried to illustrate a point about the brain drain to the United States by indicating that Lake Erie drains from north to south. Unfortunately it doesn't. Day also refused to consider he might be equally wrong thinking dinosaurs and humans lived at the same time (he was thousands of years off). He attempted to persuade voters by saying he was against medicare, against gay rights, and for creationism being taught in school. The Alliance Party failed to break into Ontario, and Chrétien and the Liberals won 173 seats.

Day stumbled merrily along until the spring of 2001, when he admitted he met a so-called spy who was going to dig up dirt on his rivals, then said he hadn't really met the spy but thought he had because reporters said so. Fed up with the bumbling, thirteen disgruntled Alliance members bolted the caucus. The next spring, in 2002, the Alliance kicked him out and chose Stephen Harper as leader.

CHAPTER 16

IDEAS SO BAD THEY DON'T FIT ANYWHERE ELSE

Just what a park needs, concrete

Massive steel mills, coke ovens, and factories on one side, highways and suburbs on the other — that's what surrounds Hamilton, Ontario. Its downtown boasts office towers, Copps Coliseum, a theatre, art galleries, a six-lane main street heading into the city, and another six-lane street heading out. In the midst of the concrete and traffic sits a small park that for a hundred years offered Hamiltonians a bit of shade and a nice place to rest from the downtown busyness, a small set of lungs that gave everyone a bit of a breather.

So naturally, in 1983, Hamilton council decided to knock it all down and add more concrete. The disastrous decision and the public outcry that followed are known in Hamilton as the Gore Park Fiasco.

The little downtown park began with a bungle and withstood attacks on its nature from the moment it was created in 1817. Two of the earliest townsfolk, George Hamilton and Nathanial Hughson, had farms on either side of the main road, called King Street. Each one owned a triangular piece of property.

Hamilton thought it might be a good idea if each man donated his portion to create a town square. Hughson agreed and Hamilton donated his land. But then Hughson backed out, deciding instead to sell his lots. The city was left with a triangular piece of land, called the Gore.

From 1817 to 1833, the Gore stood untouched but unimproved too. Residents used the Gore — dusty in the summer and a quagmire in the spring — as a dump and a place to park wagons. A well built at one end offered stages a place to water horses.

As soon as the town incorporated in 1833, politicians eyed the Gore for a market building. George Hamilton said forget it, the land was donated for a park. The politicians ignored him and started digging for the market building. George Hamilton took them to court. The politicians lost and had to fill up the holes. (Politicians 150 years later might have learned from this history lesson.)

One year after the town became a city in 1846, the politicians tried again. The Gore would be the site of a new city hall, post office, and commercial buildings. In order to stop the inevitable court action, the wily city council gave George Hamilton's son, Robert, some of the land to develop. This time surrounding landowners launched a protest. The courts again ruled the space was supposed to be left open.

But no one knew what to do with it. Wagon wheels and horses chewed up the property, water from the well turned part into muck, and woodcutters and farmers still stopped there to sell their wood and produce.

Hamiltonians pressured the politicians to get rid of the informal market and turn the place into a proper park. In 1860, the Gore became Gore Park, and trees and grass were planted, at least in the western block. The wagons and farmers simply moved to the eastern block. It took until the turn of the century and the efforts of the city's beautification society to pressure the city to turn the area into a real park.

Indeed, for 120 years, politicians made changes and Hamiltonians argued about them. Fences went up. Fences were torn down. Fountains went up. Fountains came down. Benches went in. Benches went out. Statues of Sir John A. Macdonald and Queen Victoria went up. They, at least, endured. Not so lucky was a forty-five metre iron flag pole erected in the early 1900s. The "oil derrick," as one parks board member called it, lasted twenty years.

Nonplussed, one business leader offered the city $250,000 for the rights to build a fifteen-storey building on the park's site, and simply put the park on top. Council declined the offer.

Everyone wanted to do something different with Gore Park — from paving the western half in 1951 to build a bus loading area, to putting a 1,000-car garage underneath it in 1955. The proponent of the bus plan, Alderman Jack MacDonald, suggested the park-like atmosphere could be maintained by planting a small bed of flowers on an island in the middle of the bus lanes.

With so many changes and attacks, Gore Park became a strange little place.

"It is neither particularly beautiful nor particularly ugly," stated a *Hamilton Spectator* editorial, defending the park against the attacks.

Yet it was the only place people had downtown. Every Christmas, it turned into a magic land for children, with Christmas trees, Santa's castle, lights, and live reindeer. Complaints about the reindeer droppings eventually forced council to close the petting zoo.

Oddly enough, the park survived the onslaughts of the 1950s, 1960s, and 1970s, when pavement was king, only to run head on into disaster in the 1980s when urban politicians were supposed to know better.

The 1980s were the decade of downtown action plans, and Hamilton was no exception. A major part of its plan, unveiled in 1983, was the recreation of Gore Park. A consulting firm developed three options for the park, ranging from putting a four-lane road through it to simply getting rid of the grass. Fed up with the park's reputation as a hangout for winos and teenagers, some downtown merchants liked the idea of making the park more urban. No one else seemed to pay much attention. It was simply another council with another idea, although this one was going to cost $2.8 million and include a 300-seat amphitheatre, new fountains, walkways, and concessions. Ho hum, here we go again.

Then the chainsaws roared into action. On July 18, 1983, the construction crews began bringing new life to Gore Park by cutting down a hundred-year-old maple. All the trees were to come down, shocked Hamiltonians learned.

"To make the new park more pedestrian oriented," said parks director Russ Nutley, "it was decided that the ground level would be lowered by at least a foot, avoiding the necessity of stairs to the street. You just can't go to the top of the tree and knock it deeper into the ground," he told reporters.

The new park, to be ready by November, would include even more trees. It would be great — a people place, the essence of all that is good about downtown, the city promised.

A month before it opened, politicians and residents took a closer look at what was going up in Gore. Replacing the grass and trees were a $100,000, pyramid-roofed, temple-like structure that would house displays and lead to public washrooms, and a $140,000 blue- domed, fast food concession stand.

"No one told me this Greek temple display area would be built of white plastic stucco or that the concession stand would be in eye-offending blue fibreglass," complained one alderman.

The seats in the amphitheatre, another alderman noticed, were going to be twenty centimetres high and fifty centimetres deep, hard for anyone to use, never mind seniors. The buildings weren't part of the plans shown to the public, politicians claimed.

City officials held an emergency meeting to see why the architect's vision had been altered so much by Hamilton's own building department. As politicians huddled, workers merrily continued putting up the buildings.

"Who killed Gore Park?" *The Spectator* asked. The answer: Everyone. The politicians didn't keep a close eye on the city officials doing the work. No model of the new park was ever made because staff were told to hurry up and get the thing done. After all, there was a recession going on and downtown needed help fast. Although urban planners helped the architect develop the plan for the park, the staff interpreting that plan got no help. And in their hurry, they never bothered to tell merchants what changes were being made. Eventually, no one took the blame.

But council decided in October 1983 to demolish the buildings and spent $82,000 to hire a landscape architect to come up with a new plan, and this time, build a model. City dwellers finally got a chance to say what they wanted: grass and trees.

A lot of ideas sprang up, as usual. A skating rink, a bandshell, a stage. Perhaps Ernie Seager, then sixty-nine and the former secretary to the parks board, had the best one. Of the latest ideas, and of all the ideas over the years, Seager said, "They're trying to put an elephant on a postage stamp. There is nothing wrong with a Victorian Park. We need a wrought-iron fence of elegant design, a fountain, a place to sit. There's nothing wrong with grass and flowers." Finally, in February 1984, council approved a new plan for the park, one that included a lot more grass and flowers.

The new plan hiked the cost by $750,000 to $3.5 million. About $440,000 had been wasted designing and building the concession stand, washroom, and ampitheatre. Fourteen light poles, ten flagpoles, skylights, and windows bought for the concession stand were put into storage.

And the headaches continued. Faced with budget restraints, council had to cut the washrooms out of the project. The underground washrooms had eased many a trip downtown for seventy years, and in 1981 were voted by *Today* magazine as Canada's Best Public Washroom.

Making matters worse, construction turned the park into another dusty wasteland for the second summer in a row.

"Here is natural beauty reduced to rubble and litter," *The Spectator* opined in the summer of 1984. "Here is desolation in the place of pride, the raw wound where a city's heart was ripped out. Here is the physical translation of the words, Political Bungling."

The bungling appeared to come to an end on October 19, 1984, when Gore Park finally reopened with thousands celebrating until midnight.

Three months later, a section of the interlocking bricks on King Street near the park heaved up. Whether it was frost, or faulty construction, or the fact bricks were put down to let heavy buses run over them, the problem cost taxpayers another $22,000 to fix.

Gore Park continued to attract controversy into the new millennium. The city put in new benches, but instead of facing the fountains and trees, they faced the traffic. In 1997, the deer came back to the park. This time it wasn't the droppings that sparked public ire, but the treatment of the wildlife. An animal rights group sprang up and in an effort to create an appropriate acronym, called itself Citizens Against Gore Park Exploited Deer, or CAGED. Four years later, the debate over the deer continued. No one makes a fast move on Gore Park anymore.

A shaky idea at best

After the Second World War, there was a great feeling of optimism, especially for the ability of technology to solve problems. Fuelled by the success of such earlier mega-projects as the Hoover Dam, the Americans looked to technology as the way to address a wide variety of challenges.

When the United States started forecasting to determine what their future raw material needs would be, they quickly realized they would soon need water. The population of California was growing rapidly, and water was in short supply. Canada, on the other hand, had lots of water and few people and, well, that didn't seem fair.

One proposed solution was a joint project that would dam James Bay and turn it into a big, freshwater reserve that could then be flowed back down to the United States. Ecological concerns wound up putting a stop to the idea rather early on. Even so, in the 1960s Canada considered damming South Indian Lake in Manitoba to create a lake about one quarter the size of Lake Ontario. Fears were raised about the impact on the environment and, oh yes, the tectonic plates.

Sometime after the James Bay dam idea was abandoned, the Americans learned through experience that increased weight — like that caused by a huge lake — could cause earthquakes. And "extra" water finding its way into the earth's crust could also cause unexpected slippage. At a major chemical warfare storage site near Denver, Colorado, Americans had to cease pumping nerve gas chemicals and other agents into a 4,000-metre deep shaft when hundreds of thousands of litres of liquid caused minor earthquakes.

Being bright folk, the Canadians, and the engineers before them, realized that just because you can do something, doesn't mean you should.

Did anyone remember the ice?

Rice Lake is one of the Kawartha Lakes and part of the Trent-Severn Waterway. It was a major transportation route from the lower Great Lakes to the upper Great Lakes for centuries.

Native North Americans paddled their way through on the way to Lake Simcoe and the Severn, then on to Georgian Bay and points north.

After the Hurons were decimated in the mid-1600s by the Iroquois, the latter were chased out along this corridor by the Ojibway. In fact, one of the last stands made by the Iroquois in Ontario took place in the Rice Lake area.

But in the 1800s, with the advent of the railroads, Rice Lake was no longer thought of as a route for transportation. It was, instead, a hindrance.

Big companies, like the Grand Trunk Railway, were building rail lines in all directions in a wave of expansion. Smaller lines were also flourishing. Some people were getting rich on the railroads.

The larger railways had benchmarks for the construction of their lines. Tracks were to be installed in a robust manner that would meet English standards. Whenever possible, space for a second line should be installed.

But sometimes greed and speed took over.

In Cobourg, some entrepreneurs wanted to build a line north to Peterborough to increase the trade and traffic into the area. They decided to take as direct a route as possible, so north they went and right across Rice Lake they spanned a bridge. The thing was five kilometres long and it was considered a bit of a marvel for awhile. Not long, but awhile.

In their enthusiasm and hurry to finish, they didn't quite meet the required standards — this ribbon of steel was not as robust as the links in Merry Olde England.

The Rice Lake Rail Bridge was started in 1853 and finished in November 1854, and when the rail line from Cobourg to Peterbourough was completed on December 29, a huge celebration took place. The first train, pulled by two engines with twelve cars and 1,000 people, arrived after a journey of only one hour and forty-five minutes. Harwood, the hamlet on the south side of the lake, became a boomtown almost overnight and land prices soared. The optimism was crushed, along with parts of the bridge, that winter. Apparently, when they designed this flimsy bridge, no one remembered the effects of winter on Rice Lake.

Each spring, the bridge had to be repaired. Like teeth subjected to constant wiggling, the piles holding the bridge up slowly became more and more loose. As trains rumbled over the long span, the track would sway and passengers would hold their breath. You know, in case they ended up in the water.

Bridge-phobia was underlined in 1860 when the Prince of Wales arrived for a tour of Canada. The prince was expected to ride the train across the span, but he opted instead to cross by boat, ostensibly to take in "a good view of the fir-covered

National Archives of Canada/PA-205516

When they built the Rice Lake rail bridge in 1854, they forgot about the ice. The ice gave notice of its intentions each winter and final notice several years later. The bridge was closed in 1861.

islands which picturesquely dot the lake and also the bed of the wild rice in blossom."

The following winter the bridge was closed.

Ice finished its work, and the "wonder" fell into the lake.

You can still see the remnants today. Some bits and pieces of the old bridge stick up above the surface while others rest just under the water — hampering the boat traffic.

Hardly a glowing report

The CANDU reactor, (short for CANadian Deuterium Uranium), despite being an interesting engineering achievement, does not always live up to its nickname.

It does stand apart from other nuclear reactors because it can use the cheaper and more easily accessible natural uranium, unlike others that require refined uranium, and because the waste product of the CANDU is weapons-grade uranium.

Canada has twenty-two reactors, including some at Rolphton, Pickering, and Douglas Point in Ontario and at Gentilly in Quebec. The reports aren't all glowing. Between 1952 and 2000, they have cost us $16.6 billion in subsidies. And on top of that, Ontario Hydro alone had to be relieved of $22 billion in nuclear debt prior to the province's privatization of Hydro. Eight of our reactors have been in long-term shutdown because of bent fuel rods and other problems. And there have been a few unfortunate accidents.

In Pickering in 1983, a pressure tube failed and coolant was sprayed into the reactor building. Retubing was required and it cost about $1 billion. Then, in August 1992, about 2,000 litres of heavy water (water laced with tritium, which causes cancer and birth defects) was dumped into Lake

Ontario when another tube burst. The local water treatment plant was closed down as a result, and the folks in Toronto got a dose of glowing smiles.

In 1994, around Christmas, 185 tons of heavy water was spilled at Pickering — the good news is that the emergency core cooling system kicked in successfully. A similar failure in May 1995 with a different reactor at the same plant dumped 500 tons of heavy water.

In 1995, at the Bruce Nuclear Power Plant near Kincardine, a valve failure caused a twenty-five-ton leak of radioactive heavy water into Lake Huron.

Pickering again, this time in April 1996, around Easter — 50 trillion becquerels of tritium was released into Lake Ontario. Levels of tritium in local drinking water rose to one hundred times the background levels.

On good days, when the plants are working well and not spilling stuff, they produce a lot of high-level radioactive waste. That has to be kept somewhere — safely — for a very long time. Large sums of money have been spent on finding a solution to the problem of long-term storage, about $700 million in all.

And it's not as if Canada can simply stop using the plants. Once started, it's not easy to stop a nuclear energy program. You can't just turn out the lights, lock the door, and go home. As of 2000, the cost of decommissioning the twenty-two plants and equipment and storing the radioactive waste would be $20 billion.

In addition, because the radioactive waste from CANDU reactors is fissionable, weapons-grade uranium, the sale of the reactors outside Canada can have "earth-shaking" consequences. For example, when Canada sold India its CANDU reactor (in this case called a CIRUS reactor), it extracted a promise from India that it would not use it to create nuclear weapons. Coincidentally, sometime after the purchase, India detonated its first nuclear blast, which it referred to as a "mining experiment." And China has purchased two CANDUs. At the time of the sale China was already a nuclear power, which might suggest that it understood the importance of having a ready source of weapons-grade uranium.

What all this means, of course, is that Canada faces the unpleasant prospect of not knowing which nuclear power plants will prove to be more dangerous — the ones it operates at home, or the ones it sells abroad.

I think we can take them

Despite what its name might suggest, the *Rainbow Cruiser* was a serious ship — a pre-First World War creation and one of the Royal Canadian Navy's first two fighting ships. The Liberal government, under Wilfrid Laurier, purchased the *Rainbow Cruiser* and the *Niobe* from the British to start building a navy for Canada.

The *Rainbow Cruiser* was involved in the Navy's first mission in 1914, but the Canadian Navy hardly began its existence wrapped in glory.

At the time, British Columbia had seen a large influx of immigration, especially of the non-Anglo-Saxon variety, and anti-immigrant sentiment was growing quickly. When the vessel *Komagatu Maru* was spotted making its way to the West Coast, the provincial government called on the federal government to put a stop to it.

So, in July 1914, as the world slipped into war in Europe and Canada was clamouring for manpower to meet its demands, the federal government sent half its navy to fend off 200 Sikhs.

In actual fact, the Sikhs were not planning to attack Canada. And the ship's Japanese name did not indicate any threat — Japan was on the Allies' side in the First World War.

But the *Rainbow Cruiser* sailed out of harbour and, with all its military might, faced down the immigrant ship and forced it and its 200 passengers to turn away.

Perpetually daft

In 1828, Thomas McCausland came to the hamlet that would one day be Barrie. The central Ontario community was a crossroads for transport to the Great Lakes — a place where water travel and land travel met.

McCausland, a Scottish immigrant, and his family, which included at least three children, squatted on a piece of prime real estate right next to the lake. McCausland worked hard to look after his family, but it appears that his real passion was science.

McCausland wanted to be an inventor, or, rather, *the* inventor. At the time, creating a perpetual motion machine was the Holy Grail of science, much like alchemy — turning lead into gold — had once been.

To further his dream, McCausland constructed a monstrous building on the property, apparently obstructing the view of the scion of the Upper Canada magistrate. This scion wrote a letter to his father, asking him to do something about the boor who was hiding the lake from view.

By this time, McCausland had already enjoyed some spectacular failures that had contributed to his bad reputation in the community, which, it should be noted, was full of wooden buildings.

That little detail is important because as it turned out, McCausland was never taught the trick about how to make fire by rubbing two sticks together. So he didn't understand the problems inherent in building a perpetual motion machine — or any machine, really — out of wood.

McCausland had no trouble obtaining the wood because he had his own one-mule sawmill. A mule or horse hitched to a turnstile that powered the mill provided McCausland with a small income and wood. The free wood was hammered and pegged together to form levers, wheels, and joints and soon the thing was a huge moving, whirring, creaking concern. As the moving and whirring and creaking continued, the friction between the wooden joints heated up and soon it was ablaze.

Now, a guy can only get away with this a couple of times in a town full of wooden buildings before he gets run out. And being a squatter, which McCausland apparently was, he was summarily kicked off his choice piece of real estate.

The last mention of him relates that he had moved his family into a small building used by the British Navy as a storage shed. He stayed only long enough to get kicked out of town, when he was spotted trying to rig up a small sawmill with a pony.

The throne of perfection

Once upon a time, Canada was the best place in the world. Citizens could walk the streets at any time of day in safety, children were polite, adults were hard-working, young lovers held hands in the parks, and the sun shone.

And once, almost, the toilet seats were always clean.

It wasn't that long ago that life came so close to perfection.

In 1988, Nova Scotia Premier John Buchanan surveyed his province and saw everything was good, except for one thing: dirty toilet seats. His citizens had to sit on germs whenever they needed to relieve themselves. Surely that wasn't right. Moving in the highest of circles, Buchanan had heard of a new kind of toilet seat, one that would rid the world of germs. So he had a top civil servant, Michael Zareski, the deputy minister of government services, investigate.

There are such things, Zareski reported back. But, he added, they are not practical. Oh, grey thinking civil servant! Oh, dull pusher of paper! Surely those who sit all day could appreciate clean toilet seats.

Buchanan knew better. Buchanan was a man of the people. He had not served as Conservative premier since 1978 for nothing.

Get the seats! Buchanan commanded.

Why don't we try a few experimental seats, the ordinary-thinking Zareski suggested.

Get them all, his leader said.

Shouldn't we at least read some studies about the seats, Zareski asked.

Get the seats! The people need the toilet seats! Buchanan insisted.

So Zareski signed the purchase order and the 250 seats arrived.

And what seats they were. Each one boasted a storage compartment containing plastic seat covers and a motor. At the push of a button, the motor removed one plastic seat cover and spewed out a new one. Each person, at each sitting, got his or her own hygienic toilet seat cover.

The government was pleased and ordered the seats be placed throughout its buildings and in Halifax hospitals. Once the citizens knew they were relieved forever of germs, they would demand more of the electronic seats.

Alas, more bureaucrats stepped in. The provincial health department told the government to sit on the plan. Distributing the electronic germ-stoppers could heighten fears that AIDS could be transmitted through toilet seats — a common misconception at the time. So the devices were tucked away.

Two years later, the seats were raised again. Because Buchanan had bought the toilet seats from a friend and helped out other friends in other ways, Zareski quit his job. A year later, in 1990, Zareski complained to the Nova Scotia legislature's public accounts committee about political interference and corruption. People who knew nothing about toilet seats and germs got angry. The RCMP started sniffing around. The provincial government decided to flush away the smell of scandal, selling the seats at an auction house in Ontario. Nova Scotia got a grand total of $300 for the seats then spent $424 to ship them.

Since then, the seats seem to have disappeared. No doubt they grace a country club or a resort for multimillionaires. The common man still sits on common seats. As for Buchanan, he resigned in the midst of the scandal. In September 1990, he was appointed to the Senate. There, Buchanan continued to work for the public good, helping the Tories pass the Goods and Services Tax. Only naysayers would suggest he found a new way to flush money down the toilet.

SELECTED BIBLIOGRAPHY

Alexander, Ron and Green, Larry. *A Future for the Sandbanks; a report on the sand dunes of Prince Edward County.* Prepared for Pollution Probe and Canadian Environmental Law Research Foundation. Toronto: 1972.

Auf der Maur, Nick. *The Billion-Dollar Game: Jean Drapeau and the 1976 Olympics.* Toronto: J. Lorimer, 1976.

Akrigg, G.P.V. and Akrigg, Helen B. *British Columbia Place Names.* Vancouver: UBC Press, 1997.

Bolger, Frances W.P., ed. *Canada's Smallest Province: A History of P.E.I.* Charlottetown: Prince Edward Island 1973 Centennial Commission, 1973.

Borins, Sandford with Brown, Lee. *Investments in Failure: Five Government Enterprises That Cost the Canadian Taxpayer Billions.* Toronto: Methuen, c1986.

Baldwin, Douglas. *Land of the Red Soil: A Popular History of Prince Edward Island.* Charlottetown: Ragweed, 1990.

Beattie, Owen and Geiger, John. *Frozen in Time: Unlocking the Secrets of the Franklin Expedition.* Saskatoon, SA: Western Producer Prairie Books, 1988.

Berton, Pierre. *Flames Across the Border, 1813-1814.* Toronto: McClelland and Stewart, 1981.

Berton, Pierre. *The Invasion of Canada, 1812-1813.* Toronto: McClelland and Stewart, 1980.

Berton, Pierre. *My Country: The Remarkable Past.* Toronto: McClelland and Stewart, 1976.

Berton, Pierre. *The Wild Frontier: More Tales From the Remarkable Past.* Toronto: McClelland and Stewart, 1978.

Bowering, George. *Egotists and Autocrats: The Prime Ministers of Canada.* Toronto: Viking, 1999.

Brown, J.J. *Ideas in Exile: A History of Canadian Invention.* Toronto: McClelland and Stewart, 1967.

Brown, Ron. *Ghost Towns of Ontario.* Langley, B.C.: Stagecoach Pub. Co., 1978.

Brown, Ron. *50 Unusual Things to See in Ontario*. Erin, Ont.: Boston Mills Press, 1989.

Campbell, Marjorie Wilkins. *The Saskatchewan*. Toronto: Clarke, Irwin, 1965.

Canadian Taxpayers Federation Web site: http://www.taxpayer.com/home.htm

Clark, Andrew Hill. *Three Centuries and the Island: A Historical Geography of Settlement and Agriculture in Prince Edward Island, Canada*. Toronto: University of Toronto Press, 1959.

Champlain, Samuel de. *The Works of Samuel de Champlain*, edited by H.P. Biggar. Toronto: Champlain Society, 1922-1936.

Charlottetown Examiner, April 17, 1865 (Tenants League March).

Colombo, John Robert, ed. *Colombo's Book of Canada*. Edmonton: Hurtig, 1978.

Colombo, John Robert. *Ghost Stories of Ontario*. Toronto: Hounslow Press, 1995.

Corness, Norm. "The first 9000." *The Canora Chronicle*, Vol. 15, Feb. 2002, Canadian Northern Society, Alberta.

D.L.S. *Fifty Years in Western Canada: Being the Abridged Memoirs of Rev. A.G. Morice, O.M.I.* Toronto: Ryerson Press, 1930.

Dumont, Gabriel, trans. by Michael Barnholden. *Gabriel Dumont Speaks.* Vancouver: Talonbooks, 1993.

Edmonton Journal, Oct. 17, 22, 23, 1934 (Charles Bedaux expedition).

Elofson, Warren M. *Cowboys, Gentlemen & Cattle Thieves: Ranching on the Western Frontier.* Montréal: McGill-Queen's University Press, c2000.

Elson, Harvey. "The View From the Top." *Canadian Rail,* No. 289 Feb. 1976, Canadian Railroad Historical Association, Montréal.

Ferguson, Will. *Bastards & Boneheads: Canada's Glorious Leaders, Past and Present.* Vancouver: Douglas and McIntyre, c1999.

Filey, Mike. *Toronto Sketches: The Way We Were.* Toronto: Dundurn Press, 1992.

Filey, Mike. *Toronto Sketches 4: The Way We Were.* Toronto: Dundurn Press, c1995.

The Financial Post, July 3, 1954, June 27, 1954. "New Industry Thinks in Long Terms."

The Financial Post, Sept. 23, 1961. (Avrocar)

Fredericks, H.A. with Chambers, Allan. *Bricklin.* Fredericton, N.B.: Brunswick Press, c1977.

Fryer, Mary Beacock. *Battlefields of Canada.* Toronto:

Dundurn Press, 1986.

Fryer, Mary Beacock. *More Battlefields of Canada*. Toronto: Dundurn Press, 1993.

Ganong, William Francis. *Dochet (St. Croix) Island: A Monograph*. Ottawa: J. Hope, 1902.

Geiger, John and Beattie, Owen. *Dead Silence: The Greatest Mystery in Arctic*. Toronto: Viking Press, 1993.

Globe and Mail, Jan. 13, 1975, March 17, 1977, March 7, 8, 9, 1977 (stories on community of Townsend), July 12, 1990 (Nova Scotia toilet seats), Feb. 8, 1985 (Glace Bay heavy water plant).

Gold, L.W. "Habbakuk: Building Ships of Ice," in *No Day Long Enough: Canadian Science in World War II*, edited by George R. Lindsey. Toronto: Canadian Institute of Strategic Studies, 1997.

Gouldie, D.R. "Gouldie's Perpetual Sleigh Road Supersedes the Railway." *Monetary Times*. Toronto, 1874.

Gutsche, Andrea and Bisaillon, Cindy. *Mysterious Islands: Forgotten Tales of the Great Lakes*. Toronto, Ont.: Lynx Images, c1999.

Gwyn, Richard. *Smallwood: The Unlikely Revolutionary*. Toronto: McClelland and Stewart, [1999], c1972.

Halifax Chronicle Herald, July 21, 1990 (Nova Scotia toilet seats).

Hamilton Spectator, Gore Park collection, Hamilton Public Library.

Horwood, Harold. *Joey.* Don Mills, Ont.: Stoddart, 1989.

Ketchum, Hank. "The Cost, Feasibility and Advantage of a Ship Railway Across the Isthmus of Chignecto." *Chignecto Post.* Sackville N.B., 1882

Ketchum, Hank. "The Chignecto Ship Railway." Speech to The World's Columbian Water Commerce Congress, Chicago, 1893. Boston: Damrell and Upham.

Ketchum, Hank. "The Isthmian Transit Between the Bay of Fundy and the Gulf of St. Lawrence," London: Waterloo and Sons Limited, 1884.

Kelly, L.V. *The Range Men: The Story of the Ranchers and Indians of Alberta.* New York: Argonaut Press, 1965.

Lampe, David. *Pyke: The Unknown Genius.* London: Evans Brothers, 1959.

Langley, Susan B. "Project Habbakuk, World War II Prototype Vessel." *Scientia Canadiensis.* Vol X, No. 2, Autumn/Winter, 1986.

Lescarbot, Marc. *The History of New France*, with an English translation, notes and appendices by W.L. Grant and an introduction by H.P. Biggar. Toronto: Champlain Society, 1907-1914.

Letto, Doug. *Chocolate Bars and Rubber Boots: The*

Smallwood Industrialization Plan. Paradise, Nfld.: Blue Hill Publishing, 1998.

Littleton, James. *Target Nation: Canada and the Western Intelligence Network*. Toronto: L. & O. Dennys, CBC Enterprises, c1986.

Liss, Ted and Liss, Nancy. *Curious Canadians*. Markham, Ont.: Fitzhenry and Whiteside, 2001.

Lunn, Richard and Lunn, Janet. *The County: The First Hundred Years in Loyalist Prince Edward*. Picton, Ont.: Edward County Council, 1967.

Llewelyn-Davies, Weeks. Cda Ltd. Townsend Community Plan, March 29, 1977.

MacIntyre, Linden. Five part special report, Glace Bay heavy water plant. *Halifax Chronicle Herald*, April 13-15 1971.

MacKay, Donald. *The People's Railway: A history of Canadian National*. Vancouver: Douglas and McIntyre, 1992.

MacKenzie, A.E.D. *Baldoon: Lord Selkirk's Settlement in Upper Canada*. London, Ont.: Phelps Pub. Co., 1978.

May, Gary. *Hard Oiler!: The Story of Early Canadians' Quest for Oil at Home and Abroad*. Toronto: Dundurn Press, 1998.

McGoogan, Ken. *Fatal Passage: The Untold Story of John Rae, the Arctic Adventurer Who Discovered the Fate of Franklin*. Toronto: Harper Flamingo, 2001.

Mietkiewicz, Henry and Mackowcz, Bob. *Dream Tower: The Life and Legacy of Rochdale College*. Toronto: McGraw-Hill Ryerson, 1988.

Molson, K.M. and Taylor, H.A. *Canadian Aircraft Since 1909*. Stittsville, Ont.: Canada's Wings, 1982.

Morfit, George L. Office of the Auditor General of British Columbia 1999/2000 Report 5.

A Review of the Fast Ferry Project: Governance and Risk. Victoria, B.C., October 1999.

Morritt, Hope. *Rivers of Oil: The Founding of North America's Petroleum Industry*. Kingston, Ont.: Quarry Press, c1993.

Morton, Desmond. *A Short History of Canada*. Toronto: McClelland and Stewart, 1997.

Mulhill, David. *Will to Power: The Missionary Career of Father Morice*. Vancouver: University of British Columbia Press, 1986.

Myers, Jay. *The Great Canadian Road: A History of Yonge Street*. Toronto: Red Rock Pub. Co., 1977.

Neugebauer, Peter John. *Land Use History, Landscape Change, and Resource Conflict in the Sandbanks Provincial Park Area, Prince Edward County, Ontario*. London, Ont.: Faculty of Graduate Studies, University of Western Ontario, 1974.

New York Times. "First Jet Liner Seen Here Flies from Toronto in Hour." April 19, 1950.

Northern News Service online archives: http://www.nnsl.com/ (Yellowknife dairy).

Nostbakken, Janis and Jack. *The Canadian Inventions Book: Innovations, Discoveries and Firsts.* Toronto: Greey de Pencier Books, 1976.

Peden, Murray. *Fall of an Arrow.* Toronto: Stoddart, 1987.

Read, Colin and Stagg, Ronald J. *The Rebellion of 1837 in Upper Canada: A Collection of Documents.* Toronto: Champlain Society in cooperation with the Ontario Heritage Foundation, 1985.

Regan, Honourable Mr. Justice S.O. *Royal Commission of Enquiry Into The Involvement of The Government of Newfoundland and Labrador and any of its Agencies or Corporations with Sprung Sales Limited, Sprung Environmental Space Enclosures Limited or Newfoundland Enviroponics Limited, Finding and Recommendations.* St. John's: The Commission, 1991.

Royal Canadian Air Force Web site: www.rcaf.com/database (Vickers Velos airplane).

Sauve, Roger. *Borderliners: What Canadians and Americans Should – But Don't – Know About Each Other ... A Witty, Punchy and Personal Look.* Toronto: McGraw-Hill Ryerson, 1994.

Scott, James. *The Settlement of Huron County*. Toronto: Ryerson Press, 1966.

Selkirk, Thomas Douglas, Earl of. *The Collected Writings of Lord Selkirk, 1810-1820*, edited and introduced by J.M. Bumsted. Winnipeg: Manitoba Record Society, 1988.

Sharpe, David. *Rochdale: The Runaway College*. Toronto: Anansi, 1987.

Smallwood, Joseph R. *I Chose Canada: The Memoirs of the Honourable Joseph R. "Joey" Smallwood*. Toronto: Macmillan of Canada, 1973.

St. John Morning News. Jan. 31, 1851 (Andromonon car).

St. John's Evening Telegram. May 8, 9 and 23, 1987, June 29, 1989 (Sprung greenhouse).

St. John's Telegraph Journal. Oct. 28, 1950, Oct 15, 1951 (Joey Smallwood's industrialization plan).

Starr, Richard. *Richard Hatfield: The Seventeen Year Saga*. Halifax, N.S.: Formac Pub. Co., 1987.

Stewart, Greig. *Shutting Down the National Dream: A.V. Roe and the Tragedy of the Avro Arrow*. Scarborough, Ont.: McGraw-Hill Ryerson, 1988.

Swinyard, Thomas. Reports to the Hon. the Minister of Public Works by Thomas Swinyard, on the Prince Edward Island Railway, and his correspondence with the provincial government in relation thereto, 1874-1875 [microform].

Ottawa: Maclean, Roger, 1875.

Taylor, Gordon Rattray. *The Doomsday Book*. London: Thames & Hudson, 1970.

Trial of Jones, Hazelton, Anderson, and Trevaskiss, alias Johns[t]on, for piracy and murder on board barque Saladin, with the written confessions of the prisoners, produced in evidence on the said trial. To which is added, particulars of their execution on the 30th of July. Also, the trial of Carr and Galloway for the murder of Captain Fielding and his son on board the Saladin. Compiled from the Halifax papers. Halifax, N.S.: Petheric Press, 1967. Halifax, N.S., printed and sold by S. Bowes, 1844.

Turcott, Agnes. W. *Land of the Big Goose: A History of Wawa and the Michipicoten Area, from 1622 to 1982*; with pen and ink illustrations by Jack Caldwell. Altona, Man.: Friesen Printers, 1982.

Vancouver Sun. December 7, 1995 (BC transit scandal).

van Herk, Aritha. *Mavericks: An Incorrigible History of Alberta*. Toronto: Penguin/Viking, 2001.

Vertes, Honourable Justice J.Z. *Judgement – Supreme Court of the Northwest Territories, The Commissioner of the Northwest Territories and the Northwest Territories Business Credit Corporation vs. Donald Portz (defendant)*.

Visser, Margaret. *The Rituals of Dinner: The Origins, Evolution, Eccentricities, and Meaning of Table Manners*. Toronto: HarperCollins, c1991.

Wooden, Joseph L. *A Drum to Beat Upon: The Story of St. Joseph, Ontario, the City that Never Was on the Shores of Lake Huron and Narcisse Cantin the "Wizard of St. Joseph."* Exeter : J.L. Wooden, 1971.

Zuehlke, Mark. *Scoundrels, Dreamers & Second Sons: British Remittance Men in the Canadian West.* Vancouver: Whitecap Books, c1994.

Zuk, Bill. *Avrocar: Canada's Flying Saucer: The Story of Avro Canada's Secret Projects.* Erin, Ont.: Boston Mills Press, 2001.